PORTUGAL

TOP SIGHTS, AUTHENTIC EXPERIENCES

Regis St Louis, Gregor Clark, Mark Di Duca,
Duncan Garwood, Catherine Le Nevez,
Kevin Raub and Kerry Walker

Contents

Welcome to Portugal

Medieval castles and cobblestone villages, captivating cities and golden beaches, brooding mountains and superheated plains: the Portugal experience can be many things. A vertiginous history, great seafood and idyllic scenery are just the beginning...

Celts, Romans, Visigoths, Moors and Christians all left their mark on the Iberian nation. Portugal is the sort of place where you can see the layers of history piled up on top of one another. A great way to experience the country is to base your itinerary on visiting Portugal's wonderfully preserved medieval town centres and hilltop castles.

Freshly baked bread, olives, cheese, red wine or crisp *vinho verde*, chargrilled fish, *cataplana* (seafood stew), smoked meats – the Portuguese have perfected the art of cooking simple, delicious meals, and dining is definitely one of the top reasons you might want to visit some parts of the country. Food and drink play a big part in the nation's festival calendar, meaning you can drink, dance and feast your way through all-night revelries across the land.

Outside the cities, Portugal's beauty unfolds in all its startling variety. You can go hiking amid the pristine scenery and historic villages of little-explored Beiras or enjoy a piece of the 800km of coast, the best beaches lining the laid-back Algarve. Gaze out over dramatic end-of-the-world cliffs, surf stellar breaks off dune-covered beaches or laze peacefully on sandy islands fronting calm blue seas.

> *Portugal is the sort of place where you can see the layers of history piled up on top of one another*

Ponte de Dom Luís I, Porto (p109)

Azulejo tiles, Tavira (p144)
ANDREI NEKRASSOV/SHUTTERSTOCK ©

Plan Your Trip
Portugal's Top 12

CHRISTOBOLO/GETTY IMAGES ©

Lisbon

History, culture and pumping nightlife

The capital of the Portuguese world is a fascinating place of trundling trams, breathtaking architecture and thumping nightlife. The Alfama district (pictured; p42), with its labyrinthine alleyways, hidden courtyards and curving, shadow-filled lanes, is a magical place in which to delve into the soul of the city. It's also where you are most likely to hear fado, the melancholy music of the city's old working class districts.

1

Porto

Portugal's romantic second city

It would be hard to dream up a more romantic city than Portugal's second largest. Laced with narrow pedestrian laneways, Porto (p101) is blessed with baroque churches, epic theatres and sprawling plazas. Its Ribeira district – a Unesco World Heritage Site – is just a short walk from centuries-old port wineries. A sense of renewal – in the form of modern architecture, cosmopolitan restaurants and a vibrant arts scene – is palpable.

2

CAIO PEDERNEIRAS/SHUTTERSTOCK ©

Algarve

Stunning beaches, secluded islands

Sunseekers have much to celebrate when it comes to beaches. Along Portugal's south coast, the Algarve (p135) is home to a wildly varied coastline. There are sandy islands reachable only by boat, dramatic cliff-backed shores, rugged rarely visited beaches and people-packed sands near buzzing nightlife. Days are spent playing in the waves, taking long oceanfront strolls and surfing memorable breaks. Praia Camilo, Lagos (p139)

3

Évora

Queen of the Alentejo

One of Portugal's most beautifully preserved medieval towns, Évora (p177) is an enchanting place to spend several days delving into the Portuguese past. Within the chunky, 14th-century stone walls built to protect the town from invaders, Évora's narrow, winding lanes lead to striking architectural works: an elaborate medieval cathedral and cloisters, Roman ruins and a picturesque town square. Historic and aesthetic virtues aside, Évora is also a lively university town, and its many attractive restaurants serve up excellent, hearty Alentejan cuisine.

Rio Duoro Valley

Breathtaking valley wine route

The exquisite Alto Douro wine country (p193) is the oldest demarcated wine region on earth. Its steeply terraced hills, stitched together with craggy vines that have produced luscious wines for centuries, loom either side of the Rio Douro. Whether you get here by driving the impossibly scenic back roads, or by train or boat from Porto, take the time to hike, cruise and taste. Countless vintners receive guests for tours, tastings and overnight stays, and if you find one that's still family owned, you may sample something very old and very special.

Braga

Portugal's lively third city

Portugal's third-largest city is blessed with terrific restaurants, a vibrant university and raucous festivals, but when it comes to historic sites it is unparalleled in Portugal. With a remarkable 12th-century cathedral and a 14th-century church, Braga (p209) has not one but two sets of Roman ruins, countless 17th-century plazas and an 18th-century palace-turned-museum. Then there's that splendid baroque staircase, Escadaria do Bom Jesus (pictured).

6

Coimbra

Portugal's best-known university town

Portugal's atmospheric college town, Coimbra (p223) rises steeply from the Rio Mondego to a medieval quarter housing one of Europe's oldest universities. Students roam the narrow streets clad in black capes, while strolling fado musicians give free concerts. Kids can keep busy at Portugal dos Pequenitos, a theme park with miniature versions of Portuguese monuments; grown-ups will appreciate the upper town's nightlife. Biblioteca Joanina, Velha Universidade (p226)

7

Aveiro

Portugal's answer to Venice

Every visitor to this coastal city (p239) sooner or later finds themself aboard a *moliceiro*, a traditionally fashioned boat that was once used to dredge up seaweed from the bottom of the town's canals. Retired from service many years ago, these have now been put to work as a tourist attraction. Away from the water Aveiro is a lively place of museums, great seafood restaurants and cafes selling sickly sweet *ovos moles*.

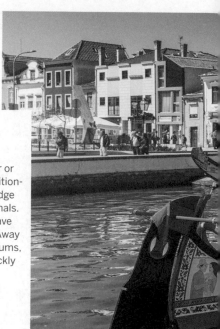

STEFANO_VALERI/SHUTTERSTOCK ©

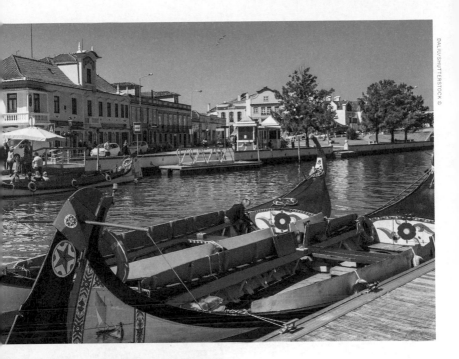

Sintra

Fairy-tale palaces and castles

Less than an hour by train from the capital, Sintra (p87) feels like another world. Like an illustration from a fairy tale, Sintra is sprinkled with stone-walled taverns and has a whitewashed palace looming over it. Forested hillsides form the backdrop to the village's storybook setting, with imposing castles, mystical gardens, strange mansions and centuries-old monasteries hidden among the woodlands. The fog that sweeps in by night adds another layer of mystery, and cool evenings are best spent fireside in one of Sintra's many charming B&Bs. From left: Palácio & Parque de Monserrate (p92); Palácio Nacional da Pena (p91)

SHAUN EGAN/GETTY IMAGES ©

Óbidos

An enchanting walled town

Wandering through the tangle of ancient streets of Óbidos (p251) is enchanting any time of year, but come during one of its festivals and you'll be in for a special treat. Whether attending a jousting match or climbing the castle walls (pictured; p254) at the medieval fair (p257), or delving into the written world at Fólio – Portugal's newest international literature festival – you couldn't ask for a better backdrop.

10

Cabo de São Vicente

The edge of the ancient world

It's thrilling to stand at Europe's most southwestern edge (p166), a headland of barren cliffs to which Portuguese sailors bid a nervous farewell during Portugal's golden years of exploration. The windswept cape is redolent of history – if you squint hard (really hard), you'll see the ghost of Vasco da Gama sailing past. These days, a fortress and lighthouse perch on the cape and a new museum beautifully highlights Portugal's maritime-navigation history.

Batalha

A marvellous monastery

This medieval Christian monument (p264) – a Unesco World Heritage Site since 1983 – constitutes one of Portugal's greatest national treasures and one of Iberia's finest chunks of Gothic architecture. The monastery has a certain magic with the whimsy of Manueline adornments and the haunting roofless shell of the unfinished Capelas Imperfeitas wowing the thousands of tourists who make a pilgrimage here every year.

Plan Your Trip
Need to Know

When to Go

Warm to hot summers, mild winters

The Douro
GO May–Sep

The Beiras
GO Jun & Sep

Lisbon
GO May & Jun

The Alentejo
GO May–Sep

The Algarve
GO Jun & Sep

High Season (Jul–Aug)
- Accommodation prices increase 30%.
- Expect big crowds in the Algarve and coastal resort areas.
- Sweltering temperatures are commonplace.
- Warmer ocean temperatures.

Shoulder (Apr–Jun & Sep–Nov)
- Mild days are ideal for hikes and outdoor activities.
- Lively festivals take place in June.
- Crowds and prices are average.
- Colder ocean temperatures.

Low Season (Dec–Mar)
- Shorter, rainier days; freezing at higher elevations.
- Lower prices, fewer crowds.
- Attractions keep shorter hours, and many beach lodgings close for winter.
- Frigid ocean temperatures, but big waves for surfers.

Currency
Euro (€)

Language
Portuguese

Visas
Generally not required for stays of up to 90 days; some nationalities will need a Schengen visa.

Money
ATMs are widely available, except in the smallest villages. Credit cards are accepted in midrange and high-end establishments.

Mobile Phones
Local SIM cards can be used in unlocked European, Australian and quad-band US mobiles.

Time
GMT/UTC in winter, GMT/UTC plus one hour in summer.

Daily Costs

Budget: Less than €50

- Dorm bed: €15–22
- Basic hotel room for two: from €35
- Lunch special at a family-run restaurant: €8–10
- Second-class train ticket from Lisbon to Faro: from €23

Midrange: €50–120

- Double room in a midrange hotel: €50–100
- Lunch or dinner in a midrange restaurant: €22–40
- Admission to museums: €3–8

Top End: More than €120

- Boutique hotel room: from €120
- Dinner for two in a top restaurant: from €80
- Three-day surf course: €150

Useful Websites

Lonely Planet (www.lonelyplanet.com/portugal) Destination information, hotel bookings, traveller forum and more.
Portugal Tourism (www.visitportugal.com) Portugal's official tourism site.
Portugal News (www.theportugalnews.com) The latest news and gossip in Portugal.
Wines of Portugal (www.winesofportugal.info) Fine overview of Portugal's favourite beverage, covering wine regions, grape varieties and wine routes.

Opening Hours

Opening hours vary throughout the year. We provide high-season opening hours; hours will generally decrease in the shoulder and low seasons.
Banks 8.30am–3pm Monday to Friday
Bars 7pm–2am
Cafes 9am–7pm

Clubs 11pm–4am Thursday to Saturday
Restaurants noon–3pm and 7–10pm
Shopping malls 10am–10pm
Shops 9.30am–noon and 2–7pm Monday to Friday, 10am–1pm Saturday

Arriving in Portugal

Aeroporto de Lisboa (Lisbon) Metro trains head downtown (€1.50, €1.33 with a Zapping card, 20 minutes, frequent departures 6.30am to 1am). AeroBus (€3.60) departs every 20 minutes from 7am to 11pm. A taxi to the centre takes 15 minutes (around €16, plus €1.60 for luggage).
Aeroporto Francisco Sá Carneiro (Porto) Metro do Porto violet line E (direction Estádio do Dragão) links to downtown Porto (one-way €2, around 45 minutes). Alternatively, daytime taxis cost €20 to €25 to the centre and take an hour.
Aeroporto de Faro (Faro) Proximo city buses 14 and 16 run to the bus station (€2.25) every 30 minutes from June to August, slightly less frequently in low season. From the bus station, it's an easy stroll to the centre. A taxi costs around €20 (20 minutes).

Getting Around

Transport in Portugal is reasonably priced, quick and efficient.

Train Extremely affordable, with a decent network between major towns from north to south. Visit Comboios de Portugal (p314) for schedules and prices.

Car Useful for visiting small villages, national parks and other regions with minimal public transport. Cars can be hired in major towns and cities. Drive on the right.

Bus Cheaper and slower than trains. Useful for more remote villages that aren't serviced by trains. Infrequent service on weekends.

For more on **getting around**, see p310

Plan Your Trip
Hotspots for...

Food & Drink

Bountiful seafood, tender roast meats, freshly baked bread, creamy custard tarts and velvety wines are key staples in the everyday feast that is eating in Portugal.

ANNA_PUSTYNNIKOVA/SHUTTERSTOCK ©

Lisbon Portugal's capital has the greatest variety when it comes to dining, with top chefs plating up imaginative creations (p70).

Alma Taste the culinary creativity at one of Lisbon's best restaurants (p72).

Douro Valley The Unesco-listed Douro Valley (p193), where Portugal's finest wines are produced, can be toured by car or scenic train line.

Quinta do Crasto Try a fabulous vintage then a tour at this renowned winery (p197).

Algarve Seafood dominates menus along the coast (p135) and this is definitely bivalve zone, with hordes of fresh clams, oysters, mussels, cockles and whelks.

O Paulo *Cataplana*, a paella-like seafood stew, is served with sea views (p161).

Aquatic Adventures

Portugal's coastline is all about getting out onto or under the water, whether that be with a surfboard, with diving gear or on a boat.

WESTEND61/GETTY IMAGES ©

Algarve Portugal's south coast is the go-to spot for all manner of water-side fun, including eco-minded boat trips (p135).

Parque Natural da Ria Formosa Look for wildlife on a boat trip (p142).

Cabo de São Vicente Surfing is as big as the Atlantic's thundering waves at Portugal's southwestern-most tip (p167).

Sagres A surfing paradise (p170) and a great après-surf scene come sundown.

Aveiro The Atlantic's chilly waters come to you in the shape of a network of canals in this coastal settlement south of Porto (p239).

Boat Tours Take a canal trip aboard a *moliceiro*, a traditional boat (p242).

Architecture

Portugal possesses a wealth of architectural treasures, from the fairy-tale castles and palaces of Sintra to the Manueline creations of the 16th century.

DIMBAR76/SHUTTERSTOCK ©

Lisbon One of Europe's most attractive capitals, is a whirl of grand plazas, art-filled churches and cutting-edge design (p35).

Porto Portugal's second city has a trove of photo-genic buildings filled with dazzling hand-painted tiles (*azulejos*, pictured; p101).

Sintra A short hop from Lisbon, this area of wooded hills has some of the finest architectural monuments in the country (p87).

Mosteiro dos Jerónimos A superlative example (p44) of the Manueline style.

São Bento Train Station Beautifully adorned railway station (p113).

Palácio Nacional de Sintra An eye-catching palace (p90) with a medley of styles.

Art & Culture

Though small, Portugal's cultural landscape is pretty diverse, from Lisbon's melancholic fado music to avant-garde street art in Porto.

GEORGES DIEGUES/ALAMY STOCK PHOTO © ARTWORK BY OKER

Lisbon Portugal has given the world a very distinct type of music – the nostalgia-induced fado (p40), a style that emerged from its working-class districts.

Porto Portugal's northern city has vibrant arts scene, including some of the country's best street art (pictured; p119).

Coimbra This fabled university town with its own unique style of fado has a dynamic cultural calendar (p223).

The Alfama The epicentre of Lisbon's fado scene with iconic spots (p81).

Travessa de Cedofeita Start your explorations on this mural-dotted street (p119).

Queima das Fitas The end of the academic year brings street revelries (p236).

Plan Your Trip
Essential Portugal

Activities

Outdoors enthusiasts will find plenty to appreciate in Portugal. With a whopping 830km of coastline, Portugal has first-rate surfing all along the Atlantic's wild coast. There are also countless opportunities for all kinds of other water sports, particularly in the Algarve. The waves are legendary, and there are many schools and surf camps where, if you've never tried surfing, you can take a few lessons. Inland, rolling cork fields, granite peaks and precipitous river gorges form the backdrop for a host of other activities – from walking and birdwatching to horse riding, mountain biking and paragliding. Football (soccer) is a national obsession and watching a match is an exhilarating experience.

Shopping

Portugal is packed with lively markets, where you can browse the local wares. In the north, Barcelos hosts a particularly famous Thursday market. Crafts to look for in Portugal include ceramics (painted bowls, mini wine jugs) and tapestries. There's also great and quite affordable wine and port to be had. Weird and wonderful creations from cork are a common memento from Évora and the Algarve. Food such as salami, olive oil, cheese and myriad sweet things also make respectable souvenirs. For self-caterers and picnickers these markets also provide a trove of fresh and sometimes exotic produce.

Entertainment

Fado, that mournful, uniquely Portuguese sound, is famous in the capital where it was born. Lisbon naturally has a good range of dinner clubs and small restaurants where you can catch live shows by some of the best performers. Outside of Lisbon, and to a lesser extent Coimbra, fado is not as common. You'll find concerts (indie rock, pop, folk) at bigger towns throughout the year. Portugal is a country of festivals with something going on in the big cities, and even in some smaller ones, throughout

ROSSHELEN/GETTY IMAGES ©

the year, but especially over the summer months. English-language theatre is rare, even in Lisbon.

Eating

Settling down to a meal with friends is one of life's great pleasures for the Portuguese, who take pride in simple but flavourful dishes. Seafood, roast meats, freshly baked bread and velvety wines are key staples in the everyday feast that is eating in Portugal. Every region has its own distinct specialities and themes – the Algarve is known for its seafood and *cataplana* (seafood stew), the north for its pork dishes, the Estramadura for its fish stews and Lisbon for its variety. One aspect of Portuguese cuisine visitors should not miss is its coffee and cake culture.

Drinking & Nightlife

Lisbon and Porto both have vibrant bars, lounges and dance clubs – Lisbon's scene is now a major European stop for all top

★ **Lisbon Fado Houses**

A Tasca do Chico (p82)

Senhor fado (p82)

Parreirinha de Alfama (p82)

Mesa de Frades (p81)

A Baiuca (p82)

international DJs. In the Algarve, there's abundant nightlife all along the coast (Lagos is the epicentre for the party crowd) – drawing mostly a foreign clientele. Smaller cities such as Coimbra, Évora and Braga have smaller scenes, with a fairly laid-back vibe during the week, and livelier celebrations on weekends. In the small towns, things are generally pretty sedate.

From left: Fans of the Portuguese football team; street dining in Ribeira (p108)

Plan Your Trip
Month by Month

MAURO RODRIGUES/ALAMY STOCK PHOTO ©

February

Winter sees fewer crowds and lower prices along with abundant rainfall, particularly in the north. Coastal temperatures are cool but mild, while inland there are frigid days. Many resorts remain shuttered until spring.

✿ Carnaval

Portugal's Carnaval features much merry-making in the pre-Lenten celebrations. Loulé boasts the best parades, but Lisbon, Nazaré and Viana do Castelo all throw a good bash.

✿ Fantasporto

Porto's world-renowned two-week international festival (www.fantasporto.com) celebrates fantasy, horror and just plain weird films.

✿ Essência do Vinho

Oenophiles are in their element at this wine gathering (www.essenciadovinhoporto.com), held in late February in the sublime setting of Palácio da Bolsa in Porto. Some 3000 wines from 350 producers are available for tasting.

April

Spring arrives, bringing warmer temperatures and abundant sunshine in both the north and the south. Late April sees a profusion of wild flowers in the south.

✿ Semana Santa

The build-up to Easter is magnificent in saintly Braga. During Holy Week, barefoot penitents walk through the streets, past rows of makeshift altars, with an explosion of jubilation at the cathedral on the eve of Easter.

✿ Festival Internacional do Chocolate

From late April to early May, Óbidos celebrates the sweet temptation of the cacao bean (www.festivalchocolate.cm-obidos.pt).

May

Lovely sunny weather and the lack of peak-season crowds make May an ideal time to visit. The beaches of the Algarve awake from their slumber and see a smattering of travellers passing through.

MAURO RODRIGUES/SHUTTERSTOCK ©

🎊 Queima das Fitas

Join the mayhem of the Burning of the Ribbons at the University of Coimbra, as students celebrate the end of the academic year with concerts, a parade and copious amounts of drinking (www.facebook.com/queimadasfitascoimbra).

🎊 Festa das Cruzes

Barcelos turns into a fairground of flags, flowers, coloured lights and open-air concerts at the Festival of the Crosses. The biggest days are 1 to 3 May. Monsanto, in the Beiras, also celebrates, with singing and dancing beside a medieval castle.

🎊 Festa do Mar

Celebrating the age-old love of the sea (and the patron saints of fishers), this lively festival brings a flotilla of fishing boats to Nazaré's harbour, as well as a colourful parade of elaborately decorated floats. There's plenty of eating and drinking.

★ Best Festivals

Carnaval, February
Serralves em Festa, May
Fado no Castelo, June
Festa de Santo António, June
Festa de São João, June

☆ Serralves em Festa

This huge cultural event runs for 50 hours non-stop over a weekend. Parque de Serralves (p118) hosts the main events, with concerts, avant-garde theatre and kids' activities. Other open-air events happen all over town.

June

Early summer is one of the liveliest times to visit, as the festival calendar is packed. Warm, sunny days are the norm, and while tourism picks up, the hordes have yet to arrive.

From left: Mercado Medieval; Carnaval, Loulé.

☆ Fado no Castelo

Lisbon's love affair with fado reaches a high point at this annual songfest held at the cinematic Castelo de São Jorge over three evenings in June.

🎎 Festa do Corpo de Deus

This religious fest happens all across northern Portugal on Corpus Christi but is liveliest in Monção, with a medieval fair, theatrical shows and over-the-top processions.

☆ Festival Med

Loulé's world-music festival (www.facebook. com/festivalmedloule), held over three days, brings more than 50 bands playing an incredible variety of music. World cuisine accompanies the global beats.

🎎 Festa de Santo António

The lively Festival of St Anthony is celebrated with fervour in Lisbon's Alfama and Madragoa districts, with feasting, drinking and dancing in some 50 *arraiais* (street parties).

🎎 Festa de São João

St John is the favourite up north, where Porto (p125), Braga and Vila do Conde celebrate with elaborate processions, music and feasting, while folks go around whacking each other with plastic hammers.

🎎 Feira de São João

Évora also hosts the feast day of São João, though plastic hammers are (thankfully) absent. The lively 10-day event kicks off in late June, and features a traditional fairground, art exhibitions, gourmet food and drink, cultural events and sporting competitions.

July

The summer heat arrives, bringing sunseekers who pack the resorts of the Algarve. Lisbon and Porto also swell with crowds and prices peak in July and August.

☆ Festival Internacional de Folclore

The week-long International Folk Festival in late July brings costumed dancers and traditional groups to Porto.

⚔ Mercado Medieval

Don your armour and head to the castle grounds for this lively two-week medieval fair (www.mercadomedievalobidos.pt) in Óbidos. Attractions include wandering minstrels, jousting matches and plenty of grog. Other medieval fairs are held in Silves and other castle towns.

August

The mercury shoots up in August, with sweltering days best spent at the beach. This is Portugal's busiest tourist month, and reserving well ahead is essential.

🎎 Festival do Marisco

Seafood-lovers should not miss this grand culinary fest (www.festivaldomarisco.com) in Olhão. Highlights include regional specialities such as chargrilled fish, *caldeirada* (fish stew) and *cataplana* (a kind of Portuguese paella); there's also live music.

☆ Folkfaro

A musician's treat, Folkfaro (www.folkfaro. com) brings local and international folk performers to the city of Faro for staged and impromptu performances across town. Street fairs accompany the event.

🎎 Festa da Ria

Aveiro celebrates its canals and *moliceiros* (traditional boats) in late August. Highlights include folk dancing and a *moliceiro* race, plus competitions for the best *moliceiro* murals.

December

Expect rain and colder temperatures, particularly in the north, but there's plenty of good cheer, with massive Nativity scenes in plazas across the country, and lively holiday markets.

🎎 New Year's Eve

Ring in the *ano novo* (new year) in Lisbon with fireworks, free concerts and DJs at this celebration down by the river.

Plan Your Trip
Get Inspired

Read

O Manual dos Inquisidores (The Inquisitor's Manual; António Lobo Antunes, 1996) Story about life under the Salazar dictatorship.

Memorial do Convento (Baltasar and Blimunda; José Saramago, 1982) Darkly comic 18th-century love story.

Livro do Desassossego (The Book of Disquiet; Fernando Pessoa, 1982) Literary masterpiece by Portugal's greatest poet.

Portugal: A Companion History (José Hermano Saraiva, 1997) An easily digestible history of the country, written for the non-expert.

Food of Portugal (Jean Anderson, 1986) One of the best English-language Portuguese cookbooks.

Watch

Lisbon Story (1994) Wim Wenders' love letter to Lisbon.

Letters from Fontainhas (1997–2006) Pedro Costa's art-house trilogy set in Lisbon.

Capitães de Abril (Captains of April; 2000) Overview of the 1974 Revolution of the Carnations.

Sangre de mi Sangre (Blood of My Blood; 2011) Oscar-nominated drama about the intricacies of life in poor suburban Lisbon.

Listen

Mariza (2018) Latest album by fado superstar Mariza.

The Art of Amália (1998) Compilation by one of fado's greats, Amália Rodrigues.

Best of Rui Veloso (2000) Portugal's legendary rock-balladeer.

10.000 Anos Depois Entre Vénus e Marte (10,000 Years Later Between Venus and Mars; 1978) José Cid's famous and oh-so '70s progressive rock album.

Above: Mariza performing live

Plan Your Trip
Five-Day Itineraries

Lisbon & Around

Base yourself in Portugal's fascinating capital and explore its Manueline architecture, fado houses and museums before heading out to the forest-lined vistas of Sintra, the walled town of Óbidos and the monastery at Batalha. This entire itinerary is possible by public transport.

③

④

Batalha (p261) A major monastery dating from the 15th century, but with many later Manueline additions making it one of the country's top architectural marvels.

④

Óbidos (p251) A quaintly beautiful walled town with heaps of architecture, interesting boutiques and a laid-back vibe.
🚌 50min to Batalha

③

Sintra (p87) A dramatic area of wooded hills, palaces and castles within easy reach of Lisbon. 🚌 40min to Lisbon then 🚌 1hr to Óbidos

②

Lisbon (p35) Two days of vintage trams, fado, thumping nightlife, monasteries and museums.
🚌 40min to Sintra

①

South Coast

Sand, seafood and surfing define Portugal's holiday coast. The Algarve is an incredibly popular destination among the British, but it's not all about Irish pubs and fish 'n' chips – there's plenty of beauty and culture to discover, too.

Lagos (p149) This busy resort city has a superb beach, great nightlife and a tightly packed historical centre.
🚌 1hr to Sagres

Sagres & Cabo de São Vicente (p163) Portugal's southwesternmost tip is a surfing centre as well as being steeped in history relating to the Age of Discoveries.

Faro (p146) Historical Faro is the buzzing gateway to the Algarve as well as the amazing Parque Natural da Ria Formosa. 🚌 2hr to Lagos

❶ Tavira (p144) This eastern Algarve town is one of the coast's most charming. Take a day trip to the Ilha de Tavira.
🚌 1hr to Faro

FROM LEFT: FRANCESCO RICCARDO IACOMINO/GETTY IMAGES ©; JOYFULL/SHUTTERSTOCK ©

Plan Your Trip
10-Day Itinerary

Porto & Around

Red wine, baroque architecture and fabulous scenery are a few highlights of this memorable ramble through Portugal's north. After getting an eyeful of beauty in Porto and Braga, hire a car for a five-day road trip through the dramatic scenery of the Douro Valley.

Braga (p209) Portugal's third-largest city is a place of narrow lanes, baroque churches, religious festivals and one remarkable cathedral.
🚗 1hr to Amarante

Porto (p101) Spend two days exploring this fascinating city, visiting historical Ribeira, azulejo-covered churches and the Museu da Misericórdia do Porto. 10min walk to Vila Nova de Gaia

Vila Nova de Gaia (p110) This hillside across the river from the city centre is where you'll find Porto's oldest wine lodges. 🚌 1hr to Braga

Amarante (p206) Visit an art-filled monastery, stroll beside pretty riverbanks and sample local delicacies.
🚗 1hr to Lamego

Pinhão (p200) A fine base for vineyard tours, nature walks and indulging in great food and wine.
🚗 1½hrs to Parque Arqueológico do Vale do Côa

Parque Arqueológico do Vale do Côa (p203) Explore the most impressive Palaeolithic site in Iberia on a guided tour.

Lamego (p205) Explore the picturesque old centre, then make the ascent up the country's most famous tile-covered stairway.
🚗 45min to Pinhão

Plan Your Trip
Two-Week Itinerary

North to South

This odyssey from north to south takes in the vast majority of Portugal's major sights, including Lisbon, Porto and the Algarve. This journey is perfectly feasible by bus and train, but a hire car will, of course, speed things up considerably.

Porto (p101) Spend at least two days sampling Porto's heady mix of port wine, *azulejos* and impressive riverside location. 🚉 1¼hr to Coimbra

Coimbra (p223) Call in at the hilltop Velha Universidade (Old University) before enjoying some student nightlife and Coimbra's own take on fado. 🚉 2hr to Lisbon

Lisbon (p35) You'll need at least three days to cover the basics in Lisbon, with regular breaks for the city's signature egg custard tarts. 🚌 2hr to Évora

Évora (p177) Few Portuguese cities boast the diversity of architecture that Évora does. A ring of defensive town walls contains Roman and medieval sites. 🚉 4hr to Faro

Sagres & Cabo de São Vicente (p163) The dramatic cliffs at Cabo de São Vicente mark Europe's most southwesterly point. It's also a big surfing location.

Faro (p146) The de facto capital of the Algarve has history, food, architecture and an easy-going vibe. 🚉 to Lagos then 🚌 to Sagres 5hr

Plan Your Trip
Family Travel

Portugal for Kids

The great thing about Portugal for children is its manageable size and the range of sights and activities on offer. There's so much to explore and to catch the imagination, even for those with very short attention spans.

The Algarve has to be the best kid-pleasing destination in Portugal, with endless beaches, zoos, water parks, zand boat trips. Kids will also be happy in Lisbon and its outlying provinces. There are trams, puppet shows, a huge aquarium, a toy museum, horse-drawn carriages, castles, parks and playgrounds.

As for fairy-tale places, Portugal has these in spades. Some children enjoy visiting churches if it means they can light a candle, and they'll enjoy the make-believe of the castles and palaces sprinkled about the country. In towns, hop-on, hop-off tours can be good for saving small legs, and miniature resort trains often cause more excitement than you would have thought possible.

Kids are welcome just about everywhere and the Portuguese are naturally very kind towards them. They can even get literary: the late Nobel Prize–winning author José Saramago wrote a charming children's fable, *The Tale of the Unknown Island*.

Portugal for Babies

o The Portuguese are generally quite laid-back about breast-feeding in public as long as some attempt at discretion is made.

o Formula (including organic brands) and disposable nappies are widely available at most pharmacies and grocery stores.

o *Turismos,* as well as most hotels and guest houses, can recommend babysitters.

o Keep your baby hydrated in the summer months, especially on the beaches of the Algarve and in big cities like Lisbon and Porto.

Eating with Kids

Portuguese restaurateurs are always glad to see junior diners. Kids portions are almost always available, a high chair can always be found somewhere and staff are very friendly

NUNO VALADAS/GETTY IMAGES ©

and forgiving towards children. Less formal cafes and bakeries are superb places to feed tots – we've yet to encounter a child in Portugal who hadn't discovered the joys of a *pastel de nata* (custard tart)! A glass of warm milk can cost as little as €0.50 and kids love the freshly squeezed juices.

Getting Around

Children aged under five years travel free; those aged five to 12 years pay half price. This is true on the trains but bus drivers on local services will often just wave you to a seat when they see a child getting on. Journeys are rarely long enough for restlessness to set in; long-distance coaches always have a toilet on board.

Annoyances

Nothing is ever perfect and there are aspects of family travel in Portugal that irk some.

o The message about kids and sugar hasn't quite reached Portugal. Often children's drinks come with extra sachets of sugar.

★ Best for Kids

Museu de Arte, Arquitetura e Tecnologia (p61) Inquisitive minds will love the scientific exhibitions here.

Oceanário de Lisboa (p63) Fishy fun in the Portuguese capital.

Museu da Marioneta (p59) Kids can play puppeteer for the day at this Lisbon puppet museum.

Algarve Beaches (p138) Sandcastle fun on Portugal's finest strands.

Aveiro Boat Trips (p242) Kids will love the brightly coloured boats and messing about on the water.

o Some Portuguese have the habit of ruffling the hair of blond children in the street – some parents may not be comfortable with this.

From left: Child enjoying Portuguese desserts; Oceanário de Lisboa (p63)

Castelo de São Jorge (p55)

LISBON

Río Tejo

Lisbon at a Glance...

Spread across steep hillsides that overlook the Rio Tejo, Lisbon has captivated visitors for centuries. Windswept vistas reveal the city in all its beauty: Roman and Moorish ruins, white-domed cathedrals, grand plazas. However, the real delight of discovery is delving into the narrow cobblestone lanes. As yellow trams clatter through tree-lined streets, lisboêtas stroll through lamp-lit old quarters. Gossip is exchanged over wine at tiny restaurants as fado singers perform in the background. In other neighbourhoods, Lisbon reveals her youthful alter ego at bohemian bars and late-night street parties. Just outside Lisbon there are woodlands, beaches and seaside villages to discover.

Two Days in Lisbon

Explore **Alfama** (p42), Lisbon's old town, on day one, perhaps taking a ride on old tram 28 part of the way. Round off with a fado performance (p40) in the evening. On day two explore Belém (p61) and the **Mosteiro dos Jerónimos** (p44). In the evening sample some of Lisbon's famous nightlife (p38).

Four Days in Lisbon

On day three hit the museums – Lisbon has plenty dedicated to a range of subjects, but one highlight is the **Museu Nacional do Azulejo** (p46) packed with traditional tiles. On day four catch the train to Sintra (p87) to spend the whole day walking through the boulder-speck-led woodlands to fairy-tale palaces.

Aeroporto de
Lisboa (1km)

Gare do Oriente
Train Station

Baixa & Rossio
The city's spiritual
heart captivates with
its must-see sights and
handsome plazas, old-
school speciality shops
and little *ginjinha* bars.

Parque das Nações
This riverside district
shines with outdoor
art, futuristic archi-
tecture and Europe's
second-biggest
aquarium.

**Museu Nacional
do Azulejo**

Santa Apolónia
Train Station

**Alfama, Castelo &
Graça**
Discover fado, char-
acterful backstreets
and viewpoints in this
trio of castle-crowned
neighbourhoods.

Cais do Sodré
Train & Metro
Station

The Alfama

Bairro Alto & Chiado
Browse boutique shops,
ride vintage funiculars
to *miradouros* and hit
Lisbon's most happen-
ing bars in these central
neighbourhoods.

Rio Tejo

Convento do Carmo (p51)

Elevador de
Santa Justa (p54)

Largo Martim Moniz

Ponte 25 de Abril (p39)

Igreja de São Roque (p47)

Marquês de Pombal & Around
Top museums, pristine gardens and some of Lisbon's best restaurants lure you to these lesser-known neighbourhoods.

Lapa & Alcântara
A world-class ancient art museum, streets with low-key, leafy charm and dockside nightlife entice in these neighbourhoods.

Sete Rios
Train Station

Rodoviário de Sete Rios

Parque Florestal de Monsanto

Campolide

Parque Eduardo VII

Belém
A Unesco-listed monastery, Manueline monuments and contemporary art await in this nautical neighbourhood by the river.

Alcântara-Terra

Belém Train Station

Mosteiro dos Jeronimos

Príncipe Real, Santos & Estrela
Serene tree-fringed neighbourhoods, dotted with boutique hotels, art galleries and antique shops.

0 2 km
0 1 mile
N

Praça do Comércio (p50)

Arriving in Lisbon

Aeroporto de Lisboa Direct flights to major international hubs including London, New York, Paris and Frankfurt.

Sete Rios bus station The main long-distance bus terminal.

Gare do Oriente bus station Bus services to the north and to Spain.

Gare do Oriente train station Lisbon's largest train station.

Santa Apolónia train station The terminal for trains from northern and central Portugal.

Where to Stay

Lisbon has an array of boutique hotels, upmarket hostels and both modern and old-fashioned guest houses. Be sure to book ahead for high season (July to September). A word to those with weak knees and/or heavy bags: many guest houses lack lifts, meaning you'll have to haul your luggage up three flights or more. If this disconcerts, be sure to book a place with a lift. For more information on the best neighbourhoods to stay, see p85.

Lisbon cabaret bar

Lisbon Nightlife

Late-night street parties in Cais do Sodré and Bairro Alto, sunset ginjinhas on Rossio's sticky cobbles, drinks with indie kids in Santa Catarina – Lisbon has one of Europe's most eclectic nightlife scenes.

Great For...

☑ **Don't Miss**

Savour a craft cocktail at **Cinco Lounge** (Map p60; www.cincolounge.com; Rua Ruben António Leitão 17; ⊘9pm-2am) courtesy of an award-winning, London-born mixologist.

Cais do Sodré

For years Cais do Sodré was the haunt of whisky-slugging sailors craving after-dark sleaze. In late 2011, the district went from seedy to stylish. Rua Nova do Carvalho was painted pink and the call girls were sent packing, but the edginess and decadence on which Lisbon thrives remains. Now party central, it hass boho bars, live-music venues and burlesque clubs that are perfect for a late-night bar crawl. When someone refers to Pink Street, they mean here.

Bairro Alto & Harbour Area

Bairro Alto is the epicenter of Lisbon's liveliest street party, gathering a wide cross section of revelers to its narrow lanes each evening. At dusk, the nocturnal hedonist rears its head with bars trying

Rua Nova do Carvalho

MAICASAA/SHUTTERSTOCK ©

ⓘ Need to Know

Top nightlife neighbourhoods are Cais do Sodré, Bairro Alto, Alfama and the harbour area.

✕ Take a Break

There are countless places to eat amid the revelry. On bar-lined Rua Nova do Carvalho, **Povo** (Map p52; ☏213 473 403; www.povolisboa.com; Rua Nova do Carvalho 32; small plates €7.50-16; ⊗6pm-2am Sun-Wed, to 4am Thu-Sat) serves excellent Portuguese *petiscos* (tapas), and there's often live music.

★ Top Tip

Locals don't even think about showing up at a club before 2am.

to out-decibel each other, hash peddlers lurking in the shadows and kamikaze taxi drivers forcing kerbside sippers to leap aside. For a more sophisticated and more artistically minded crowd, head a few blocks south to Bica.

The dockside duo of Doca de Alcântara and Doca de Santo Amaro harbour wall-to-wall bars with a preclubbing vibe. Many occupy revamped warehouses, with terraces facing the river and the lit-up **Ponte 25 de Abril**. Most people taxi here, but you can take the train from Cais do Sodré to Alcântara Mar or catch tram 15 from Praça da Figueira.

Clubbing Tips

Though getting into clubs is not as much of a beauty contest as it is in other capitals,

you'll stand a better chance of slipping past the fashion police if you dress smartish and don't rock up on your lonesome. Most clubs charge entry (around €5 to €20, which usually includes a drink or two) and some operate a card-stamping system to ensure you spend a minimum amount. Many close Sunday and Monday.

Keep in mind club security has the right to dramatically inflate cover charges (€250 in some cases!) in order to discourage entry for those they deem to be potential trouble, whether due to level of intoxication or any other reason. Yes, it's discriminatory, but unfortunately it's perfectly legal.

Something Different

Nightlife in Alfama revolves mostly around fado – the neighbourhood packs in a wide variety of atmospheric live-music venues. Just north of Bairro Alto, Príncipe Real is the epicentre of Lisbon's gay scene and home to some quirky drinking dens.

Fado singer Pedro Galveias performing in Mouraria

PATRICIA DE MELO MOREIRA/AFP/GETTYIMAGES ©

Fado

Portugal's most famous style of music is fado (Portuguese for 'fate'), a simple, wistful genre that emerged in the 19th-century working-class neighbourhoods of Lisbon.

Great For...

☑ Don't Miss

The greatest fadista, Amália Rodrigues, was given a place in the Panteão Nacional.

Soulful Sounds

No visit to the Portuguese world is complete without an evening of fado music, the traditional music of Lisbon. A performance in a typical fado house provides an insight into the Portuguese soul, the lilting guitar and vocals evoking a melancholic yearning for the past.

A Fado Primer

Although fado is something of a national treasure – in 2011 it was added to Unesco's list of the World's Intangible Cultural Heritage – it's really the music of Lisbon (Coimbra has its own, slightly different version). Fados are traditionally sung by one performer accompanied by a 12-string Portuguese *guitarra* (pear-shaped guitar). When two *fadistas* (singers of traditional

Traditional Portuguese guitar

MAURO RODRIGUES/SHUTTERSTOCK ©

classes took an interest and brought it into the mainstream. Fado's popularity slipped in the post-revolution days, when the Portuguese were eager to make a clean break with the past. (Salazar spoke of throwing the masses the three Fs – fado, football and Fátima – to keep them happily occupied.) The 1990s, however, saw a resurgence of fado's popularity, with the opening of new fado houses and the emergence of new performers.

Amália Rodrigues

One singer who played a major role in its popularisation was Amália Rodrigues, the 'queen of fado', who became a household name in the 1940s. Born to a poor family in 1920, Amália took the music from the tavern to the concert hall, and then into households via radio and onto film screens, starring in the 1947 film *Capas Negras* (Black Capes).

Cover Charges & Menus

Most fado places have a minimum cover charge of €15 to €25, though a fixed menu can cost up to €50. The quality of food can be hit and miss; if in doubt, it might be worth asking whether you can just order a bottle of wine.

Portuguese song) perform, they sometimes engage in *desgarrada*, a bit of improvisational one-upmanship where the singers challenge and play off one another. At fado houses there are usually a number of singers, each one traditionally singing three songs.

History of Fado

No one quite knows fado's origins, though African and Brazilian rhythms, Moorish chants and the songs of Provençal troubadours may have influenced the sound. What is clear is that by the 19th century fado could be heard all over the working-class neighbourhoods of Mouraria and Alfama. It was the anthem of the poor and it maintained an unsavoury reputation until the late 19th century, when the upper

Walking Tour: Exploring Alfama

This scenic route starts on tram 28 from Largo Martim Moniz or the Baixa, taking in the city's best tram route and avoiding uphill slogs. Take the tram up to Largo da Graça. From here, stroll north and turn left behind the barracks to Miradouro da Senhora do Monte.

Start Miradouro da Senhora do Monte
Distance 3km
Duration Two to three hours

1 The views of the city's red roofs from Lisbon's highest lookout point, **Miradouro da Senhora do Monte**, are simply breathtaking.

4 Towering dramatically above Lisbon, the mid-11th-century hilltop fortifications of **Castelo de São Jorge** sneak into almost every snapshot. One of the city's top attractions.

Take a Break...
Cruzes Credo Café (Rua Cruzes da Sé 29; ⊘ noon-midnight) is a handy stop for a drink.

6 The 12th-century, fortress-like **Sé de Lisboa** was built on the site of a mosque soon after Christians recaptured the city from the Moors.

7 The urban space, **Praça do Comércio**, claims to be Europe's largest square, though it has many rivals.

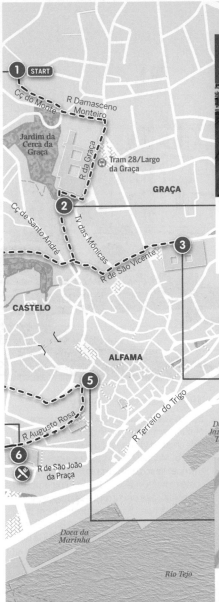

Cç do Monte

R Damasceno
Monteiro

Jardim da
Cerca da
Graça

R da Graça

Tram 28/Largo
da Graça

GRAÇA

Cç de Santo André

Tv das Mónicas

R de São Vicente

CASTELO

Santa
Apolónia

ALFAMA

R Terreiro do Trigo

R Augusto Rosa

R de São João
da Praça

Doca do
Jardim do
Tabaco

Doca da
Marinha

Rio Tejo

Classic Photo
An old yellow tram 28 hauling itself
up to Largo da Graça.

2 From the Miradouro da Senhora
do Monte walk south and right to
pine-shaded **Miradouro da Graça**,
where central Lisbon spreads out
before you.

3 The exquisitely tiled interiors of
Mosteiro de São Vicente de Fora
house an eerie mausoleum holding
the tombs of Portugal's last kings.

5 There are more fine vistas from
bougainvillea-clad lookout point
Miradouro de Santa Luzia.

0 — 400 m
0 — 0.2 miles

SAIKO3P/SHUTTERSTOCK ©

Mosteiro dos Jerónimos

One of Lisbon's top attractions, this photogenic Unesco-listed monastery is a dazzling example of the elaborate Manueline style looming large in the seaside district of Belém.

Great For...

☑ Don't Miss

The main entrance doorway (*portal principal*) with its exquisite carvings of Catholic saints and Portuguese royals.

The Monastery's Story

Belém's undisputed heart-stealer is the stuff of pure fantasy: a fusion of Diogo de Boitaca's creative vision and the spice and pepper dosh of Manuel I, who commissioned it to trumpet Vasco da Gama's discovery of a sea route to India in 1498. The building embodies the golden age of Portuguese discoveries and was funded using the profits from the spices Vasco da Gama brought back from the subcontinent. It was begun in 1502 but not completed for almost a century. Wrought for the glory of God, Jerónimos was once populated by monks of the Order of St Jerome, whose spiritual job for four centuries was to comfort sailors and pray for the king's soul. The monastery withstood the 1755 earthquake but fell into disrepair when the order was dissolved in 1833. It was later used as a school and orphanage until about 1940.

CASSINGA/GETTY IMAGES ©

❶ Need to Know

Map p62; www.mosteirojeronimos.pt; Praça do Império; adult/child €10/5, free Sun until 2pm for Portuguese citizens/residents only; ◷10am-6.30pm Tue-Sun Jun-Sep, to 5.30pm Oct-May

✕ Take a Break

Enoteca de Belém (Map p62; 🖉213 631 511; www.travessadaermida.com; Tv do Marta Pinto 10; mains €17-20; ◷1-11pm; 🛜) serves modernised Portuguese classics, matched by an excellent wine selection.

★ Top Tip

On Sundays and holidays, admission is free from 10am to 2pm.

In 2007 the now much-discussed Treaty of Lisbon was signed here.

The Church

On entering the church through the western portal, you'll notice tree-trunk-like columns that seem to grow into the ceiling, which is itself a spiderweb of stone. Windows cast a soft golden light over the church. Superstar Vasco da Gama is interred in the lower chancel, just left of the entrance, opposite venerated 16th-century poet Luís Vaz de Camões. From the upper choir, there's a superb view of the church; the rows of seats are Portugal's first Renaissance woodcarvings.

Vasco Da Gama

Born in Alentejo in the 1460s, Vasco da Gama was the first European explorer to reach India by ship. This was a key moment in Portuguese history as it opened up trading links to Asia and established Portugal's maritime empire, the wealth from which made the country into a world superpower. Da Gama died from malaria on his third voyage to India in 1524.

The Cloisters

There's nothing like the moment you walk into the honey-stone Manueline cloisters, which drip with organic detail in their delicately scalloped arches, twisting auger-shell turrets and columns intertwined with leaves, vines and knots. It will simply wow. Keep an eye out for symbols of the age such as the armillary sphere and the cross of the Military Order, plus gargoyles and fantastical beasties on the upper balustrade.

MARCIN JAMROWSKI/ADVENTURE PICTURES/ALAMY STOCK PHOTO ©

Azulejos & Museu Nacional do Azulejo

Few visitors fail to be impressed by the exquisite tiles the Portuguese have traditionally used to decorate their buildings. There's even a museum that tells the story of these azulejos.

Great For...

☑ **Don't Miss**

The museum shop has a superb range of ceramic souvenirs and beautiful coffee-table books.

Azulejos

Portugal's favourite decorative art is easy to spot. Polished painted tiles called *azulejos* (after the Arabic *al zulaycha*, meaning 'polished stone') cover everything from churches to train stations. The Moors introduced the art, having picked it up from the Persians, but the Portuguese wholeheartedly adopted it.

Portugal's earliest tiles are Moorish, from Seville. These were decorated with interlocking geometric or floral patterns. After the Portuguese captured Ceuta in Morocco in 1415, they began exploring the art themselves. The 16th-century Italian invention of maiolica, in which colours are painted directly onto wet clay over a layer of white enamel, gave works a fresco-like brightness.

Mosteiro de São Vicente de Fora (p59)

ⓘ Need to Know

☏ 218 100 340; www.museudoazulejo.pt; Rua Madre de Deus 4; adult/child €5/free; ⊙10am-6pm Tue-Sun

✕ Take a Break

You can enjoy classic Portuguese dishes, savoury crepes and desserts at the museum's on-site restaurant.

★ Top Tip

Pick up the audio guide for a deeper understanding of the art and history of the *azulejo*.

The earliest home-grown examples date from the 1580s, and may be seen in churches such as Lisbon's Igreja de São Roque, providing an ideal counterbalance to fussy baroque.

The late 17th century saw a fashion for huge panels depicting everything from saints to seascapes. As demand grew, mass production became necessary and the Netherlands' blue-and-white Delft tiles started appearing.

Portuguese tile makers rose to the challenge of this influx, and the splendid work of virtuosos António de Oliveira Bernardes and his son Policarpo in the 18th century springs from this competitive creativity. You can see their work in Évora, in the Igreja de São João (p181).

By the end of the 18th century, industrial-scale manufacture began to affect quality.

There was also massive demand for tiles after the 1755 Lisbon earthquake. From the late 19th century, the art nouveau and art deco movements took *azulejos* by storm, providing fantastic facades and interiors for shops, restaurants and residential buildings. Today, *azulejos* still coat contemporary life.

The Museum

Housed in a sublime 16th-century convent, Lisbon's **Museu Nacional do Azulejo** covers the entire *azulejo* spectrum. Star exhibits feature a 36m-long panel depicting pre-earthquake Lisbon, a Manueline cloister with web-like vaulting and exquisite blue-and-white *azulejos* and a gold-smothered baroque chapel. Here you'll find every kind of *azulejo* imaginable, from early Ottoman geometry to zinging altars, and from scenes of lords a-hunting to Goan intricacies. Bedecked with food-inspired *azulejos* – ducks, pigs and the like – the restaurant opens onto a vine-clad courtyard

ALLAN BAXTER/GETTY IMAGES ©

Lisbon's Trams

For a quintessentially Lisbon experience, don't leave the city without riding one of the city's typical yellow trams. Tram 28, which climbs through Alfama, is a must for every visitor.

Great For...

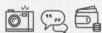

☑ **Don't Miss**

In addition to tram 28, other city-centre tram routes include 12, 15, 18 and 25.

Lisbon's Old Trams

Lisbon's vintage yellow trams are a nostalgic throwback to the early days of urban public transport and would have long since been pensioned off to a transport museum in most other European countries. They have survived largely because they were specially designed for a specific task – to trundle up and down central Lisbon's steep gradients (just like their San Francisco cousins) and would be much too expensive to replace. These roller-coaster trams date from the 1930s and are called *remodelados* (remodelled). The name comes from the fact that the cars were slightly upgraded in the 1990s to include such luxuries as late 20th-century brakes. There were once 27 lines in the city, but after the construction of the metro, the system went into decline. Today

KIEVVICTOR/SHUTTERSTOCK ©

there are only five lines left – *remodelados* run on all of them.

Tram Stops & Fares

Lisbon's tram stops are marked by a small yellow *paragem* (stop) sign hanging from a lamp post or from the overhead wires. You'll pay more for a tram ride if you buy your ticket on board rather than purchasing a prepaid card. On-board one-way prices are €2.85, but a day pass costs just €6 and is valid on all of the city's public transport for 24 hours.

Pickpockets

With groups of tourists crammed into a small space, sadly tram 28 is a happy hunting ground for pickpockets. Take the usual precautions to avoid being parted from your possessions.

Tram 28

Famous tram 28, Lisbon's longest tram route, is extremely popular with tourists as it heads through Baixa, Graça, Alfama and Estrela, climbing the steep hill from Baixa to the castle and Alfama as well as three of the city's seven other hills en route. There are 34 stops between Campo Ourique in the west of the city centre to Martim Monique, though the most interesting section is between Estrela and Graça. Trams depart every 11 minutes, though the last leaves fairly early (around 9pm). The experience on the museum-piece tram can be an uncomfortable one for some, with varnished wooden benches, steps and crowds of tourists getting in each other's way. But it's worth it for the ride, there's no cheaper tour in town and it's a great option to take when the weather is not playing ball.

◉ SIGHTS

On Lisbon's riverfront is the grand Praça do Comércio. Behind it march the pedestrian-filled streets of Baixa (lower) district, up to Praça da Figueira and Praça Dom Pedro IV (aka Rossio). From Baixa it's a steep climb west, through swanky shopping district Chiado, into the narrow streets of nightlife-haven Bairro Alto. The Unesco World Heritage Sites of Belém lie further west along the river – an easy tram ride from Praça do Comércio. Eastwards from the Baixa it's another climb to Castelo de São Jorge and the Moorish, labyrinthine Alfama district around it.

◉ Baixa & Rossio

Arco da Rua Augusta   Landmark

(Map p52; Rua Augusta 2-10; €3; ☉9am-8pm)
This triumphal arch was built in the wake of the 1755 earthquake. A lift whisks you to the top, where fine views of Praça do Comércio, the Rio Tejo and Castelo de São Jorge await. Admission for kids under five years is free.

**Núcleo Arqueológico
da Rua dos Correeiros**   Ruins

(Map p52; ✆211 131 004; http://ind.millennium bcp.pt; Rua Augusta 96; ☉10am-noon & 2-5pm Mon-Sat) **FREE** Hidden under the Millennium BCP bank building are layers of ruins dating from the Iron Age, discovered on a 1991 parking-lot dig. Fundacao Millennium runs fascinating archaeologist-led tours (booking ahead is highly recommended) that descend into the depths – in English or Portuguese (departing on the hour and depending on bookings). The extremely well-done site is now rightfully a National Monument.

Praça do Comércio   Plaza

(Terreiro do Paço; Map p52; Praça do Comércio)
With its grand 18th-century arcades, lemon-meringue facades and mosaic cobbles, the riverfront Praça do Comércio is a square to out-pomp them all. Everyone arriving by boat used to disembark here, and it still feels like the gateway to Lisbon, thronging with activity and rattling trams.

Basílica da Estrela (p59)

ARTFOTOSS/GETTY IMAGES ©

Igreja de São Domingos — Church
(Map p52; www.patriarcado-lisboa.pt; Largo de São Domingos; ⓘ7.30am-7pm) **FREE** It's a miracle that this baroque church dating to 1241 still stands, having barely survived the 1755 earthquake, then fire in 1959. Its sea of tea lights illuminates gashed pillars, battered walls and ethereal sculptures in its musty yet enchanting interior. Note the Star of David memorial outside, marking the spot of a bloody anti-Semitic massacre in 1506.

Museu de Design e da Moda — Museum
(Mude; Map p52; www.mude.pt; Rua Augusta 24; ⓘ10am-6pm Tue-Sun) This Baixa star, set in a cavernous former bank, contains furniture, industrial design and couture dating from the 1930s. It was closed for renovations at the time of writing and will reopen with an admission fee (it was previously free). Highlights include iconic furniture by Charles Eames, Frank Gehry and Brazil's Campana Brothers, plus haute couture by the likes of Givenchy, Christian Dior and Balenciaga.

Museu do Dinheiro — Museum
(Map p52; www.museudodinheiro.pt; Largo de São Julião; ⓘ10am-6pm Wed-Sat) **FREE** Pop into Banco do Portugal's money museum to see the stunning €34-million interior renovation of the once-mighty São Julião church (closed in 1933), and the more notable **Interpretation Centre for King Dinis' Wall**, a preserved 30m expanse of the 13th-century medieval city wall, located in the church's former crypt and discovered during a 2010 excavation.

Lisbon Story Centre — Museum
(Map p52; www.lisboastorycentre.pt; Praça do Comércio 78-81; adult/child €7/3; ⓘ10am-8pm) This museum takes visitors on a 60-minute journey through Lisbon's history, from its early foundation (pre-ancient Roman days) to modern times. An audio guide and multimedia exhibits describe key episodes, including New World discoveries, the terrifying 1755 earthquake (with a vivid film re-enacting the horrors) and the ambitious reconstruction that followed.

Neighbourhoods in a Nutshell

Baixa, near the riverfront, and Rossio, just north of there, are the heart of old Lisbon, with pedestrian streets and picturesque plazas. Follow the rattling trams to the east and you'll reach Alfama, with its medina-like lanes, and tiny, fado-filled restaurants. Above Alfama looms the ramparts of an ancient castle, with great viewpoints here and in other parts of the aptly named Castelo neighbourhood.

A steep climb west of Baixa leads into the swanky shopping and dining district of Chiado; further uphill lie the narrow streets of nightlife-haven Bairro Alto. Nearby, Santa Catarina, with its tiny bars and old-fashioned funicular, has a more laid-back vibe. Further downhill towards the river is Cais do Sodré, a red-light-district-turned-hipster centre, with late-night bars and eateries.

The Unesco World Heritage Sites of Belém lie further west along the river – an easy tram ride from Baixa or Cais do Sodré.

Baixa
SAM74100/GETTY IMAGES ©

◎ Bairro Alto & Chiado

Convento do Carmo & Museu Arqueológico — Ruins
(Map p52; www.museuarqueologicodocarmo.pt; Largo do Carmo; adult/child €4/free; ⓘ10am-7pm Mon-Sat Jun-Sep, to 6pm Oct-May) Soaring above Lisbon, the skeletal Convento do Carmo was all but devoured by the 1755 earthquake, and that's precisely what makes it so captivating. Its shattered pillars and wishbone-like arches

Bairro Alto, Chiado, Baixa & Rossio

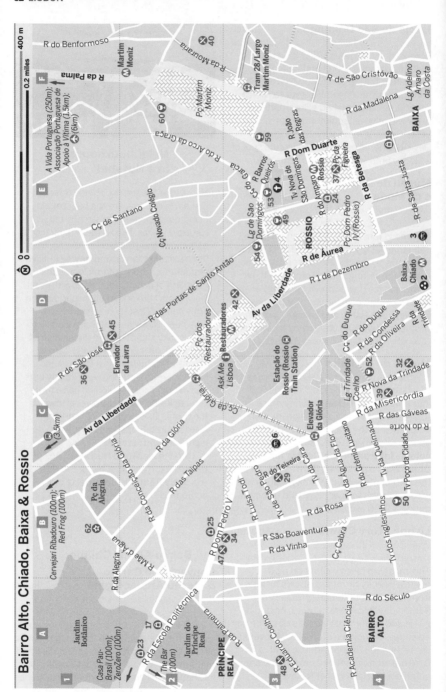

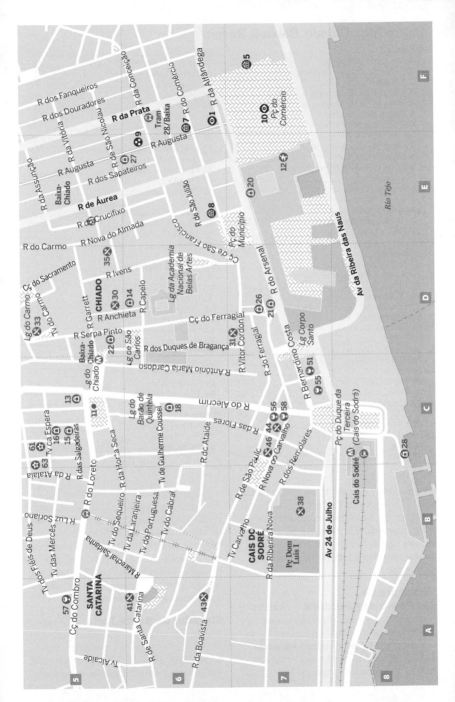

Bairro Alto, Chiado, Baixa & Rossio

are completely exposed to the elements. The Museu Arqueológico shelters archaeological treasures, such as 4th-century sarcophagi, griffin-covered column fragments, 16th-century *azulejo* (hand-painted tile) panels and two gruesome 16th-century Peruvian mummies.

Miradouro de São Pedro de Alcântara   Viewpoint

(Map p52; Rua São Pedro de Alcântara; ⊙viewpoint 24hr, kiosk 10am-midnight Sun-Wed, to 2am Thu-Sat) Hitch a ride on vintage **Ascensor da Glória** (www.carris.pt/pt/ascensores-e-elevador; Praça dos Restauradores; return €3.80;

⊙7.15am-11.55pm Mon-Thu, to 12.25am Fri, 8.45am-12.25am Sat, 9.15am-11.55pm Sun) from Praça dos Restauradores, or huff your way up steep Calçada da Glória to this terrific hilltop viewpoint. Fountains and Greek busts add a regal air to the surroundings, and the open-air kiosk doles out wine, beer and snacks, which you can enjoy while taking in the castle views and live music.

Elevador de Santa Justa   Viewpoint

(Map p52; www.carris.pt/en/elevators; cnr Rua de Santa Justa & Largo do Carmo; return trip €5.30; ⊙7am-11pm Mar-Oct, to 9pm Nov-Feb) If the lanky, wrought-iron Elevador de Santa

Justa seems uncannily familiar, it's probably because the neo-Gothic marvel is the handiwork of Raul Mésnier, Gustave Eiffel's apprentice. It's Lisbon's only vertical street lift, built in 1902 and steam-powered until 1907. Get here early to beat the crowds and zoom to the top for sweeping views over the city's skyline.

⦿ Alfama, Castelo & Graça

Castelo de São Jorge   Castle
(Map p56; www.castelodesaojorge.pt; adult/student/child €8.50/4/free; ⏰9am-9pm Mar-Oct, to 6pm Nov-Feb) Towering dramatically above Lisbon, these mid-11th-century hilltop fortifications sneak into almost every snapshot. Roam its snaking ramparts and pine-shaded courtyards for superlative views over the city's red rooftops to the river. Three guided tours daily (in Portuguese, English and Spanish), at 10.30am, 1pm and 4pm, are included in the admission price (additional tours available).

These smooth cobbles have seen it all – Visigoths in the 5th century, Moors in the 9th century, Christians in the 12th century, royals from the 14th to 16th centuries, and convicts in every century.

Inside the **Tower of Ulysses**, a camera obscura offers a unique 360-degree view of Lisbon, with demos every 20 minutes. There are also a few galleries displaying relics from past centuries, including traces of the Moorish neighbourhood dating from the 11th century at the **Archaeological Site**. But the standout is the view – as is the feeling of travelling back in time amid fortified courtyards and towering walls. There are a few cafes and restaurants in which you can while away time as well.

Bus 737 from Sé or Praça da Figueira goes right to the gate. Tram 28E also passes nearby. A set of escalators traversing the hill from Praça Martim Moniz opened in 2018.

Jardim da Cerca da Graça   Park
(Map p56; Calçada Do Monte 46; 🚻) Closed for centuries, this 1.7-hectare green space opened again in 2015 and is Lisbon's second-biggest park, offering a lush transition between the neighbourhoods of Graça and Mouraria. There are superb city and castle views from several points and a shady picnic

Castelo de São Jorge

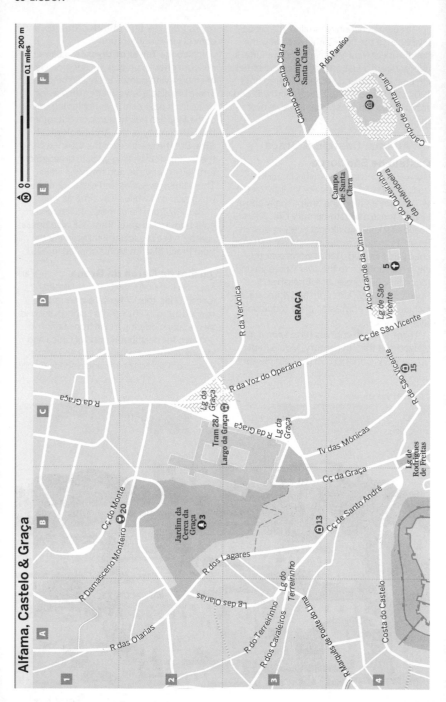

Alfama, Castelo & Graça

R das Olarias

R Damasceno Monteiro

Cç do Monte ⓜ 20

Jardim da Cerca da Graça 🌳 3

R dos Lagares

Lg das Olarias

R do Terreirinho

R dos Cavaleiros

Lg do Terreirinho

R Marquês de Ponte do Lima

ⓜ 13

Cç de Santo André

Costa do Castelo

R da Graça

R da Graça

Tram 28/ Largo da Graça ⓜ

Lg da Graça

R da Voz do Operário

Lg da Graça

R da Graça

Tv das Mónicas

Cç da Graça

Lg de Rodrigues de Freitas

R da Verónica

GRAÇA

Cç de São Vicente

R de São Vicente

Arco Grande da Cima

Lg de São Vicente

ⓜ 5

Lg do Outeirinho da Amendoeira

ⓜ 15

Campo de Santa Clara

Campo de Santa Clara

Campo de Santa Clara

Campo de Santa Clara

R do Paraíso

🏛 9

N

0 ——— 200 m
0 ——— 0.1 miles

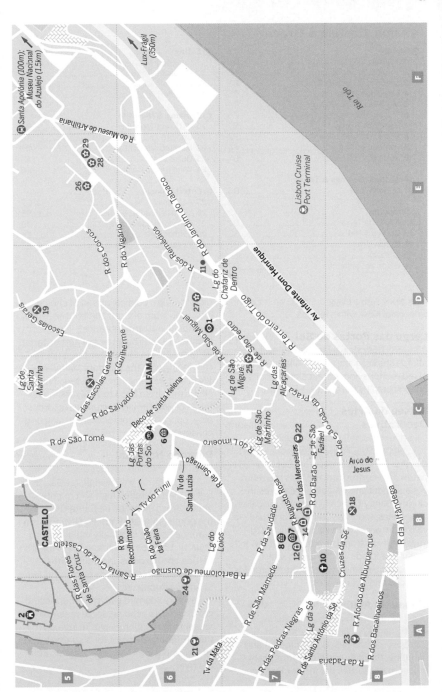

Alfama, Castelo & Graça

park along with a playground, an orchard and a peaceful kiosk with a terrace.

Largo das Portas do Sol   Viewpoint

(Map p56) This original Moorish gateway affords stunning angles over Alfama's jumble of red rooftops and pastel-coloured houses, underscored by the true blue Rio Tejo.

Museu de Artes Decorativas   Museum

(Museum of Decorative Arts; Map p56; www. fress.pt; Largo das Portas do Sol 2; adult/child €4/free; ⊙10am-5pm Wed-Mon) Set in a petite 17th-century palace, this museum creaks under the weight of treasures including blingy French silverware, priceless Qing vases and Indo-Chinese furniture – a collection amassed by a wealthy Portuguese banker from the age of 16. It's worth a visit just to admire the lavish apartments, embellished with baroque *azulejos*, frescoes and chandeliers.

Museu do Aljube   Museum

(Map p56; www.museudoaljube.pt; Rua de Augusto Rosa 42; adult/child €3/free, free Sun until 2pm; ⊙10am-6pm) Both poignant and haunting, this new and highly important museum has turned the former Portuguese dictatorship's political prison of choice into a museum of truth and consequence, memorial and remembrance – it's a must-see. Disturbing tales of authoritarian dictatorship are found over three floors (beginning with the *Ditadura Militar* in 1926, and evolving into the *Estado Novo*, or New State, from 1933 to 1974), including those of government torture, eavesdropping, oppression, coercion, informing and censorship.

Panteão Nacional   Museum

(Map p56; www.panteaonacional.gov.pt; Campo de Santa Clara; €4; ⊙10am-6pm Tue-Sun, to 5pm Oct-Mar) Perched high and mighty above Graça's Campo de Santa Clara, the porcelain-white Panteão Nacional is a baroque beauty. Originally intended as a church, it now pays homage to Portugal's heroes and heroines, including 15th-century explorer Vasco da Gama and *fadista* Amália Rodrigues.

Lavishly adorned with pink marble and gold swirls, its echoing dome resembles an enormous Fabergé egg. Trudge up to the 4th-floor viewpoint for a sunbake and vertigo-inducing views over Alfama and the river.

Sé de Lisboa — Cathedral

(Map p56; Largo de Sé; ⊘9am-7pm Tue-Sat, to 5pm Sun & Mon) FREE The fortress-like Sé de Lisboa is one of Lisbon's icons, built in 1150 on the site of a mosque soon after Christians recaptured the city from the Moors. It was sensitively restored in the 1930s. Despite the masses outside, the rib-vaulted interior, lit by a rose window, is calm. Stroll around the cathedral to spy leering gargoyles above the orange trees.

Mosteiro de São Vicente de Fora — Church

(Map p56; Largo de São Vicente; adult/child €3/free; ⊘10am-6pm Tue-Sun) Graça's Mosteiro de São Vicente de Fora was founded in 1147 and revamped by Italian architect Felipe Terzi in the late 16th century. Since the adjacent church took the brunt of the 1755 earthquake (the church's dome crashed through the ceiling of the sacristy, but emerged otherwise unscathed), elaborate blue-and-white azulejos dance across almost every wall, echoing the building's architectural curves.

Museu do Teatro Romano — Museum

(Roman Theatre Museum; Map p56; www.museudelisboa.pt; Rua de São Mamede 3A; adult/child €3/free, free Sun until 2pm; ⊘10am-6pm Tue Sun) The ultramodern Museu do Teatro Romano, reopened in 2015 after a two-year renovation and further excavation, catapults you back to Emperor Augustus' rule in Olisipo (Lisbon). The star attraction is a ruined **Roman theatre**, extended in AD 57, buried in the 1755 earthquake and finally unearthed in 1964 (you can enter for free).

◉ Príncipe Real, Santos & Estrela

Basílica da Estrela — Church

(Map p60; Praça da Estrela; basilica free, nativity scene €2, roof €3; ⊘basilica 9.30am-1pm & 3-7.30pm, terrace 10am-6.40pm, presépio 10-11.30am & 3-5pm, closed Mon, Sat & Sun morning, Wed afternoon) The curvaceous, sugar-white dome and twin belfries of Basílica da Estrela are visible from afar. The echoing interior is awash with pink-and-black marble, which

ⓘ Top Tips for Visiting Lisbon

o Plan your museum-going for Sunday mornings when some museums are free (until 2pm).

o Reserve well ahead at popular restaurants. Without reservations, you'll often be turned away at hotspots, even in low season or midweek.

o Those tempting olives, cheeses and bread baskets your server slaps down on your table unsolicited? Those are not free! Send them back if you do not want them.

NATALIA MYLOVA/SHUTTERSTOCK ©

creates a kaleidoscopic effect when you gaze up into the cupola. The neoclassical beauty was completed in 1790 by order of Dona Maria I (whose tomb is here) in gratitude for a male heir.

Casa Museu de Amália Rodrigues — Museum

(Map p60; www.amaliarodrigues.pt; Rua de São Bento 193; adult/child under 5yr €6/free; ⊘10am-6pm) A pilgrimage site for fado fans, this is where the Rainha do Fado (Queen of Fado) Amália Rodrigues (1920-99) lived; note the *calçada portuguesa* (Portuguese sidewalk design) announcing 'Amália'. Short tours take in portraits, glittering costumes and crackly recordings of her performances.

Museu da Marioneta — Museum

(Puppet Museum; Map p60; www.museudamarioneta.pt; Rua de Esperança 146; adult/child €5/3, free before 2pm Sun; ⊘10am-6pm Tue-Sun; ⏲) Discover your inner child at the

Lapa, Alcântara, Príncipe Real, Santos & Estrela

Lapa, Alcântara, Príncipe Real, Santos & Estrela

surprisingly enchanting Museu da Marioneta, a veritable Geppetto's workshop housed in the 17th-century Convento das Bernardas. Alongside superstars such as impish Punch and his Portuguese equivalent Dom Roberto are rarities: Vietnamese water puppets, Sicilian opera marionettes and intricate Burmese shadow puppets. Check out the fascinating exhibit of the making of the animation film *A Suspeita*.

Jardim da Estrela   Gardens
(Map p60; Praça da Estrela; ⊙7am-midnight; ﹙⬦﹚)
FREE Seeking green respite? Opposite the Basílica da Estrela, this 1852 green space is perfect for a stroll, with paths weaving past pine, monkey-puzzle and palm trees, rose and cacti beds, and the centrepiece – a giant banyan tree. Kids love the duck ponds and animal-themed playground. There are several open-air cafes where you can recharge.

> *With paths weaving past pine, monkey-puzzle and palm trees, rose and cacti beds*

◎ Lapa & Alcântara

Museu Nacional de Arte Antiga — Museum

(National Museum of Ancient Art; Map p60; www.museudearteantiga.pt; Rua das Janelas Verdes; adult/child €6/free, with themed exhibitions €10/free, free Sun until 2pm for Portuguese citizens/residents only; ⊙10am-6pm Tue-Sun) Set in a lemon-fronted, 17th-century palace, the Museu Nacional de Arte Antiga is Lapa's biggest draw. It presents a star-studded collection of European and Asian paintings and decorative arts.

Museu do Oriente — Museum

(Map p60; www.museudooriente.pt; Doca de Alcântara; adult/child €6/2, free 6-10pm Fri; ⊙10am-6pm Tue-Thu, Sat & Sun, to 10pm Fri) The beautifully designed Museu do Oriente highlights Portugal's ties with Asia, from colonial baby steps in Macau to ancestor worship. The cavernous museum occupies a revamped 1940s *bacalhau* (dried salt-cod) warehouse – a €30-million conversion. Strikingly displayed in pitch-black rooms, the permanent collection focuses on the Portuguese presence in Asia, and Asian gods.

◎ Marquês de Pombal & Around

Museu Calouste Gulbenkian – Coleção do Fundador — Museum

(Founder's Collection; www.gulbenkian.pt; Av de Berna 45A; Coleção do Fundador/Coleção Moderna combo ticket adult/child €10/free, temporary exhibitions €3-6, free Sun from 2pm; ⊙10am-6pm Wed-Mon) Famous for its outstanding quality and breadth, the world-class Founder's Collection at Museu Calouste Gulbenkian showcases an epic collection of Western and Eastern art – from Egyptian treasures to Old Master and Impressionist paintings. Admission includes the separately housed Coleção Moderna.

◎ Belém

Torre de Belém — Tower

(Map p62; www.torrebelem.pt; Av de Brasília; adult/child €6/3, free Sun until 2pm for Portuguese citizens/residents only; ⊙10am-6.30pm Tue-Sun May-Sep, to 5.30pm Oct-Apr) Jutting out onto the Rio Tejo, this Unesco World Heritage–listed fortress epitomises the Age of Discoveries. You'll need to breathe in to climb the narrow spiral staircase to the tower, which affords sublime views over Belém and the river.

Museu Coleção Berardo — Museum

(Map p62; www.museuberardo.pt; Praça do Império; adult/student/child under 6yr €5/2.50/free, free Sat; ⊙10am-7pm) Culture fiends can get their contemporary-art fix at Museu Coleção Berardo, the star of the Centro Cultural de Belém. The ultrawhite, minimalist gallery displays billionaire José Berardo's eye-popping collection of abstract, surrealist and pop art, including Hockney, Lichtenstein, Warhol and Pollock originals.

Museu Nacional dos Coches — Museum

(Map p62; www.museudoscoches.pt; Av da Índia 136; €8, combined ticket with Antigo Picadeiro Real €10, free Sun to 2pm for Portuguese citizens/residents only; ⊙10am-6pm Tue-Sun) Cinderella wannabes delight in Portugal's most visited museum, which dazzles with its world-class collection of 70 17th- to 19th-century coaches in an ultramodern (and some might say inappropriately contrasting) space that debuted in 2015. Don't miss Pope Clement XI's stunning ride, the scarlet-and-gold *Coach of the Oceans*, or the old royal riding school, **Antigo Picadeiro Real** (Map p62; Praça Afonso de Albuquerque; €4, combined ticket with Museu Nacional dos Coches €10), across the street.

Museu de Arte, Arquitetura e Tecnologia — Museum

(MAAT; Art, Architecture & Technology Museum; Map p62; www.maat.pt; Av de Brasília, Central

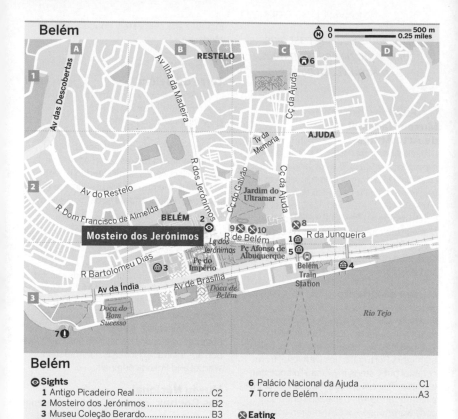

Belém

◎ Sights
1 Antigo Picadeiro Real C2
2 Mosteiro dos Jerónimos B2
3 Museu Coleção Berardo........................... B3
4 Museu de Arte, Arquitetura e
     Tecnologia D3
5 Museu Nacional dos Coches.................. C3
6 Palácio Nacional da Ajuda C1
7 Torre de Belém A3

⊗ Eating
8 Alecrim & Manjerona C2
9 Antiga Confeitaria de Belém................... C2
10 Enoteca de Belém..................................... C2

Tejo; admission with/without Central Tejo
€9/5; ⊙11am-7pm Wed-Mon) Lisbon's latest
riverfront star is this low-rise, glazed-tiled
structure that intriguingly hips and sways
into ground-level exhibition halls. Visitors
can walk over and under its reflective
surfaces, which play with water, light and
shadow, and pay homage to the city's
intimate relationship with the sea.

Palácio Nacional da Ajuda Palace
(Map p62; www.palacioajuda.gov.pt; Largo da
Ajuda; adult/child €5/free, free Sun until 2pm for
Portuguese citizens/residents only; ⊙10am-6pm
Thu-Tue) Built in the early 19th century, this
staggering neoclassical palace served as
the royal residence from the 1860s until the
end of the monarchy (1910). You can tour
private apartments and state rooms, getting
an eyeful of gilded furnishings and exquisite
artworks dating back five centuries, as well
as the queen's chapel, home to Portugal's
only El Greco painting.

It's a long uphill walk from Belém, or you
can take tram 18E or several buses from
downtown, including 760 from Praça do
Comércio.

◎ Parque das Nações

Oceanário de Lisboa   Aquarium

(www.oceanario.pt; Doca dos Olivais; adult/
child €15/10, incl temporary exhibition €18/12;
☺10am-8pm, to 7pm in winter) The closest
you'll get to scuba diving without a wetsuit,
Oceanário is mind-blowing. With 8000
marine creatures splashing in 7 million litres
of seawater, no amount of hyperbole does it
justice. Huge wrap-around tanks make you
feel as if you're underwater, as you eyeball
zebra sharks, honeycombed rays, gliding
mantas and schools of neon fish.

Pavilhão do Conhecimento   Museum

(Pavilion of Knowledge; www.pavconhecimento.
pt; Largo José Mariano Gago 1; adult/child €9/6;
☺10am-6pm Tue-Fri, 11am-7pm Sat & Sun; 👪)
Kids won't grumble about science at the
interactive Pavilhão do Conhecimento,
where they can run riot in the adult-free
unfinished house, get dizzy on a high-wire
bicycle or have fun whipping up tornadoes
and blowing massive soap bubbles.

✪ ACTIVITIES

ViniPortugal   Wine

(Map p52; www.winesofportugal.info; Praça do
Comércio; ☺11am-7pm Apr-Oct, closed Sun
Nov-Mar) Under the arcades on Praça do
Comércio, this viticultural organisation
offers €6 themed wine tastings, if booked
in advance. Otherwise, pop in and grab a
€3 enocard, which allows you to taste at
least three Portuguese wines, from Alentejo
whites to full-bodied Douro reds (glasses
are €1 to €8).

Kiss the Cook   Cooking

(Map p60; ☎968 119 652; www.kissthecook.pt;
Rua Rodrigues de Faria 103, LX Factory; classes
€65) If you're into Portuguese food in a big
way and fancy picking up a few tips and
tricks from the experts, why not pass by
Kiss the Cook? Here you can prepare (and
devour) traditional dishes. The cookery
classes are totally hands-on, and the price
includes lunch and wine.

Palácio Nacional da Ajuda

PETER DELUIS/ALAMY STOCK PHOTO ©

Factory of the Arts

Tune into Lisbon's creative pulse at LX Factory, housed in a cavernous 19th-century industrial complex. Abandoned warehouses have been transformed into spaces for art studios, galleries, workshops and printing and design companies. Creative restaurants, bars and shops have added to the energy, and today LX Factory is a great spot to check out an alternative side of Lisbon. It's liveliest on weekend nights, though it's also worth stopping by the open-air market (vintage clothes, crafts) held on Sundays from 11am to 7pm. Get there on tram 15E or 18E.

FRANZ12/SHUTTERSTOCK ©

Culinary Backstreets   Food & Drink

(☑963 472 188; www.culinarybackstreets.com/culinary-walks/lisbon; 3/6hr tour €83/118) *Eat Portugal* co-author Célia Pedroso leads epic culinary walks through Lisbon, a fantastic way to take in some of the best treats in town. Try *ginjinha* (cherry liqueur) then *pastéis de nata* (custard tarts) and artisanal sheep cheese, paired with killer local wines. Tours are mostly available Tuesday to Saturday. Expect tantalising multiple foodgasms followed by a debilitating food coma.

We Hate Tourism Tours   Tours

(Map p60; ☑913 776 598; www.wehatetourism tours.com; Rua Rodrigues de Faria 103, 4th fl, LX Factory; per person from €30; ⊗2-6pm) One memorable way to explore Lisbon is aboard an open-topped UMM (a Portuguese 4WD once made for the army). In addition to the weekend King of the Hills tour, this

alternative outfit organises innovative lunch and dinner tours, longer city tours and excursions to Sintra and Cascais.

Lisbon Walker   Walking

(Map p56; ☑218 861 840; www.lisbonwalker.com; Rua do Jardim do Tabaco 126; 3hr walk adult/child €15/free; ⊗10am) This excellent company, with well-informed, English-speaking guides, offers themed walking tours of Lisbon. Note that these normally depart at 10am from the northwest corner of Praça do Comércio (p50).

Sandemans New Lisbon   Walking

(Map p52; www.newlisbontours.com; ⊗10am, 11am & 2pm) For the inside scoop on the city, Sandemans' fun, informative and free 2½-hour walking tours of downtown Lisbon are hard to beat. You'll do the rounds of all the major landmarks and get versed in history and city tips as you stroll. The tours begin at the scheduled times (book online) at the monument on Praça Luís de Camões.

Lisbon Bike Tour   Cycling

(☑912 272 300; www.lisbonbiketour.com; adult/child €32.50/15; ⊗9.30am-1pm) It's all downhill on this 3½-hour guided bike ride from Marquês de Pombal to Belém.

🅐 SHOPPING

Le freak, c'est retro *chic* in grid-like Bairro Alto, which attracts vinyl lovers and vintage devotees to its cluster of late-opening boutiques. Elegant Chiado is the go-to place for high-street and couture shopping, to the backbeat of buskers. Alfama, Baixa and Rossio have frozen-in-time stores dealing exclusively in buttons and gloves, tawny port and tinned fish.

🅐 Baixa & Rossio

Garrafeira Nacional   Wine

(Map p52; ☑218 879 080; www.garrafeira nacional.com; Rua de Santa Justa 18; ⊗9.30am-7.30pm Mon-Fri, to 7pm Sat) This Lisbon landmark has been selling Portuguese wine since 1927 and is easily the best spot to pick up a bevy of local wines and spirits. It is especially helpful and will steer you towards lesser-known boutique wines and vintage ports in addition to the usual suspects. The small museum features vintages dating to the 18th century.

Typographia   Clothing

(Map p52; www.typographia.com; Rua Augusta 93; ⏱10am-7pm) With stores in Porto and Madrid as well, this high-design T-shirt shop is one of Europe's best. It features a select, monthly changing array of clever and artsy, locally designed T-shirts (€23.95), which no one else will be wearing back home.

Manteigaria Silva   Food

(Map p52; www.manteigariasilva.pt; Rua Dom Antão de Almada 1D; ⏱9am-7.30pm Mon-Sat) Specialising in the best of the best and in business for more than a century, Manteigaria Silva does a brisk trade in staunchly curated Portuguese ham, cheese, wine and *bacalhau*.

Lisbon Shop   Gifts & Souvenirs

(Map p52; www.askmelisboa.com; Rua do Arsenal 15; ⏱9.30am-7.30pm) Housed in the Pombaline Pátio da Galé complex, this shop is crammed with Portuguese gifts, from tram T-shirts, cockerel mugs and cork bags to speciality foods. It's run by Ask Me Lisboa, the public face of Lisbon tourism.

🔒 Bairro Alto & Chiado

A Vida Portuguesa   Gifts & Souvenirs

(Map p52; www.avidaportuguesa.com; Rua Anchieta 11; ⏱10am-8pm Mon-Sat, from 11am Sun) A flashback to the late 19th century with its high ceilings and polished cabinets, this former warehouse and perfume factory lures nostalgics with its all-Portuguese products, from retro-wrapped Tricona sardines to Claus Porto soaps, and heart-embellished Viana do Castelo embroideries to Bordalo Pinheiro porcelain swallows. There's also a location in **Intendente** (www.avidaportuguesa. com; Largo do Intendente 23; ⏱10.30am-7.30pm).

Loja das Conservas (p66)

THOMAS DEMARCZYK/GETTY IMAGES ©

Torre de Belém (p61)

Loja das Conservas   Food

(Map p52; www.facebook.com/lojadas
conservas; Rua do Arsenal 130; ⊙10am-8pm
Mon-Sat, from noon Sun) What appears to be a
gallery is, on closer inspection, a fascinating temple to tinned fish (or *conservas*
as the Portuguese say) – the result of an
industry on its deathbed revived by a savvy
marketing about-face and new generations of hipsters. The retro-wrapped tins,
displayed along with the history of each
canning factory, are artworks.

Loja do Burel   Clothing

(Map p52; www.burelfactory.com; Rua Serpa
Pinto 15B; ⊙10am-8pm Mon-Sat, 11am-7pm Sun)
Once a clothing staple of Serra da Estrela
mountain-dwelling shepherds, Burel, a
Portuguese black wool, was all but left to
disappear until this company single-
handedly resurrected the industry, giving
it a stylish makeover fit for 21st-century
fashion. The colourful blankets, handbags,
jackets, hats and other home decor items
aren't like anything anyone has back home.

Cork & Company   Gifts & Souvenirs

(Map p52; www.corkandcompany.pt; Rua das
Salgadeiras 10; ⊙11am-7pm Mon-Sat, from 5pm
Sun) 🖋 At this elegantly designed shop,
you'll find cork put to surprisingly imaginative uses, with well-made and sustainable
cork handbags, pens, wallets, journals,
candleholders, hats, scarves, place mats,
umbrellas, iPhone covers and even chaise
longues!

Fábrica Sant'Ana   Arts & Crafts

(Map p52; www.santanna.com.pt; Rua do Alecrím
95; ⊙9.30am-7pm Mon-Sat) Handmaking and
painting *azulejos* (from €5) since 1741,
this is the place to get some eye-catching
porcelain tiles for your home.

Underdogs Public Art Store   Art

(Map p52; www.under-dogs.net; Rua da Cintura
do Porto de Lisboa, Armazém A; ⊙11am-7pm
Tue-Sun) Witness the strength of street
knowledge at this part gallery, part
Montana-street-art paint store and cafe behind Cais do Sodré. Underdogs specialises
in high-profile public art and offers Lisbon's
best public-art tours on a sporadic,

by-appointment-only basis (tours from
€35). Good coffee is available, too.

A Carioca
Food

(Map p52; Rua da Misericórdia 9; ☺9am-7pm
Mon-Fri, to 1pm Sat) Little has changed since
this old-world store opened in 1924: brass
fittings still gleam, the coffee roaster is
still in action, and home blends, sugared
almonds and toffees are still lovingly
wrapped in green paper.

El Dorado
Vintage, Clothing

(Map p52; ☏213 423 935; Rua do Norte 23;
☺1-9pm Mon-Thu, to 11pm Fri & Sat, 3-9pm Sun)
A gramophone plays vinyl classics as divas
grab vintage styles, from psychedelic prints
to 6in platforms and pencil skirts, at this
Bairro Alto hipster place. There's also a
great range of club wear.

Storytailors
Clothing

(Map p52; www.storytailors.pt; Calçada do
Ferragial 8; ☺11am-7pm Tue-Sat) Mirror,
mirror...undoubtedly one of Lisbon's fairest
boutiques is this chandelier-lit enchanted
forest of fashion, where design duo Luís
Sanchez and João Branco bewitch with
fairy-tale dresses, floaty ruffle skirts,
quirky reversible coats and their latest
catwalk creations (for women, men and
the gender-fluid).

🔒 Alfama, Castelo & Graça

Cortiço & Netos
Homewares

(Map p56; www.corticoenetos.com; Calçada de
Santo André 66; ☺10am-1pm & 2-7pm Mon-Sat)
A wonder wall of fabulous *azulejos* greets
you as you enter this very special space. It's
the vision of brothers Pedro, João, Ricardo
and Tiago Cortiço, whose grandfather
dedicated more than 30 years to gathering,
storing and selling discontinued Portuguese
industrial tiles. Reviving the family trade, the
brothers are experts on the *azulejo* and how
it can be interpreted today.

A Arte da Terra
Gifts & Souvenirs

(Map p56; www.aartedaterra.pt; Rua de Augusto
Rosa 40; ☺11am-8pm) In the stables of a
centuries-old bishop's palace, A Arte da

Great Escapes

Some of Lisbon's greenest and most
peaceful *praças* (town squares) are
perfect for a crowd-free stroll or picnic.
A few of our favourites:

Praça da Alegria Swooping palms and
banyan trees shade tranquil Praça da
Alegria, which is actually more round
than square. Look out for the bronze
bust of 19th-century Portuguese painter
and composer Alfredo Keil.

Praça do Príncipe Real A century-old
cedar tree forms a giant natural parasol
at the centre of this palm-dotted square,
popular among grizzled card players by
day and gay cruisers by night. There's a
kids playground and a relaxed cafe with
alfresco seating.

Praça das Flores Centred on a fountain,
this romantic, leafy square has cobbles,
pastel-washed houses and enough
doggie-do to make a Parisian proud.

Campo dos Mártires da Pátria Framed
by elegant buildings, this grassy square
is dotted with pine, weeping willow and
jacaranda trees, with a pond for ducks
and a pleasant indoor-outdoor cafe.
Lisboêtas in search of cures light candles
before the statue of Dr Sousa Martins,
who was renowned for his healing work
among the poor.

Praça do Príncipe Real

Terra brims with authentic Portuguese
crafts including Castello Branco embroideries, nativity figurines, hand-painted *azulejos,*
fado CDs and quality cork goods (umbrellas,

aprons, writing journals). Some goods are beautifully lit in former troughs.

Garbags
Fashion & Accessories

(Map p56; www.garbags.eu; Rua São Vicente 17; ⊙11am-7pm) A second outlet of the ecofriendly **Graça shop** (Map p56; Calçada da Graça 16; ⊙10am-8pm) 🌠 hawking all manner of gear (wallets, phone cases, handbags) fashioned from recycled coffee sacks, crisp bags, juice containers and other materials.

O Voo da Andorinha
Gifts & Souvenirs

(Map p56; www.facebook.com/ovooda andorinha; Rua do Barão 22; ⊙11am-7.30pm Mon-Sat) Candy-bright beads, hand-stitched swallows, embroidered accessories and quirky furnishings made with recycled castaways such as cassette tapes, floppy discs, computer keys and old vinyl – you'll find all of this and more at this adorable boutique representing some 50 Lisbon-area artists near the cathedral.

Fabula Urbis
Books

(Map p56; www.fabula-urbis.pt; Rua de Augusto Rosa 27; ⊙11am-1.30pm & 3-8pm Thu-Sat) A great little bookshop that celebrates works about Portugal, by both home-grown and expat authors. All the best books by Lobo Antunes, Saramago, Pessoa, Richard Zimler and Robert C Wilson are here – available in English, French, Spanish, Italian, German and, of course, Portuguese.

🅐 Príncipe Real, Santos & Estrela

Embaixada
Shopping Centre

(Map p52; www.embaixadalx.pt; Praça do Príncipe Real 26; ⊙noon-8pm Mon-Fri, 11am-7pm Sat & Sun, restaurants to 2am) Take an exquisite 19th-century neo-Moorish palace and fill it with fashion, design and concept stores on the cutting edge of cool and you have one of Lisbon's most exciting new shopping experiences: Embaixada. Centred on a grand sweeping staircase and courtyard are boutiques selling everything from vintage records to organic cosmetics,

Embaixada

Ler Devagar (p70)

eco-homewares, contemporary Portuguese ceramics and catwalk styles.

Solar — Antiques
(Map p52; www.solar.com.pt; Rua Dom Pedro V 70; ⊙10am-7pm Mon-Fri, to 1pm Sat) Hawking antique *azulejos* for seven decades, Solar offers row after row and pile after pile of precious Portuguese tiles dating from the 1500s to 1900s, many of which were salvaged from old churches and palaces.

Verso Branco — Design
(Map p60; www.versobranco.pt; Rua da Boavista 132-134; ⊙11.30am-8pm Tue-Sat) 'Free verse' is the name of this split-level design store, where Fernando has a story for every object. The high-ceilinged space showcases Portuguese contemporary arts, crafts and furnishings, from Burel's quality wool creations to limited-edition La.Ga bags by designer Jorge Moita – the beautifully crafted bags made from Tyvek weigh just 40g and can hold 55kg.

Casa Pau-Brasil — Design
(Rua da Escola Politécnica 42; ⊙noon-8pm Mon-Sat, to 6pm Sun) Inside the 18th century Castilho Palace, this high-design Brazilian concept store divvies up space among 18 Brazilian brands and designers, including Granado cosmetics, iconic furniture by Sérgio Rodrigues, swimwear by Lenny and interior design by Campana. Brazilian accents fill the trendy space.

Loja Real — Design
(Map p52; www.facebook.com/lojareal.Lisboa; Praça do Príncipe Real 20; ⊙10.30am-8pm) A showcase largely for Portuguese designers, Loja Real features a wide assortment of unique, high-quality products that run the gamut of home decor (cushions, teapots, vases), fashion (clothing, jewellery) and artwork to items for children (clothing, books and toys). The emphasis is 'slow retail': nothing is mass-produced or made with plastics or cheap materials.

Mercado da Ribeira

🔒 Lapa & Alcântara

Ler Devagar Books

(Map p60; 📞213 259 992; www.lerdevagar.com; Rua Rodrigues de Faria 103, LX Factory; ⏰11am-9pm Sun-Mon, to 11pm Tue-Thu, to 1am Fri & Sat) Late-night bookworms and anyone who enjoys a good read will love this floor-to-ceiling temple of books. Foreign-language titles and books on art and culture are well represented.

✖ EATING

Creative new-generation chefs at the stove, first-rate raw ingredients and a generous pinch of world spice have transformed Lisbon into a buzzing culinary capital. Reservations, even early in the week and in low season, are a good idea – getting turned away without them is all too common.

✖ Baixa & Rossio

Mercado da Baixa Market €

(Map p52; www.adbaixapombalina.pt/mercado-da-baixa; Praça da Figueira; ⏰10am-10pm Fri-Sun last weekend of month) This tented market and glorious food court has featured cheese, wine, smoked sausages and other gourmet goodies since 1855. It's fantastic fun to stroll the stalls, eating and drinking yourself into a gluttonous mess.

Pinóquio Portuguese €€

(Map p52; 📞213 465 106; www.restaurant epinoquio.pt; Praça dos Restauradores 79; mains €17-26; ⏰noon-midnight; 📶) Busy Pinóquio is easy to miss as it's tucked into a *praça* corner partially obstructed by a souvenir kiosk. Dressed in white tablecloths against pea-green walls, it's distinctly old school, with indomitable waiters slinging a stunning slew of classic dishes: *arroz de pato* (duck rice), seafood *feijoada*, *arroz de bacalhau* (codfish rice), and pork chops with almonds and coriander.

Solar dos Presuntos Portuguese €€€

(Map p52; 📞213 424 253; www.solardos presuntos.com; Rua das Portas de Santo Antão 150; mains €16-27.50, seafood per kg €29-98; ⏰12.30-3.30pm & 7-11pm Mon-Sat; 📶) Don't be fooled by the smoked *presunto* (ham) hanging in the window; this iconic restaurant is renowned for its excellent seafood too. Start with the *pata negra* (cured ham), *paio* smoked sausage and cheese *couvert* (stew), then dig into a fantastic lobster *açorda*, delectable seafood paella or crustacean curry. Go easy on their homespun piri-piri (hot sauce) – it bites back!

Bairro Alto & Chiado

Mercado da Ribeira   Market €

(Map p52; www.timeoutmarket.com; Av 24 de Julho; ⊙10am-midnight Sun-Wed, to 2am Thu-Sat, traditional market 6am-2pm Mon-Sat; 🛜) Doing trade in fresh fruit and veg, fish and flowers since 1892, this domed market hall has been the word on everyone's lips since *Time Out* transformed half of it into a gourmet food court in 2014. Now it's Lisbon in chaotic culinary microcosm: Garrafeira Nacional wines, Café de São Bento steaks, Manteigaria Silva (p65) cold cuts and Michelin-star chef creations from Henrique Sá Pessoa.

Pistola y Corazon   Mexican €

(Map p52; www.pistolaycorazon.com; Rua da Boavista 16; tacos €7-10; ⊙6pm-midnight Mon & Sat, noon-3pm & 6pm-midnight Tue-Fri, noon-3pm & 7pm-1am Sun; 🛜) This lively hipster taqueria is a godsend of authentic Mexican street tacos (*carnitas, cochinita pibil, carne asada, al pastor* etc), served among tweaked *El Tri* kitsch (Frida Kahlo rocking a Daft Punk T-shirt!). The creative mescal- and tequila-laced cocktail list is equally outstanding. Write your name on the wait list – it's always packed.

Ao 26 – Vegan Food Project   Vegan €

(Map p52; ☑967 989 184; www.facebook. com/ao26veganfoodproject; Rua Vítor Cordon 26; mains €5.50-7.50; ⊙12.30-6.30pm & 7.30-11pm Tue-Sat; 🛜🥗) So good it even lures in devout carnivores, this small, hip and bustling place offers two elaborate, daily-changing chalkboard specials (eg Manchurian meatballs with tomato, coconut and masala). There's a fixed menu of loaded lentil burgers, beet burgers and veg sandwiches on *bolo do caco* (round

bread cooked on a basalt stone slab), plus Lisbon craft beer.

Bairro de Avillez   Portuguese €€

(Map p52; ☑215 830 290; www.bairrodo avillez.pt; Rua Nova da Trindade 18; small plates €2-16.50, mains €7-18.50; ⊙noon-midnight; 🛜) Step into the latest culinary dream by Portugal's most famous chef – Michelin-starred maestro José Avillez – who has set up his gastronomic dream destination: a 'neighbourhood' featuring several dining environments, including everything from a traditional tavern to an avant-garde gourmet cabaret.

Boa-Bao
Asian €€

(Map p52; ☑919 023 030; www.boabao.pt; Largo Rafael Bordalo Pinheiro 30; small plates from €6.50, mains €12-19; ⊘noon-11.30pm Sun-Wed, to 12.30am Thu-Sat; 🛜) The food at this trendy spot will transport you to Laos, Cambodia, Malaysia and Vietnam, but the ceramic swallows draped across the exposed brick archway (the most famous artwork of Rafael Bordalo, the artist for which the beautiful Chiado plaza is named) are undeniably Portuguese.

Taberna Tosca
Tapas €€

(Map p52; ☑218 034 563; www.taberna tosca.com; Praça São Paulo 21; tapas €4-13; ⊘noon-midnight, to 2am Fri-Sat) A peaceful retreat from the nearby Rua Nova do Carvalho mayhem, Tosca is an enticing spot for Portuguese tapas and bold Douro reds (but don't be afraid to spring for a pitcher of fabulous port sangria). Open-air seating is on leafy Praça São Paulo in front, opposite an 18th-century church, making it feel like a hidden Lisbon highlight.

Pharmacia
Mediterranean €€

(Map p52; ☑213 462 146; www.chef-felicidade. pt; Rua Marechal Saldanha 2; tapas €10-15; ⊘noon-1am; 🛜) At this wonderfully quirky restaurant in Lisbon's apothecary museum, chef Susana Felicidade (Algarvian grandmother-trained!) dispenses tasting menus and tapas singing with flavours that are both market-fresh and Mediterranean influenced. Appetisers served in test tubes, cabinets brimming with pill bottles and flacons – it's all part of the pharmaceutical fun. The terrace is a great spot for cocktails.

Fábulas
Cafe €€

(Map p52; www.fabulas.pt; Calçada Nova de São Francisco 14; mains €11-17; ⊘11am-11pm Sun-Thu, to 11.45pm Fri & Sat; 🛜🍴) Exposed stone walls, soft lighting, vaulted ceilings and twisting corridors that open onto cosy nooks do indeed conjure a *fábula* (story-book fable). Vintage armchairs and sofas are fine spots for a snack, drink or classic dishes such as black-pork cheeks. There's a divine drinking patio outside for warm weather, and the vibe is delightfully mellow.

Mercantina
Pizza €€

(Map p52; ☑231 070 013; www.mercantina. pt; Rua da Misericórdia 114; pizza €8-14, pasta €11-13.50; ⊘noon-3.30pm & 7.30-11.30pm Mon-Thu, 12.30-3.30pm & 7pm-midnight Fri-Sun; 🛜) You'll find some of Lisbon's best pizza – uncut, certified by Napoli's strict *Associazione Verace Pizza Napoletana* – at this cosy Chiado hotspot whose hardwood-heavy decor vaguely approaches ski-lodge territory. The spicy *diavola* (tomato, mozzarella, ventricina sausage, Parmesan and basil) and *mercantina* (tomato, mozzarella, ham, salami, mushrooms and Parmesan) are both show-stoppers, but don't discount the phenomenal lasagne. Reserve ahead online.

Alma
Modern Portuguese €€€

(Map p52; ☑213 470 650; www.almalisboa.pt; Rua Anchieta 15; mains €32-36, tasting menus €110-120; ⊘noon-3pm & 7-11pm Tue-Sun; 🛜) Two-Michelin–starred Henrique Sá Pessoa's flagship Alma is one of Portugal's destination restaurants and, in our humble opinion, Lisbon's best gourmet dining experience. The casual space exudes understated style amid the original stone flooring and gorgeous hardwood tables, but it's Pessoa's outrageously good nouveau Portuguese cuisine that draws the foodie flock from far and wide.

100 Maneiras
Fusion €€€

(Map p52; ☑910 307 575; www.restaurante 100maneiras.com; Rua do Teixeira 35; tasting menu €60, with classic/premium wine pairing €95/120; ⊘7pm-2am; 🛜) How do we love 100 Maneiras? Let us count the 100 ways... The 10-course tasting menu changes twice yearly and features imaginative, delicately prepared dishes. The courses are all a surprise – part of the charm – though somewhat disappointingly, the chef will only budge so far to accommodate special diets and food allergies. Reservations are essential for the elegant and small space.

Fábulas

🪑 Alfama, Castelo & Graça

Ti-Natércia Portuguese €

(Map p56; 📞218 862 133; Rua Escola Gerais 54; mains €5.50-12; ⊙7pm-midnight Tue-Fri, noon-3pm & 7pm-midnight Sat) 'Aunt' Natércia and her downright delicious Portuguese home cooking is a tough ticket: there are only six tables and they fill up fast. She'll talk your ear off (and doesn't mince words – some have been rubbed the wrong way, vegetarians in particular should avoid) while you devour her excellent take on the classics. Reservations are essential. Cash only.

Pois Café Cafe €

(Map p56; www.poiscafe.com; Rua de São João da Praça 93; mains €7-10; ⊙noon-11pm Mon, from 10am Tue-Sun; 🛜) Boasting a laid-back vibe under dominant stone arches, atmospheric Pois Café has creative salads, sandwiches and fresh juices, plus a handful of heartier daily specials (such as salmon quiche and sirloin steak). Its sofas invite lazy afternoons spent reading novels and sipping coffee, but you'll fight for space with the laptop brigade.

O Zé da Mouraria Portuguese €€

(Map p52; 📞218 865 436; Rua João do Outeiro 24; mains for 2 €16.50-33.50; ⊙noon-4pm Mon-Sat; 🛜) Don't be fooled by the saloon-like doors, there's a typical Portuguese *tasca* (tavern) inside: homey local cuisine, blue-and-white-tiled walls, chequered tablecloths – and it's one of Lisbon's best. The house-baked cod loaded with chickpeas, onions, garlic and olive oil is rightfully popular, and daily specials (duck rice on Wednesday!) make return trips tempting. Service is a lost cause, however.

Os Gazeteiros European €€

(Map p56; 📞939 501 211; www.osgazeteiros.pt; Rua das Escolas Gerais 114-116; prix-fixe dinners €35; ⊙7.30-10pm Tue-Sat; 🛜) 🍽 French chef David Eyguesier honed his skills at Pois Café, then at his own underground restaurant at home before opening this sorely needed Alfama gem, whose name loosely translates as 'the Truants' (he 'skipped' culinary school!). His daily-changing, market-fresh four-course set menus delight under a spiderweb of modern lighting,

Off the Beaten Track: Madragoa

The neighbourhood of Madragoa, west of Baixa, with its narrow lanes and charming restaurants, is reminiscent of Alfama, but with a fraction of the tourists. Take tram 25 from Praça do Comércio to get there.

Traditional houses in Madragoa
MAURICIO ABREU/GETTY IMAGES ©

beautiful geometric cabinetry and an open kitchen. No microwave, no freezer!

⊗ Príncipe Real, Santos & Estrela

Gelataria Nannarella   Gelato €

(Map p60; www.nannarella.pt; Rua Nova da Piedade 68; small/medium/large €2.50/3/3.50; ⊘noon-10pm) Seatless Nannarella is squeezed into little more than a doorway and serves up Lisbon's best gelato. Roman transplant Constanza Ventura churns out 34 perfect, spatula-slabbed flavours of traditional gelato and sorbet daily (18 fixed, 10 daily-changing, four seasonal) to anxious lines of *lisboêtas*. Nailing both consistency and flavour, this sweet, sweet stuff seemingly emerges straight from Ventura's kitchen.

Coyo Taco   Mexican €€

(Map p52; ☑210 529 201; http://coyotaco. pt; Rua Dom Pedro V 65; tacos €7.50-9; ⊘noon-midnight Sun-Wed, to 2am Thu-Sat; 🛜) Straight outta Miami, where it is reportedly Barack Obama's favourite taqueria, Coyo brings fierce taco authenticity to one of Lisbon's most gourmand streets.

Handmade tortillas stuffed with duck carnitas, chicken and pork *al pastor* and *cochinita pibil*, along with excellent shrimp quesadillas and easy-drinkin' margaritas (served out of a window to the street), help fill a long-empty Mexican niche.

Tapisco   Fusion €€

(Map p52; ☑213 420 681; www.tapisco.pt; Rua Dom Pedro V 81; tapas €5-18, mains €16-29; ⊘noon-midnight; 🛜) Michelin-starred Lisbon chef Henrique Sá Pessoa's venture into Príncipe Real may seem obvious (trans-Iberian tapas) but in reality Spain and Portugal don't often share more than the peninsula. Washing down *tapiscos* (Spanish tapas and Portuguese *petiscos* – get it?) with traditional vermouth never felt so novel.

ZeroZero   Pizza €€

(☑213 420 091; www.pizzeriazerozero.pt; Rua da Escola Politécnica 32; pizza €10-19; ⊘noon-midnight Sun-Thu, to 1am Fri & Sat; 🛜) Just arriving at your table here is a memorable ride, sliding past an enormous illustration by Ana Gil, a beautiful prosecco bar and minimalist copper lamps and muted grey walls leading to an impressive, oak-fired pizza oven. Attention to Italian detail is fierce, and the thin-crusted, uncut pies make an impression. And the patio is a bougainvillea-draped haven for pizza lovers.

Taberna da Esperança   Fusion €€

(Map p60; ☑213 962 744; www.tabernada esperanca.com; Rua da Esperança 112-114; small plates €7-12, mains €17-19; ⊘7.30pm-2am Tue-Fri, 11-4pm & 7pm-midnight Sat & Sun) In a cosy, atmospheric dining room, Taberna da Esperança wows diners with flavourful dishes that blend Alentejan recipes with a modern edge. The inventive menu changes often and features plates designed for sharing. Favourites include fava beans with sausages, sautéed mushrooms with chestnuts, and *bacalhau* rice with rosemary. Reserve ahead. Cash only for nonresidents.

There's a wine bar between here and **Petiscaria Ideal** (Map p60; ☑213 971 504; www.petiscariaideal.com; Rua da Esperança

100; small plates €3-9, mains €9-14; ⊘7pm-2am Mon-Sat; 🛜), where you can sip carefully selected juice and craft beers while you wait.

Terra   Vegetarian €€

(Map p52; www.restauranteterra.pt; Rua da Palmeira 15; buffet €13-16; ⊘12.30-3.30pm & 7.30-11.30pm Tue-Sun; 🛜🌿) 🍃 Vegetarians sing the praises of Terra for its superb buffet (including vegan options) of salads, kebabs and curries, plus organic wines and juices. A fountain gurgles in the tree-shaded courtyard, lit by twinkling lights after dark.

⊗ Lapa & Alcântara

Cafetaria Village   Cafe €

(Map p60; www.vulisboa.com; Rua Primeiro de Maio 103, Village Underground Lisboa; mains €2.50-7; ⊘noon-8pm Apr-Sep, to 6pm Tue-Sun Oct-Mar; 🛜♿) Located inside a raised antique double-decker city bus resting on shipping containers, this small cafe is part of Village Underground Lisboa, a London cultural-hub concept sprung up in Lisbon inside the grounds of the Carris complex in Alcântara. It does fantastic *tostas* and salads, good weekend brunches, and monthly specials such as *feijoada* and *cozida portuguesa,* both types of Portuguese stews.

Último Porto   Seafood €€

(Map p60; 📞308 808 939; Estação Marítima da Rocha do Conde de Óbidos; mains €8.50-17; ⊘8am-4.30pm Mon-Sat) An absolute local's secret for a reason, this top seafooder takes an act of God to find. Hidden among the shipping-container cranes of the Port of Lisbon, its fantastically simple grilled fish paired with top Alentejan and Douro wines draws locals in droves. With shipping containers and departmental port buildings framing the ambience, María do Céu oversees a parking-lot-style grill.

⊗ Marquês de Pombal & Around

Jesus é Goês   Indian €€

(Map p52; 📞211 545 812; Rua de São José 23; mains €8-18.50; ⊘noon-3pm & 7-11pm

Coyo Taco

Tue-Sat; 🛜) At one of Lisbon's best Indian restaurants, jovial chef Jesus Lee whips up contemporary Goan delicacies. Rice-sack tablecloths and colourful murals (note the playful Christian-Hindu imagery) set the scene for starters such as onion-coriander chickpea fritters or potato bhaji with puri, followed by mushroom and chestnut or shrimp curries, or 11-spices goat – all fiery-fantastic. Bookings are essential – it's tiny. Cash only.

Cervejaria Ribadouro
Seafood €€

(📞213 549 411; www.cervejariaribadouro.pt; Rua do Salitre 2; mains €11-30, seafood per kg €42.50-147; 🕑noon-1.30am; 🛜) Bright, noisy and full to the gills, this bustling beer hall is popular with local seafood fans, some of whom just belly up to the bar, chase their fresh shrimp and *tremoços* (lupin beans) with an ice-cold *imperial* (draught beer) and call it a night. The shellfish are plucked fresh from the tank, weighed and cooked to lip-smacking perfection.

✖ Belém

Antiga Confeitaria de Belém
Pastries €

(Pastéis de Belém; Map p62; www.pasteisde belem.pt; Rua de Belém 84-92; pastries from €1.10; 🕑8am-11pm Oct-Jun, to midnight Jul-Sep) Since 1837 this patisserie has been transporting locals to sugar-coated nirvana with heavenly *pastéis de Belém*. The crisp pastry nests are filled with custard cream, baked at 200°C for that perfect golden crust, then lightly dusted with cinnamon. Admire *azulejos* in the vaulted rooms or devour a still-warm tart at the counter and try to guess the secret ingredient.

Alecrim & Manjerona
Cafe €

(Map p62; www.facebook.com/alecrim manjeronamercearia; Rua do Embaixador 143; light meals & lunches €2.75-8; 🕑10am-6pm Mon-Fri) Tucked away from the crowds on a side street, Alecrim & Manjerona ('Rosemary & Marjoram') is a cute grocery store, cafe, deli and wine bar rolled into one. Besides delicious homemade cakes

Pensão Amor (p78)

HORACIO VILLALOBOS · CORBIS/CORBIS VIA GETTY IMAGES ©

Wine Bar do Castelo (p79)

and tarts, it rustles up wallet-friendly specials – from quiches to *bacalhau espiritual* (codfish gratin).

🎯 Parque das Nações

Casa Bota Feijão Portuguese €

(☎218 532 489; www.restaurantebotafeijao. pt, Rua Conselheiro Lopo Vaz 5; half/whole portions €8.50/12; ☺8am-8pm Mon-Fri) Don't be fooled by the nondescript decor and railroad-track views. When a tucked-away place is this crowded with locals at lunchtime midweek, it must be doing something right. Everyone's here for one thing and one thing only: Bairrada-style *leitão* – suckling pig spit-roasted on an open fire until juicy and meltingly tender, doused in a beautiful, peppery garlic sauce.

🍷 DRINKING & NIGHTLIFE

Late-night street parties in Cais do Sodré and Bairro Alto, sunset *ginjinhas* on Rossio's sticky cobbles, drinks with indie kids in Santa Catarina – Lisbon has one of Europe's most eclectic nightlife scenes.

🎯 Baixa & Rossio

TOPO Martim Moniz Cocktail Bar

(Map p52; www.facebook.com/pg/topolisboa; Centro Comercial Martim Moniz, 6th fl, Praça Martim Moniz; ☺12.30pm-midnight Sun-Wed, to 1am Thu, to 2am Fri & Sat) This hipster hang-out is an excellent rooftop lounge with extraordinary views over lively Praça Martim Moniz and the whole of Lisbon. It features loungey open-air wooden benches for cocktails (€8 to €14), coffee and light bites, and a covered indoor lounge. It's all set to a vibey soundtrack, often courtesy of DJs.

Rooftop Bar Bar

(Map p52; www.hotel-mundial.pt; Praça Martim Moniz 2, Hotel Mundial; ☺4-11pm) Grab a table at sundown on the Hotel Mundial's roof terrace for a sweeping view of Lisbon and its hilltop castle. The backlit bar, white sofas and ambient sounds set the stage for evening drinks and sharing plates.

Memmo Alfama

🍷 Bairro Alto, Chiado & Cais do Sodré

Park   Bar

(Map p52; www.facebook.com/parklisboa
official; Calçada do Combro 58; ⊘1pm-2am
Tue-Sat, to 8pm Sun; 🛜) If only all multistorey
car parks were like this... Take the lift to
the 5th floor, and head up and around to
the top, which has been transformed into
one of Lisbon's hippest rooftop bars, with
sweeping views reaching right down to the
Rio Tejo and over the bell towers of Igreja
de Santa Catarina.

Pensão Amor   Bar

(Map p52; www.pensaoamor.pt; Rua do Alecrím
19; ⊘2pm-3am Sun-Wed, to 4am Thu-Sat) Set
inside a former brothel, this cheeky bar
pays homage to its lascivious past with
colourful wall murals, a library of erotically
tinged works and a small stage where you
can sometimes catch burlesque shows.

BA Wine Bar do Bairro Alto   Wine Bar

(Map p52; 📋213 461 182; bawinebar@gmail.
com; Rua da Rosa 107; ⊘6-11pm Tue-Sun; 🛜)

Reserve ahead unless you want to get shut
out of Bairro Alto's best wine bar, where
the genuinely welcoming staff will offer
you three fantastic tasting choices based
on your wine proclivities (wines from €5;
tasting boards for one/four €13/47). The
cheeses (from small artisanal producers)
and charcuterie (melt-in-your-mouth
black-pork *presuntos*) are not to be missed,
either. Reservations are essential.

Duque Brewpub   Craft Beer

(Map p52; www.duquebrewpub.com; Duques
da Calçada 49; ⊘3pm-midnight Sun-Wed,
to 1am Thu, to 2am Fri & Sat; 🛜) Lisbon's
inaugural brewpub features 12 taps of
Portuguese-only craft brews, a few of which
are dedicated to on-site suds (under the
banner of Cerveja Aroeira), brewed in true
craft-beer style: no two batches are the
same. Additional taps feature invitees such
as Dois Corvos, Musa and Letra.

O Bom O Mau e O Vilão   Cocktail Bar

(Map p52; www.thegoodthebadandtheuglybar.com;
Rua do Alecrím 21; ⊘7pm-2am Mon-Thu, to 3am Fri
& Sat) 'The Good, the Bad and the Ugly' is an

artsy drinking den sprung from a refurbished Pombaline town house. It's divided among several rooms draped in contemporary artworks and period furnishings. DJs throw down funk, soul, acid jazz and vintage beats to an eclectic, easy-on-the-eyes crowd that is mingle-friendly and more highbrow than average for the neighbourhood.

Crafty Corner · Craft Beer

(Map p52; www.facebook.com/craftycorner lisboa; Tv Corpo Santo 15; ⊙4pm-2am Mon-Sat, to 11.45pm Sun; 🖘) An Irishman well versed in Cais do Sodré bars – he owns **Hennessy's Irish pub** (Map p52; www.hennessys-pub.com; Rua Cais do Sodré 32-38; ⊙noon-2am Sun-Thu, to 3am Fri & Sat; 🖘) as well – has stepped up the neighbourhood's bar game with this refined lounge dedicated to Lisbon craft beer. There are 12 taps and plenty of atmospheric ambience: leather sofas in the loft, stools fashioned from emptied kegs and original wooden ceilings.

🌀 Alfama, Castelo & Graça

Wine Bar do Castelo · Wine Bar

(Map p56; 📞218 879 093; www.facebook.com/ winebardocastelo; Rua Bartolomeu de Gusmão 13; ⊙1-10pm) Located near the entrance to the Castelo de São Jorge (p55), this laid-back wine bar serves more than 150 Portuguese wines by the glass (€4 to €30), along with gourmet smoked meats, cheeses, olives and other tasty accompaniments. Nuno, the multilingual owner, is a welcoming host and a fount of knowledge about all things wine-related.

Memmo Alfama · Bar

(Map p56; www.memmoalfama.com; Tv das Merceeiras 27; ⊙noon-midnight; 🖘) Wow, what a view! Alfama unfolds like origami from the stylishly decked roof terrace of the **Memmo Alfama hotel** (📞210 495 660; www.memmoalfama.com; Tv Merceeiras 27; d €200-350, ste €300-450; 🕸🖘🌊). It's a perfect sundowner place, with dreamy vistas over the rooftops, spires and down to the Rio Tejo (and, unfortunately, the new cruise-ship terminal). Cocktails cost €7.50 to €10.

🍷 Ginjinha Bars

Come dusk, the area around Largo de São Domingos and the adjacent Rua das Portas de Santo Antão buzzes with locals getting their cherry fix in a cluster of *ginjinha* (cherry liqueur) bars. **A Ginjinha** (Map p52; Largo de Saõ Domingos 8; ⊙9am-10pm) is famous as the birthplace of the sugary-sweet tipple, thanks to a quaffing friar from Igreja de Santo António who revealed the secret to an entrepreneurial Galician by the name of Espinheira. Order your €1.40 *ginjinha sem* (without) or – our favourite – *com* (with) the alcohol-soaked cherries. Other postage-stamp-sized bars nearby include **Ginjinha Sem Rival** (Map p52; www.facebook.com/ginjasemrivaleeduardino; Rua das Portas de Santo Antão 7; ⊙8am-midnight Mon-Fri, from 9am Sat & Sun) and **Ginjinha Rubi** (Map p52; Rua Barros Queirós 27; ⊙7am-10.30pm Mon-Sat).

A Ginjinha
STOCKPHOTOSART/SHUTTERSTOCK ©

Lux-Frágil · Club

(www.luxfragil.com; Av Infante D Henrique, Armazém A, Cais de Pedra; ⊙11pm-6am Thu-Sat) Lisbon's ice-cool, must-see club, glammy Lux hosts big-name DJs spinning electro and house. It was started by late Lisbon nightlife impresario Marcel Reis and is part-owned by John Malkovich. Grab a spot on the terrace to see the sun rise over the Rio Tejo, or chill like a king or queen on the throne-like giant interior chairs.

Outro Lado
Craft Beer

(Map p56; www.facebook.com/OutroLado Lisboa; Beco do Arco Escuro 1; ⏰3pm-midnight Tue-Thu, to 2am Fri & Sat, 2-11pm Sun; 📶) An Egyptian-Polish couple took over and seriously upgraded Lisbeer, one of Lisbon's loungiest and least beer-geeky craft-beer bars, in late 2018. Sé's Outro Lado now offers 15 artisanal brews on draught and 200 or so by the bottle/can, with an emphasis on Portugal's rising scene and the freshest options from Europe, the USA and Canada.

8ª Colina Taproom
Craft Beer

(Map p56; www.oitavacolina.pt; Rua Damasceno Monteiro 8a; ⏰noon-11pm Tue-Thu & Sun, to 1am Fri & Sat) One of the top brewers in Lisbon's microbrew scene, 8ª Colina's long-awaited taproom opened with spectacularly framed castle views straight from its 10 taps in 2018. The minimalist, slate-grey space is a nod to industrial design; and there's good pub grub (pulled pork, banh mi, bratwurst) to pair with its lagers, IPAs and porters.

Chapitô
Bar

(Map p56; 📞218 875 077; www.chapito.org; Costa do Castelo 7; ⏰terrace 7am-1pm, restaurant 7pm-2am; 📶) There are fantastic views from this bar at an alternative theatre and circus school occupying a former female prison. It's a top choice for sundowners or late-night drinks overlooking the city. More serious foodies will want to book a table at **Chapitô à Mesa** (Map p56; Rua Costa do Castelo 7; mains €19-21; ⏰noon-midnight Mon-Fri, 7.30-11pm Sat & Sun; 📶), the restaurant in the hands of Bertílio Gomes, one of the city's top chefs.

🍺 Príncipe Real, Santos & Estrela

Cerveteca Lisboa
Craft Beer

(Map p60; www.cervetecalisboa.com; Praça das Flores 62; ⏰3.30pm-1am Sun-Thu, to 2am Fri & Sat; 📶) Lisbon's best craft-beer bar is a boozy godsend: 14 oft-changing taps (including two hand pumps) focusing on local and Northern European artisanal brews, including numerous local microbreweries. Not only will hopheads rejoice at IPAs from Lisbon

Fado performance in Lisbon

Foxtrot

including standouts such as Dois Corvos and 8ª Colina, but having choice alone inspires cartwheels. *Adeus,* tasteless lagers!

Foxtrot
Bar

(Map p60; www.barfoxtrot.com; Tv Santa Teresa 28; ☺6pm-2am Mon-Thu, to 3am Fri & Sat, 8pm-2am Sun; 🛜) A cuckoo-clock doorbell announces new arrivals to this dark, decadent slither of art-nouveau glamour, in the bar business since 1978. Foxtrot keeps the mood mellow with jazzy beats and intensely attentive mixology detailed on a tracing-paper menu (cocktails €7 to €15). It's a wonderfully atmospheric spot for a drink.

The Bar
Cocktail Bar

(Tv Monte do Carmo 1; ☺7pm-midnight Tue-Thu, to 2am Fri & Sat; 🛜) Australian Teresa Ruiz runs a one-woman cocktail show at this fantastic bar that puts tasty spins on classics in a heavily concreted environment spruced up with an eye-catching she-wolf street mural by Tamara Alves. Negronis are her thing (traditional, with mezcal or with Aperol) but there's something for everyone,

including Aussies missing Bondi Beach (No 9 – vodka, Campari and OJ).

🍺 Marquês de Pombal & Around

Red Frog
Cocktail Bar

(www.facebook.com/redfrogspeakeasy; Rua do Salitre 5A; ☺6pm-2am Mon-Thu, to 3am Fri & Sat) In true speakeasy fashion, Red Frog is accessed via a 'Press for Cocktails' doorbell and a list of rules. Enter a sophisticated mixology world of craft cocktails and appropriate glassware, dress and behaviour. The exquisite seasonal cocktail menu (€10 to €14.50) is perfectly balanced, and the dark and classy room, plus the intriguing secret one, are perfect accompaniments. Connoisseurs only.

⭐ ENTERTAINMENT

Lisbon entertains with high culture, experimental art and everything in between, from sumptuous strings and street theatre in Chiado, to the melancholic soul of fado in Alfama's atmospheric lanes.

Hot Clube de Portugal
Jazz

(Map p52; ☎213 460 305; www.hcp.pt; Praça da Alegria 48; ⏰10pm-2am Tue-Sat) As hot as its name suggests, this small, poster-plastered cellar (and newly added garden) has staged top-drawer jazz acts since the 1940s. It's considered one of Europe's best.

Mesa de Frades
Live Music

(Map p56; ☎917 029 436; www.facebook.com/mesadefradeslisboa; Rua dos Remédios 139A; prix-fixe shows €50; ⏰8pm-2.30am Mon-Sat) A magical place to hear fado, tiny Mesa de Frades used to be a chapel. It's tiled with exquisite *azulejos* and has just a handful of tables, including a dark and sexy mezzanine level. Shows begin at around 10.30pm.

Tasca Bela
Live Music

(Map p56; ☎926 077 511; www.facebook.com/bela.vinhosepetiscos; Rua dos Remédios 190; ⏰8.30pm-3am Tue-Sun) This intimate spot features live fado on Wednesday, Friday, Saturday and Sunday, and eclectic cultural fare (jazz, poetry readings) on other nights. Although there is a €19 minimum spend, at Tasca Bela you won't have to buy a pricey meal (unlike most fado houses), because it's more an appetisers-and-drinks kind of place. Fado begins at 9.30pm.

A Baiuca
Live Music

(Map p56; ☎218 867 284; Rua de São Miguel 20; ⏰8pm-midnight Thu-Mon) On a good night, walking into A Baiuca is like gatecrashing a family party. It's a special place with *fado vadio*, where locals take a turn and spectators hiss if anyone dares to chat during the singing. There's a €25 minimum spend, which is as tough to swallow as the food, though the fado is spectacular. Reserve ahead.

Senhor Fado
Live Music

(Map p56; ☎914 431 971; www.sr-fado.com; Rua dos Remédios 176; ⏰8pm-2am Wed-Sat) Small and lantern-lit, this is a cosy spot for *fado vadio* (street fado). *Fadista* Ana Marina and guitarist Duarte Santos make a great double act.

Parreirinha de Alfama
Live Music

(Map p56; ☎218 868 209; www.parreirinha dealfama.com; Beco do Espírito Santo 1; minimum €30; ⏰8pm-2am Tue-Sun) Owned by fado

Estádio da Luz

legend Argentina Santos, this place offers good food amid candlelit ambience; it attracts an audience that often falls hard for the top-quality *fadistas* (three singers and two guitarists per night, sometimes appearing straight out of the crowd). Book by 4pm.

A Tasca do Chico
Live Music

(Map p52; 961 339 696; www.facebook.com/atasca.dochico; Rua do Diário de Notícias 39; ☉7pm-1.30am Sun-Thu, to 3am Fri & Sat) This crowded dive (reserve ahead), full of soccer banners and spilling over with people of all ilks, is a fado free-for-all. It's not uncommon for taxi drivers to roll up, hum a few bars, and hop right back into their cabs, speeding off into the night.

Zé dos Bois
Live Music

(ZDB; Map p52; www.zedosbois.org; Rua da Barroca 59; cover €6-10; ☉expositions 6-11pm Wed-Sat, concerts from 10pm) Focusing on tomorrow's performing-arts and music trends, Zé dos Bois is an experimental venue with a graffitied courtyard and an eclectic line-up of theatre, film, visual arts and live music.

Estádio da Luz
Stadium

(Estádio do Sport Lisboa e Benfica; 707 200 100; www.slbenfica.pt; Av General Norton de Matos; tour/museum €12.50/10) SL Benfica play at this 65,000-seat stadium in the northwestern Benfica district, which also houses the club's well-done **museum** (https://museubenfica.slbenfica.pt), where you can visit the soaring bald eagle mascot, Vitória. The stadium hosted the 2014 Champions League final and was voted the most beautiful stadium in Europe the same year by French sporting newspaper, *L'Équipe*. Seeing a match here is epic.

ℹ INFORMATION

Ask Me Lisboa (Map p52; 213 463 314; www.askmelisboa.com; Praça dos Restauradores, Palácio Foz; ☉9am-8pm) Lisbon's largest and most helpful tourist office faces Praça dos Restauradores inside the Palácio Foz. Has maps and information, and books accommodation and rental cars.

ℹ GETTING THERE & AWAY

AIR

Situated around 6km north of the centre, the ultramodern **Aeroporto de Lisboa** (Lisbon Airport; 218 413 500; www.ana.pt/pt/lis/home; Alameda das Comunidades Portuguesas) operates direct flights to major international hubs including London, New York, Paris and Frankfurt. Low-cost carriers (Norwegian, easyJet, Ryanair, Transavia, Blue Air and Wizz Air) leave from the less efficient Terminal 2 – you'll need to factor in extra time for the shuttle ride if arriving at the airport on the metro.

BUS

Lisbon's main long-distance bus terminal is **Terminal Rodoviário de Sete Rios** (Praça General Humberto Delgado, Rua das Laranjeiras), adjacent to both Jardim Zoológico metro station and Sete Rios train station. The big carriers, **Rede Expressos** (707 223 344; www.rede-expressos.pt; Praça General Humberto Delgado, Terminal Rodoviário de Sete Rios; ☉info booth 9am-1pm & 2-6pm Mon-Sat, 10am-2pm & 3-7pm Sun) and **Eva** (707 223 344; www.eva-bus.com; Praça General Humberto Delgado, Terminal Rodoviário de Sete Rios), run frequent services to almost every major town in Portugal.

Intercentro/Internorte (707 200 512; www.intercentro.pt; Av Dom João II, Gare do Oriente; ☉9am-6pm) runs coaches to destinations all over Europe, beginning at Sete Rios and stopping at Gare do Oriente 15 minutes later. In addition to Madrid (from €40, 9¼ hours), there are direct connections to Seville (€45, 7¾ hours) and Paris (€95, 27 hours).

Domestic services:

Coimbra €13.80, 2½ hours, 49 daily

Évora €11.90, 1¾ hours, 27 daily

Faro €18.50, 4 hours, 19 daily

Porto €19, 4¼ hours, 40 daily

TRAIN

Lisbon is linked by train to other major cities. Check the website of **Comboios de Portugal** (707 210 220; www.cp.pt) for schedules – cheaper promo fares are often available online.

MSTEPANPHOTOGRAPHER/SHUTTERSTOCK © ARCHITECT SANTIAGO CALATRAVA

Gare do Oriente

Express services from Gare do Oriente (the biggest of several train stations) include the following:

Coimbra €23.50–33.70, 2 hours, 10–20 daily

Évora €12.40–16.50, 1½ hours, 3–4 daily

Faro €21.90–30.70, 3 hours, 3–6 daily

Porto €25–43.60, 3 hours, 7–20 daily

❶ GETTING AROUND

BUS, TRAM & FUNICULAR

Companhia Carris de Ferro de Lisboa (☎213 500 115; www.carris.pt) operates all transport in Lisbon proper except the metro. Its buses and trams run from about 5am or 6am to about 10pm or 11pm; there are some night bus and tram services.

Pick up a transport map, Rede de Transportes de Lisboa, from tourist offices. The Carris website has timetables and route details.

Board tram 28 at Praça Martim Moniz. You'll increase your chances of a seat and avoid waiting at heavier trafficked tourist areas where packed trams skip stops.

METRO

The **metro** (☎213 500 115; www.metrolisboa.pt; single/day ticket €1.50/6.40; ☺6.30am-1am) is useful for short hops and to reach the Gare do Oriente and nearby Parque das Nações.

Buy tickets from metro ticket machines, which have English-language menus. The Lisboa Card is also valid.

Entrances are marked by a big red 'M'. Useful signs include *correspondência* (transfer between lines) and *saída* (exit to the street).

TICKETS & PASSES

On-board one-way prices are €2 for buses and €3 for trams. One-way tickets for funicular rides are not available; these are €3.80 return. A day pass costs €6.40. You can also purchase Zapping cards (€0.50 from metro-station kiosks) and load them with credit in €5 denominations for use on trams, buses and the metro (around €1.35 per ride for each).

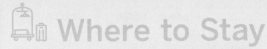

Where to Stay

You're spoilt for choice when it comes to places to unpack your valise in the Portuguese capital. Each neighbourhood has its own noise level so choose carefully. Room rates tend to be lower than in most of Western Europe.

Marquês de Pombal & Around

Baixa & Rossio

Príncipe Real, Santos & Estrela

Alfama, Castelo & Graça

Bairro Alto, Chiado & Cais do Sodré

Doca de Alcântara

Rio Tejo

Neighbourhood	For	Against
Baixa & Rossio	Very central; great public-transport links.	Very touristy; the 24-hour buzz can disrupt sleep.
Bairro Alto, Chiado & Cais do Sodré	Chiado boasts top-end trendies, boutique options galore, world-class shopping; Bairro Alto oozes historical charm.	Chiado is pricey; Bairro Alto is rowdy-nightlife central.
Alfama, Castelo & Graça	Castelo and Graça offer dramatic views; Alfama is Lisbon's most cinematic neighbourhood.	Alfama can be noisy near fado houses. Castelo and Graça require steep climbs for those on foot. Limited public transport.
Príncipe Real, Santos & Estrela	Bohemian Príncipe Real is tops for cutting-edge local fashion, shopping, restaurants and the LGBT community; Santos and Estrela are ideal for escapists who prefer pin-drop peace to central bustle.	Príncipe Real is one of Lisbon's highest neighbourhoods – it's a climb to reach it on foot. Santos and Estrela sit a tad outside the action.
Marquês de Pombal & Around	Home to Lisbon's finest restaurants and designer boutiques.	Big avenues; high-rise dwellings lack charm.

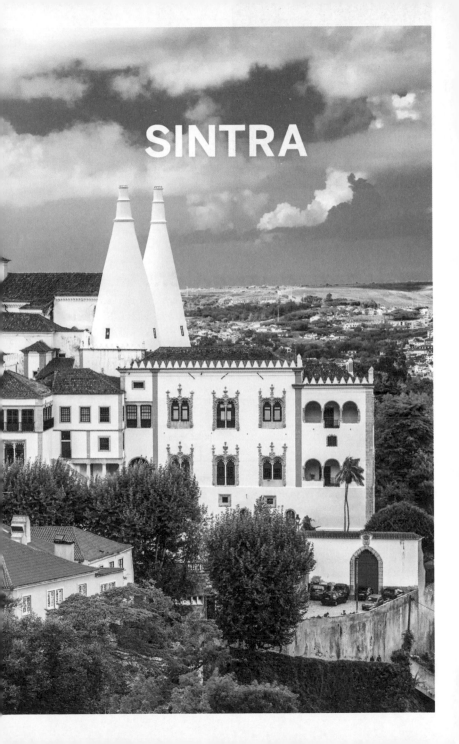

SINTRA

Sintra at a Glance...

With its rippling mountains, dewy forests thick with ferns and lichen, exotic gardens and glittering palaces, Sintra is like a page torn from a fairy tale. Its Unesco World Heritage–listed centre, Sintra-Vila, is dotted with pastel-hued manors folded into luxuriant hills that roll down to the blue Atlantic.

Celts worshipped their moon god here, the Moors built a precipitous castle, and 18th-century Portuguese royals swanned around its dreamy gardens. Even Lord Byron waxed lyrical about Sintra's charms: 'Lo! Cintra's glorious Eden intervenes, in variegated maze of mount and glen', which inspired his epic poem Childe Harold's Pilgrimage.

Two Days in Sintra

Two days in Sintra is just enough to get a taste of its grand buildings and idyllic landscapes. Start with the **Castelo dos Mouros** (p91) and the **Palácio Nacional da Pena** (p91) on day one, followed by the **Palácio Nacional de Sintra** (p90) and **Quinta da Regaleira** (p94) on day two.

Four Days in Sintra

On day three, visit the **Convento dos Capuchos** (p93) set amid lush forest and the manicured gardens and striking architecture of the **Palácio & Parque de Monserrate** (p92). On day four, take a detour out to Cabo da Roca for dazzling views over towering sea cliffs. End the Sintra stay with Portuguese tapas and red wine at **Nau Palatina** (p96).

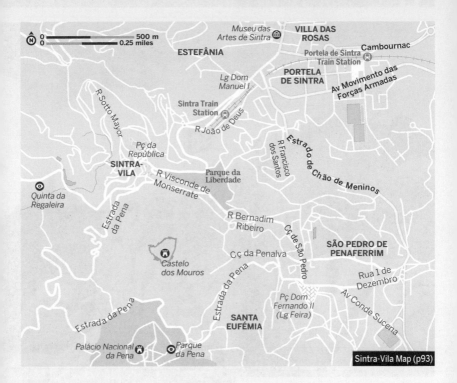

Sintra-Vila Map (p93)

Arriving in Sintra

Both buses and trains arrive at Sintra train station. If arriving by train, go to the last stop – Sintra – from where it's a pleasant 1km walk (or short bus ride) into the village. **Comboios de Portugal** (p314) runs trains (€2.25, 40 minutes) half-hourly between Sintra and Lisbon's Rossio station (hourly on weekends),

Where to Stay

It's worth staying overnight as Sintra has some magical guest houses, from quaint villas to lavish manors. Book (way) ahead in summer.

There's a dense concentration of accommodation in the village itself as well as around the train station. Other options are dotted around the area, with many offering wonderful views of the wooded hills.

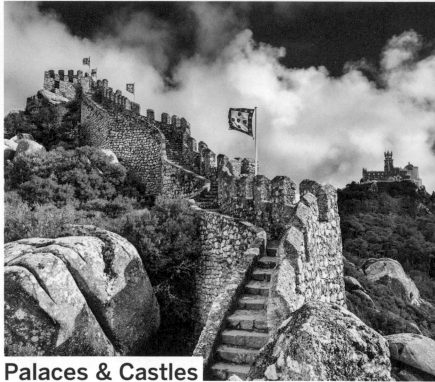

Castelo dos Mouros

SEAN PAVONE/SHUTTERSTOCK ©

Palaces & Castles

There's so much to see in Sintra it can be difficult to know where to start. Here we give you the low-down on three not-to-be-missed historic sights.

Great For...

☑ Don't Miss

The surreal descent into the underworld via a fairy-lit well at the Quinta da Regaleira (p94).

Palácio Nacional de Sintra

The star of Sintra-Vila is this **palace** (Map p93; www.parquesdesintra.pt; Largo Rainha Dona Amélia; adult/child €10/8.50; ⏱9.30am-7pm), with its iconic twin conical chimneys and lavish, whimsical interior, which is a mix of Moorish and Manueline styles, with arabesque courtyards, barley-twist columns and 15th- and 16th-century geometric *azulejos* (hand-painted tiles) that figure among Portugal's oldest.

Of Moorish origins, the palace was first expanded by Dom Dinis (1261–1325), enlarged by João I in the 15th century (when the kitchens were built), then given a Manueline twist by Manuel I in the following century.

Highlights include the octagonal Sala dos Cisnes (Swan Room), adorned with frescoes of 27 gold-collared swans; and the Sala das

Palácio Nacional da Pena

ANDREI NEKRASSOV/SHUTTERSTOCK ©

Palácio Nacional da Pena

Rising from a thickly wooded peak and often enshrouded in swirling mist, **Palácio Nacional da Pena** (www.parquesdesintra.pt; combined ticket with Parque da Pena adult/child €14/12.50; ☺9.45am-7pm) is a wacky confection of onion domes, Moorish keyhole gates, writhing stone snakes and crenellated towers in pinks and lemons. It is considered the greatest expression of 19th-century romanticism in Portugal.

The eclectic, extravagant interior is equally unusual, brimming with precious Meissen porcelain, Portuguese-style furniture, trompe l'œil murals and Dom Carlos' unfinished nudes of buxom nymphs.

There are daily guided tours at 2.30pm. Buses depart from the entrance to the palace every 15 minutes (€3), otherwise it's a 10- to 15-minute walk uphill.

Pegas (Magpie Room), with its ceiling emblazoned with magpies. Other standouts are the wooden Sala dos Brasões, bearing the shields of 72 leading 16th-century families, the shipshape Galleon Room and the Palatine chapel featuring an Islamic mosaic floor.

Castelo dos Mouros

Soaring 412m above sea level, this mist-enshrouded ruined **castle** (www.parquesdesintra.pt; adult/child €8/6.50; ☺9.30am-8pm) looms high above the surrounding forest. When the clouds peel away, the vistas over Sintra's palace-dotted hill and dale, across to the glittering Atlantic are – like the climb – breathtaking. The 10th-century Moorish castle's dizzying ramparts stretch across the mountain ridges and past moss-clad boulders the size of small buses.

◎ SIGHTS

Palácio & Parque de Monserrate   Palace

(www.parquesdesintra.pt; adult/child €8/6.50; ☺9.30am-7pm) At the centre of a lush, 30-hectare park, a manicured lawn sweeps up to this whimsical, Moorish-Gothic-Indian *palácio,* the 19th-century romantic folly of English millionaire Sir Francis Cook. The wild and rambling gardens were created in the 18th century by wealthy English merchant Gerard de Visme, then enlarged by landscape painter William Stockdale (with help from London's Kew Gardens).

Its wooded hillsides bristle with exotic foliage, from Chinese weeping cypress to dragon trees and Himalayan rhododendrons. Seek out the Mexican garden nurturing palms, yuccas and agaves, and the bamboo-fringed Japanese garden abloom with camellias.

The park is 3.5km west of Sintra-Vila.

Parque da Pena   Gardens

(☏219 237 300; www.parquesdesintra.pt; adult/child €7.50/6.50, combined ticket with Palácio Nacional da Pena €14/12.50; ☺9.30am-8pm) Nearly topped by King Ferdinand II's whimsical Palácio Nacional da Pena (only Cruz Alta, at 529m, is higher), these romantic gardens are filled with tropical plants, huge redwoods and fern trees, camellias, rhododendrons and lakes (note the castle-shaped duck houses for web-footed royalty!).

While the crowds descend on the palace, another less-visited but fascinating site within the park is the *Snow White & the Seven Dwarfs*–evoking **Chalet da Condessa d'Edla** (adult/child €9.50/8.50), an alpine-inspired summer getaway cottage commissioned by King Ferdinand II and his future second wife, Elise Hensler (the Countess of Edla).

Buses to the park entrance leave from Sintra train station and near Palácio Nacional de Sintra, among other spots around town. A taxi costs around €10 one-way. The steep, zigzagging walk through pine and eucalyptus woods from Sintra-Vila is around 3km to 4km.

Parque da Pena

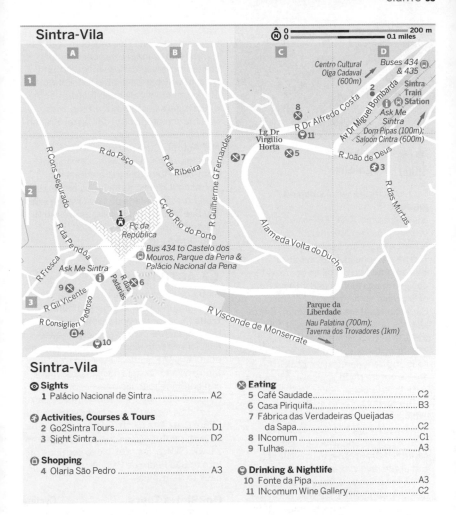

Sintra-Vila

Convento dos Capuchos Monastery

(Capuchin Monastery; ☏ 219 237 300; www.
parquesdesintra.pt; adult/child €7/5.50;
⊙ 9.30am-8pm) Hidden in the woods is this
bewitchingly hobbit-hole-like convent,
which was originally built in 1560 to house
friars, who lived in incredibly cramped
conditions, in tiny cells with low, narrow
doors. Byron mocked the monastery
in his poem *Childe Harold's Pilgrimage*,
referring to recluse Honorius, who spent a
staggering 36 years here (before dying at
age 95 in 1596).

It's often nicknamed the Cork Convent,
as its minuscule cells are lined with cork.
Visiting here is an *Alice in Wonderland*
experience, as you squeeze through to
explore the warren of cells, chapels, kitchen
and cavern. The monks lived a simple,
touchingly well-ordered life in this idyllic yet
spartan place, hiding up until 1834 when
it was abandoned after all religious orders
were abolished. Worthwhile audio guides
are available for €3.

You can walk here – the monastery is
7.3km from Sintra-Vila (5.1km from the

Quinta da Regaleira

Exploring this magical **villa and gardens** (www.regaleira.pt; Rua Barbosa du Bocage; adult/child €6/4, tours €12/8; ⊙9.30am-7pm Apr-Sep, to 5pm Oct-Mar) is like delving into another world. The neo-Manueline extravaganza was dreamed up by Italian opera-set designer Luigi Manini under the orders of Brazilian coffee tycoon, António Carvalho Monteiro, aka Monteiro dos Milhões (Moneybags Monteiro). Enter the villa to begin the surreal journey, with ferociously carved fireplaces, frescoes and Venetian-glass mosaics. Keep an eye out for mythological and Knights Templar symbols.

The playful gardens are fun to explore – footpaths wriggle through the dense foliage to follies, fountains, grottoes, lakes and underground caverns. All routes seem to eventually end at the revolving stone door leading to the initiation well, **Poço Iniciático**, plunging some 27m. You walk down the nine-tiered spiral (three by three – three being the magic number) to mysterious hollowed-out underground galleries, lit by fairy lights.

DALE JOHNSON/500PX ©

turn-off to Parque da Pena) along a remote, wooded road. There is no bus connection to the convent. Taxis charge around €35 return; arrange a pick-up.

Museu das Artes de Sintra   Museum

(MU.SA; www.cm-sintra.pt/musa-museu-das-artes-de-sintra; Avenida Heliodoro Salgado; adult/child €1/free; ⊙10am-8pm Tue-Fri, from 2pm Sat & Sun) This museum features a small and manageable collection of contemporary and modern art, around 80% of which is dedicated to local works. The permanent collection features some of Portugal's best-known artists, most notably sculptor Dorita de Castel-Branco and painters Columbano Bordalo Pinheiro and António Carneiro.

Temporary exhibitions run the gamut from war photography to abstract art. Permanent highlights include Carneiro's *Maria Josefina,* Maria do Céu Crispim's *Can You See Me?* (made of nails), and several paintings from various artists of Sintra's 18th-century glory days.

🚴 ACTIVITIES

Sintra is a terrific place to get out and stride around, with waymarked **hiking trails** (look for red and yellow stripes) that corkscrew up into densely wooded hills strewn with giant boulders. Justifiably popular is the gentle 50-minute trek from Sintra-Vila to Castelo dos Mouros. You can continue to Palácio Nacional da Pena (another 15 minutes). From here you can ascend Serra de Sintra's highest point, the 529m Cruz Alta (High Cross), named after its 16th-century cross, with amazing views all over Sintra. It's possible to continue on foot to São Pedro de Penaferrim and loop back to Sintra-Vila.

Go2Sintra Tours   Cycling

(Map p93; ☎917 855 428; www.go2cintra.com; Avenida Dr Miguel Bombarda 37; ⊙10am-7pm) Offers highly recommended electric-bike tours (from €35) as well as eBike rental (take our word for it – you'll want the motorised option in Sintra!). A full day's rental with support starts at €30. Its office is across from the Sintra train station inside the SintraCan shop.

Also offers wi-fi–equipped Twizy e-vehicles that can go all the way to the coast (€25 to €75).

Café Saudade

MuitAvenutra   Adventure
(📱967 021 248; www.muitaventura.com; Rua
Marquês Viana 31, São Pedro de Penaferrim) This
adventure outfitter has a regular schedule
of organised activities, including mountain
biking, rappelling, jeep tours, trekking and
night-time hikes.

✖ EATING

Much of Sintra's dining options are geared
towards making a quick buck off day
trippers, but hang around and you'll be
treated to a decent selection of authentic
tabernas, old-school restaurants and
scrumptious *pastelarias* (pastry shops)
slinging the city's famous sweet treats.
More recently, a few worthwhile contemporary culinary hotspots have cropped up,
giving the dining scene a much-needed
boost.

Café Saudade   Cafe €
(Map p93; www.facebook.com/CafeSaudade;
Avenida Dr Miguel Bombardo 6; mains €5.50-
8; ⊘8.30am-7pm; 🛜) This former bakery,
where Sintra's famous *queijadas* (crisp

pastry shells filled with a marzipan-like mix
of fresh cheese, sugar, flour and cinnamon)
were made, has cherub-covered ceilings
and a rambling interior. It's a fine spot for
pastries (the massive scones are a travel
highlight in the making), lighter fare or an
evening glass of wine.

A gallery in back features changing art
exhibitions. It also runs a refined guest
house, Chalet Saudade, nearby.

INcomum   Portuguese €€
(Map p93; 📱219 243 719; www.incomumby
luissantos.pt; Rua Dr Alfredo Costa 22;
mains €12.50-15.50, tasting menu €37.50;
⊘noon-midnight Mon-Fri & Sun, from 4.30pm
Sat; 🛜) Chef Luis Santos shakes up
Sintra's culinary scene with his modern
upgrades to Portuguese cuisine, served
amid the muted greys and greens of his
synchronic dining room. INcomum quickly
establishes itself as the anti-traditional
choice among serious foodies, first by
dangling an unbeatable €11 three-course-
lunch carrot, then by letting the food seal
the deal.

Sweet Dreams: Sintra Desserts

Sintra is famous for its luscious sweeties. **Fábrica das Verdadeiras Queijadas da Sapa** (Map p93; www.facebook.com/queijadasdasapa; Alameda Volta do Duche 12; pastries from €0.85; ⊙9am-6pm Tue-Fri, 9.30am-6.30pm Sat & Sun) has been fattening up royalty since 1756 with bite-sized *queijadas* – crisp pastry shells filled with a marzipan-like mix of fresh cheese, sugar, flour and cinnamon. Since 1952, **Casa Piriquita** (Map p93; www.piriquita.pt; Rua das Padarias 1-5; travesseiros €1.40; ⊙9am-8pm Thu-Tue) has been serving another kind of sweet dream: the *travesseiro* (pillow), a light puff pastry turned, rolled and folded seven times, then filled with delicious almond-and-egg-yolk cream and lightly dusted with sugar.

Travesseiro
SOPOTNICKI/SHUTTERSTOCK ©

The Swiss-trained chef does memorable things with chestnuts, and the seasonally changing menu isn't afraid to buck convention (duck magret with figs, cocoa and carrot purée, for example). Not much that's underwhelming emerges from his kitchen. Don't miss the **INcomum Wine Gallery** (Map p93; Rua Dr Alfredo Costa 18; ⊙noon-midnight Mon-Fri & Sun, from 4.30pm Sat; 🛜), either. A holiday highlight.

Nau Palatina   Portuguese €€
(☏219 240 962; www.facebook.com/barnaupalatina; Calçada São Pedro 18, São Pedro de Penaferrim; tapas €1.50-11.90; ⊙6pm-midnight Tue-Sat; 🛜) Sintra's friendliest and most welcoming restaurant is a travel-highlight star in the making. Congenial owner Zé's creative tapas are as slightly off-centre as his location, a worthwhile 1km walk from Sintra centre in São Pedro de Penaferrim. Spice Route undertones are weaved throughout the small but tasty menu of tidbits, strongly forged from local and regional ingredients.

Paired with an excellent house Setúbal red and Zé's convivial nature, you have yourself an evening to remember. Don't miss the pork cheeks!

Dom Pipas   Portuguese €€
(www.restaurantedompipas.pt; Rua João de Deus 62; mains €9.50-16.75; ⊙noon-3pm & 7-10pm Tue-Sun; 🛜) A consistently buzzing local favourite, Dom Pipas serves excellent Portuguese dishes amid *azulejos* and rustic country decor. It's behind Sintra's train station (left out of the station, first left, then left again to the end) – a fair way outside the hubbub.

Tulhas   Portuguese €€
(Map p93; www.restaurantetulhas.pt; Rua Gil Vicente 4; mains €12-20; ⊙noon-11pm, to 10pm in winter; 🛜) This converted grain warehouse is dark, tiled and quaint, with wrought-iron chandeliers and a relaxed, cosy atmosphere. It's rightfully renowned for its *bacalhau com nata* (creamy béchamel with shredded cod, served *au gratin*) but experiences here are hit and miss.

🍷 DRINKING & NIGHTLIFE

Saloon Cintra   Bar
(www.facebook.com/barsaloon.cintra; Avenida Movimento das Forças Armadas 5, Portela de Sintra; ⊙8pm-2am Mon-Fri, from 3pm Sat & Sun; 🛜) Sintra's best bar isn't in Sintra-Vila, but that shouldn't stop seasoned drinkers from checking it out. A potpourri of antiques and Portuguese bric-a-brac hovering over numerous mismatched vintage sofas makes for an atmospheric spot to take in the Belgian-heavy beer list (including Mc Chouffe on tap), good cocktails and the

cool local crowd. It's 700m east of Sintra train station.

Smoking is allowed.

Fonte da Pipa
Bar

(Map p93; www.facebook.com/barfonte dapipa; Rua Fonte da Pipa 11-13; ☺9pm-3am) A tiled bar, Fonte da Pipa has craggy, cave-like rooms and comfy seats. It's a Sintra mainstay that's especially popular with students and twenty-somethings.

🟢 ENTERTAINMENT

Taverna dos Trovadores
Live Music

(📞967 050 536; www.tavernadostrovadores.pt; Praça Dom Fernando II 18, São Pedro de Penaferrim; ☺noon-3.30pm & 7-10.30pm Mon-Sat, bar to 2am Fri & Sat) This atmospheric restaurant and bar features live music (folk and acoustic) on Friday and Saturday nights – an institution that's been around for more than two decades. Concerts run from 11pm to 2am. Nearby, its new Sabores de Sintra offers dinner and fado. It's in São Pedro de Penaferrim.

Festival de Sintra

Usually beginning in May or June, the three-week-long Festival de Sintra features classical recitals, ballet and modern dance, world music and multi-media events, plus concerts for kids.

National Palace of Queluz, a venue for the festival
NIKOLPETR/SHUTTERSTOCK ©

Centro Cultural Olga Cadaval
Performing Arts

(📞219 107 110; www.ccolgacadaval.pt; Praça Francisco Sá Carneiro) Sintra's major cultural venue stages concerts, theatre and dance.

Fonte da Pipa

Speedy Transport

If you have limited time and you'd like to see some of the attractions beyond Sintra-Vila, **Sight Sintra** (Map p93; ☑219 242 856; www.facebook.com/SightSintra; Rua João de Deus; tour €35-45; ☺9am-8pm Apr-Oct, 9.30am-6pm Nov-Mar) rents out tiny two-person buggies that guide you by GPS along one of three different routes. The most popular takes you to Castelo dos Mouros and Palácio Nacional da Pena, among other sites. It's located around the corner from the Sintra train station. You can also create your own itinerary, and hire a buggy for €25 per hour.

 INFORMATION

Ask Me Sintra (Map p93; ☑219 231 157; www.visitlisboa.com; Praça da República 23; ☺9.30am-6pm), near the centre of Sintra-Vila, is a helpful multilingual office with expert insight into Sintra and the surrounding areas. There's also a small branch at **Sintra train station** (Map p93; ☑211 932 545; www.visitlisboa.com; Av Miguel Bombarda, Sintra train station; ☺9am-7pm), often overrun by those arriving by rail.

Parques da Sintra – Monte da Lua (☑219 237 300; www.parquesdesintra.pt; Largo Sousa Brandão; ☺9.30am-6pm Apr-Oct, 10am-5pm Nov-Mar), which manages the majority of top Sintra sites, has a friendly information and ticket centre (along with a smaller one next to the Sintra-Villa post office).

 GETTING THERE & AWAY

Comboios de Portugal (p83) runs trains (€2.25, 40 minutes) half-hourly between Sintra and Lisbon's Rossio station (hourly on weekends), and every 20 minutes to Lisbon's less-convenient Oriente station (half-hourly on weekends). If arriving by train, go to the last stop – Sintra – from where it's a pleasant 1km, sculpture-peppered walk into the village.

Centro Cultural Olga Cadaval

Palácio & Parque de Monserrate (p92)

❶ GETTING AROUND

From the train station it's a 1km walk into Sintra-Vila, or you can grab the hop-on, hop-off **bus 435** (Map p93; Avenida Dr Miguel Bombarda), which goes from the station to Sintra-Vila (€5). This bus continues on to Quinta da Regaleira, and Palácio and Parque de Monserrate.

Scotturb bus 434 (Map p93; Praça da República) is handy for accessing Castelo dos Mouros (€6.90), which runs frequently from the train station via Sintra-Vila to the castle (10 minutes), Palácio Nacional da Pena (15 minutes) and back. One ticket gives you hop-on, hop-off access (in one direction; no backtracking).

You can also purchase a daily €12 hop-on, hop-off Scotturb ticket that works across the entire network and is valid in any direction until midnight. Be prepared to wait – even in winter the bus lines outside major attractions can be long.

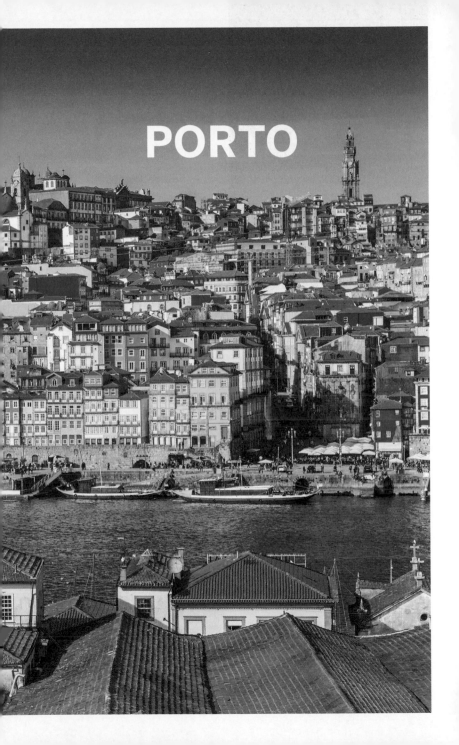

Porto at a Glance...

Opening up like a pop-up book from the Rio Douro at sunset, humble yet opulent Porto entices with its higgledy-piggledy medieval centre, divine food and wine, and charismatic locals. Porto's charms are as subtle as the nuances of an aged tawny port, best savoured slowly on a romp through the hilly backstreets of Miragaia, Ribeira and Massarelos. It's the quiet moments of reflection and the snapshots of daily life that you'll remember most: the slosh of the Douro against the docks or the sound of wine glasses clinking. The city also has some of Portugal's top festivals and restaurants.

Two Days in Porto

Spend day one exploring the Ribeira's knot of alleyways, churches and palaces, including the Romanesque **Sé** (p108), the **Palácio da Bolsa** (p112) and **Igreja de São Francisco** (p108). On day two take a culinary tour of the city and draw in more of its architecture, spotting *azulejos* (hand-painted tiles) as you go. End the day at a pavement cafe on the Cais da Ribeira, followed by dinner.

Four Days in Porto

Take your taste buds on day three across the Rio Douro to the Vila Nova de Gaia (p110) where you'll discover many old port-wine cellars, some still belonging to the original British merchant families who established them. Spend day four exploring some of Porto's other superb attractions such as the exquisitely tiled **São Bento Train Station** (p113) and the waterfront.

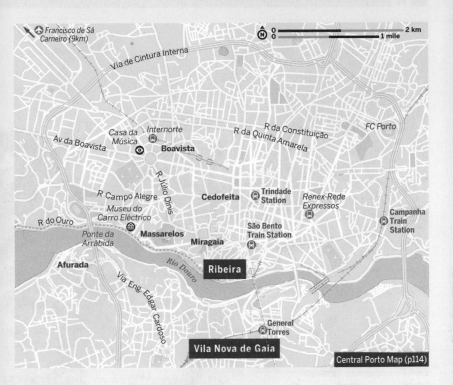

Central Porto Map (p114)

Arriving in Porto

Francisco de Sá Carneiro Airport
Linked to many European hubs.

Bus station There is no central bus station – bus companies arrive and depart from a variety of places throughout the city.

Campanhã train station Sits 3km east of the city centre – handles long-distance trains.

São Bento train station Local train services.

Where to Stay

Porto's sleeping scene has experienced an incredible renaissance in recent years, due to the influx of weekend visitors arriving on low-cost flights. Time-worn guest houses are slowly being replaced, and hipsterish hostels, retro-cool B&Bs, boutique hotels and slickly modern apartments (look for the 'AL' sign) are now plentiful. For more information on the best neighbourhoods to stay, see p133.

Pastéis de nata

STRELNIKAND/SHUTTERSTOCK ©

Wine, Tiles & Custard Tarts

The cultural trinity that intrigues every visitor to Portugal's second city is its unique wines, eye-catching tiles and addictive custard tarts.

Great For...

☑ **Don't Miss**

The exquisite *azulejos* at the city's São Bento train station.

Port

You can't say you've been to Porto until you've tasted the Douro's oak-barrel-aged nectar. Ever since the 17th century, lodges in Vila Nova de Gaia have been the nerve centre of port production. It was probably Roman soldiers who first planted grapes in the Douro Valley. According to legend, British merchants invented port when they added brandy to the wine to preserve it for shipment back to England. Something about the fortification of the wine and the time it spent in hot barrels at sea turned the wine into the wonderful beverage we know today. Madeira's famous dessert wine was 'accidentally' produced in the same way.

Azulejos

TIPHAINE_BUCCINO/GETTY IMAGES ©

Train Station (p113), a veritable ode to tile art with over 20,000 *azulejos* adorning the station's vestibule. Dating from 1905 to 1916, they are the romantic work of tile painter Jorge Colaço and depict scenes from Portugal's history. Another of Colaço's *azulejos* masterpieces in Porto is the facade of the **Igreja de Santo Ildefonso** (Map p114; Praça da Batalha; ◷3-6.30pm Mon, 9am-noon & 3-6.30pm Tue-Sun).

Wine Tasting

For an insightful primer on port, hook onto a tasting at Touriga (p122), where the learned owners give an enlightening lesson with each glass they pour, or sample fine ports by the glass at Prova (p129). From here, head across the Douro to Vila Nova de Gaia, the steep banks of which are speckled with grand port-wine lodges.

Azulejos

Azulejos greet you at almost every corner in Porto. One of the delights of taking a stroll through the centre is the tiles you will encounter. Old and new, utilitarian and decorative, plain and geometrically patterned. Some of the finest grace Porto's churches, but Porto's crowning *azulejos* glory is undoubtedly the resplendent São Bento

Pastel de Nata

Though native to Lisbon, Porto is as good a place as any to try the ubiquitous *pastel de nata*, often rather drearily translated into English as 'custard tart', which barely does this irresistible treat justice. It's made with egg custard and cinnamon and baked in a cup of flaky pastry, and once you've tried one you'll be hooked – many develop a 'one-a-day' habit throughout their time in Portugal. It doesn't help that they are so cheap as well – you'll have overpaid if you part with more than €1.50 for this most typical of Portuguese temptations. Porto's cafes are, of course, brimming with other traditional cakes and pastries, ideal for a cheap and filling breakfast accompanied by a cup of smooth and frothy Portuguese coffee.

Porto City Centre

This walking tour winds its way through the city centre, skirting the edge of the Ribeira before running along the river to Porto's main river bridge. The route takes in some of the city's architectural highlights and two of the best waterfront dining areas.

Start Torre dos Clérigos
Distance 2km
Duration Two to three hours

1 Begin at the baroque **Torre dos Clérigos** (p117), which offers unrivalled views over Porto from its 76m-high tower.

4 Near the end of Rua das Flores stands Nicolau Nasoni's baroque masterpiece, the **Igreja da Misericórdia**, part of the Museu da Misericórdia do Porto (p112).

5 At the neoclassical **Palácio da Bolsa** (p112) check out the main courtyard (once Porto's stock exchange) for free, or stay on for a tour.

6 Just next door to the Palácio da Bolsa is the **Igreja de São Francisco** (p108), a severe Gothic facade hiding a jaw-dropping golden interior.

7 In Rua da Alfândega you'll find the medieval **Casa do Infante** (p112), the birthplace of Henry the Navigator and the site of some remarkable Roman ruins.

2 Admire the beaux arts splendour of **Avenida dos Aliados**; most of the grand buildings are hotels and banks; the palatial town hall stands at one end.

3 One of Porto's architectural highlights, the French-inspired **São Bento Train Station** (p113) boasts some astounding *azulejos* in its main hall.

Take a Break... Just off the route, Jimão (p125) is a great place for tapas and wine, or afternoon coffee and snacks.

RIBEIRA

Classic Photo
Porto's waterfront

8 The **Waterfront Esplanade** is a great place to grab an outdoor table at one of its cafes and enjoy the splendid city views across the Douro.

Igreja de São Francisco

ALEXANDRE FERNANDEZ PHOTOGRAPHE/GETTY IMAGES ©

Ribeira

Ribeira is Porto's biggest heart stealer, with its Unesco World Heritage maze of medieval alleys that zigzag down to the Douro River. Exploring this postcard-perfect neighbourhood is a must for every visitor.

Great For...

☑ Don't Miss

Ponte de Dom Luís I – admire, photograph and walk across Porto's architecturally striking main bridge.

Churches & Palaces

Sitting on Praça Infante Dom Henrique, **Igreja de São Francisco** (Map p114; Jardim do Infante Dom Henrique; adult/child €6/5; ⊘9am-8pm Jul-Sep, to 7pm Mar-Jun & Oct, to 5.30pm Nov-Feb) looks from the outside to be an austerely Gothic church, but inside it hides one of Portugal's most dazzling displays of baroque finery. Hardly an inch escapes unsmothered, as otherworldly cherubs and sober monks are drowned by nearly 100kg of gold leaf. If you see only one church in Porto, make it this one.

Porto's **Sé** (Map p114; Terreiro da Sé; cloisters adult/student €3/2; ⊘9am-7pm Mon-Sat & 9.30am-12.30pm & 2.30-7pm Sun Apr-Oct, 9am-6pm Mon-Sat & 9am-12.30pm & 2.30-6pm Sun Nov-Mar) is a hulking, hilltop fortress of a cathedral, founded in the 12th century though largely rebuilt a century later and extensively

Cais da Ribeira

FABRIZIO TROIANI/ALAMY STOCK PHOTO

ℹ️ Need to Know

The local metro stop is São Bento (Praça Almeida Garrett), yellow metro line D.

✕ Take a Break

Centrally located **Mercearia das Flores** (Map p114; Rua das Flores 110; petiscos €2.50-8.50; ⊘11am-9pm Mon-Thu, to 10pm Fri-Sat, 11.30am-8pm Sun; 🛜) is a delicatessen and food store serving tea from the Azores and light lunches.

★ Top Tip

Take a vintage boat tour to see the sights of Ribeira and Vila Nova de Gaia from the water.

altered during the 1700s. You can still make out the church's Romanesque origins in the barrel vaulted nave. Inside, a rose window and a 14th-century Gothic cloister also remain from its early days.

The splendid neoclassical Palácio da Bolsa (p112) honours Porto's past and present money merchants. Just past the entrance is the glass-domed Pátio das Nações (Hall of Nations), where the exchange once operated. But this pales in comparison with rooms deeper inside; to visit these, join one of the half-hour guided tours (every 30 minutes).

Ponte de Dom Luís I

Completed in 1886 by a student of Gustave Eiffel, this bridge's top deck is now reserved for pedestrians, as well as one of the city's metro lines; the lower deck bears regular traffic and narrow walkways for those on foot. The views of the river and Old Town are simply stunning, as are the daredevils who leap from the lower level. The bridge's construction was significant, as the area's foot traffic once navigated a bridge made from old port boats lashed together. To make matters worse, the river was wild back then, with no upstream dams.

Cais da Ribeira

This riverfront promenade is postcard Porto, taking in the whole spectacular sweep of the city, from Ribeira's pastel houses, stacked like Lego bricks, to the *barcos rabelos* (flat-bottomed boats) once used to transport barrels of port from the Douro. Early evening buskers serenade crowds and chefs fire up grills in the hole-in-the-wall fish restaurants and *tascas* (taverns) in the old arcades.

Barrels at the Cálem winery

Vila Nova de Gaia

Vila Nova de Gaia (simply 'Gaia' to locals) takes you back to the 17th-century beginnings of port-wine production, when British merchants transformed wine into the post-dinner tipple of choice.

Great For...

☑ Don't Miss

A tasting session at Graham's, Porto's finest port-wine lodge.

Wine Lodges

One of the main reasons to head to Porto is to sample port wine, and the place to do this is Gaia. A good place to start is the Espaço Porto Cruz (p117), a swanky emporium inside a restored 18th-century riverside building that celebrates all things port. In addition to a shop where tastings are held (€9.50 for three ports), there are exhibition halls, a rooftop terrace with panoramic views and a restaurant. **Graham's** (Map p114; ☑ 223 776 490, 223 776 492; www.grahams-port.com; Rua do Agro 141; tours incl tasting from €15; ⊙9.30am-6.30pm Apr-Oct, to 6pm Nov-Mar) is one of the original British-founded Gaia wine cellars, established way back in 1820. The complex has been totally revamped and now features a small museum. It's a big name and a popular choice for tours (30 minutes), where you can dip into atmospheric barrel-lined cellars

Port in Graham's cellar

❶ Need to Know

Metro line D runs through the Jardim do Morro stop.

✕ Take a Break

Taberninha Do Manel (p128) serves up Portuguese classics a short stroll from the Ponte Dom Luís I.

★ Top Tip

The artwork-filled 14th-century Convento Corpus Christi is a peaceful spot for a post port-sipping stroll.

and conclude with a tasting of three to eight port wines.

British-run **Taylor's** (☎223 772 973; www. taylor.pt; Rua do Choupelo 250; tours incl tasting adult/child €15/6; ☺10am-6pm) boasts lovely, oh-so-English grounds with tremendous views of Porto. Its audio-guide tours include a tasting of two top-of-the-range port wines. The 300-year-old cellars are simply staggering, piled to the rafters with huge barrels, including the big one containing 100,000L of late bottled vintage. **Sandeman** (Map p114; ☎223 740 533; www.sandeman. com; Largo Miguel Bombarda 3; museum free, guided tours incl tasting €12-40; ☺10am-8pm Mar-Oct, 10am-12.30pm & 2-6pm Nov-Feb) and **Cálem** (Map p114; ☎916 113 451; www.calem. pt; Avenida Diogo Leite 344; tours incl tasting €12; ☺10am-7pm May-Oct, to 6pm Nov-Apr) are other recommended places.

Teleférico de Gaia

Don't miss a ride on the **Teleférico de Gaia** (Map p114; www.gaiacablecar.com; Calçada da Serra 143; one way/return €6/9; ☺10am-8pm May-Sep, to 6pm Oct-Mar), an aerial gondola that provides fine views over the Douro and Porto on its short jaunt between the southern end of the Ponte de Dom Luís I and the riverside. At the bridge end of the teleférico is a hilltop park called the Jardim do Morro (p117), which can also be reached by crossing the upper level of Ponte de Dom Luís I.

Mosteiro da Serra de Pilar

Watching over Gaia is this 17th-century hilltop **monastery** (Map p114; Rampa do Infante Santo; adult/child €4/2; ☺10am-6.30pm Tue-Sun Apr-Oct, to 5.30pm Nov-Mar), with its striking circular cloister, church with gilded altar and stellar river views from its cupola – it's one of the few places where you can glimpse the Ponte de Dom Luís I from above. Requisitioned by the future Duke of Wellington during the Peninsular War (1807–14), it still belongs to the Portuguese military.

⊙ SIGHTS

With the exception of the blockbuster Museu de Arte Contemporânea, Porto's must-sees cluster in the compact centre and are easily walkable. Many of the big-hitters huddle in the Unesco-listed Ribeira district and Aliados, while hilltop Miragaia has some peaceful pockets of greenery and knockout views. For port-wine lodges aplenty, cross the river to Vila Nova de Gaia.

⊙ Ribeira

Palácio da Bolsa   Historic Building

(Stock Exchange; Map p114; www.palacioda bolsa.com; Rua Ferreira Borges; tours adult/ child €10/6.50; ⊘9am-6.30pm Apr-Oct, 9am-12.30pm & 2-5.30pm Nov-Mar) This splendid neoclassical monument (built from 1842 to 1910) honours Porto's past and present money merchants. Just past the entrance is the glass-domed **Pátio das Nações** (Hall of Nations), where the exchange once operated. But this pales in comparison with rooms deeper inside; to visit these, join one of the half-hour guided tours, which set off every 30 minutes.

Museu da Misericórdia do Porto   Church, Museum

(MMIPO; Map p114; www.mmipo.pt; Rua das Flores 5; adult/child €5/2.50; ⊘10am-6.30pm Apr-Sep, to 5.30pm Oct-Mar) The Museu da Misericórdia do Porto harmoniously unites cutting-edge architecture, a prized collection of 15th- to 17th-century sacred art and portraiture, and one of Ribeira's finest churches, **Igreja da Misericórdia**. Bearing the hallmark of Italian baroque architect Nicolau Nasoni, the church's interior is adorned with blue-and-white *azulejos*. The museum's biggest stunner is the large-scale Flemish Renaissance painting *Fons Vitae* (Fountain of Life), depicting Dom Manuel I and family around a fountain of blood from the crucified Christ.

Casa do Infante   Historic Building

(Map p114; Rua Alfândega 10; adult/child €2.20/ free; ⊘10am-5.30pm Tue-Sun) In this handsomely renovated medieval town house, according to legend, Henry the Navigator was born in 1394. The building later served as Porto's first customs house. Today it boasts three floors of exhibits. In 2002 the complex was excavated, revealioundations

Igreja da Misericórdia

KIEVVICTOR/SHUTTERSTOCK ©

Livraria Lello

and some remarkable mosaics – all of which are now on display.

Jardim do Infante Dom Henrique
Gardens

(Map p114; Rua Ferreira Borges) Presided over by the late-19th-century market hall **Mercado Ferreira Borges** and neoclassical Palácio da Bolsa (p112), these gardens are named after the centrepiece statue. Lifted high on a pedestal, the monument depicts Prince Henry the Navigator (1394–1460) – a catalyst in the Age of Discoveries and pioneer of the caravel, who braved the battering Atlantic in search of colonies for Portugal's collection.

Museu das Marionetas
Museum

(Map p114; www.marionetasdoporto.pt; Rua de Belomonte 61; €2; ⊘11am-1pm & 2-6pm; ⊕) Porto's marionette museum turns the spotlight on the remarkable puppet creations that have taken to the stage at the **Teatro Marionetas do Porto** (Map p114; ☑222 089 175; www.marionetasdoporto.pt; Rua de Belmonte 57) over the past 25 years. Rotating exhibitions present marionettes

from productions such as *Macbeth, Faust* and *Cinderella*.

◎ Aliados & Bolhão

Livraria Lello
Historic Building

(Map p114; www.livrarialello.pt; Rua das Carmelitas 144; €5; ⊘10am-7.30pm Mon-Fri, to 7pm Sat, 11am-7pm Sun; ⊕) Ostensibly a bookshop, but even if you're not after books, don't miss this exquisite 1906 neo-Gothic confection, with its lavishly carved plaster resembling wood and a stained-glass skylight. Feels magical? Its intricately wrought, curiously twisting staircase was supposedly the inspiration for the one in the Harry Potter books, which JK Rowling partly wrote in Porto while working here as an English teacher from 1991 to 1993.

The €5 entry is redeemable if you buy a book.

São Bento Train Station
Historic Building

(Map p114; Praça Almeida Garrett; ⊘5am-1am) One of the world's most beautiful train stations, beaux arts São Bento wings you

Central Porto

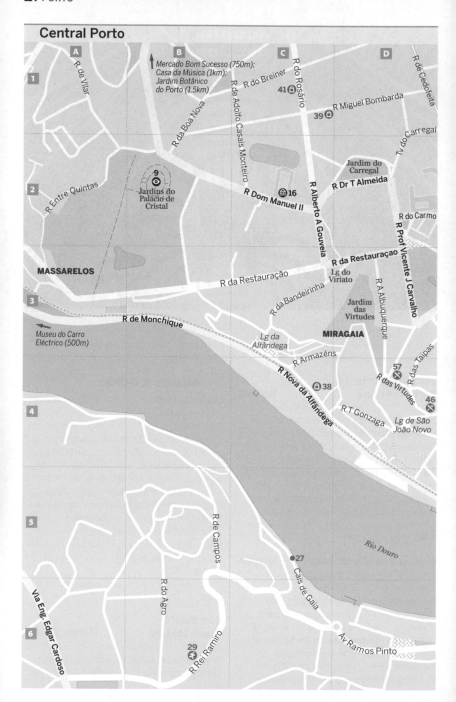

A

B

C

D

1

R de Vilar

Mercado Bom Sucesso (750m);
Casa da Música (1km);
Jardim Botânico
do Porto (1.5km)

R do Breiner

R do Rosário

R de Cedofeita

R da Boa Nova

R de Adolfo Casais Monteiro

41

39

R Miguel Bombarda

Tv do Carregal

Jardim do
Carregal

9

R Entre Quintas

2

Jardins do
Palácio de
Cristal

R Dom Manuel II

16

R Alberto A Gouveia

R Dr T Almeida

R do Carmo

R Prof Vicente J Carvalho

MASSARELOS

R da Restauração

R da Restauração

R da Restauração

Lg do
Viriato

R A Albuquerque

3

R de Monchique

R da Bandeirinha

Jardim
das
Virtudes

MIRAGAIA

Museu do Carro
Eléctrico (500m)

Lg da
Alfândega

R Armazéns

R Nova da Alfândega

57

R das Virtudes

R das Taipas

46

38

R T Gonzaga

Lg de São
João Novo

4

5

R de Campos

27

Rio Douro

Cais de Gaia

6

Via Eng. Edgar Cardoso

R do Agro

29

R Rei Ramiro

Av Ramos Pinto

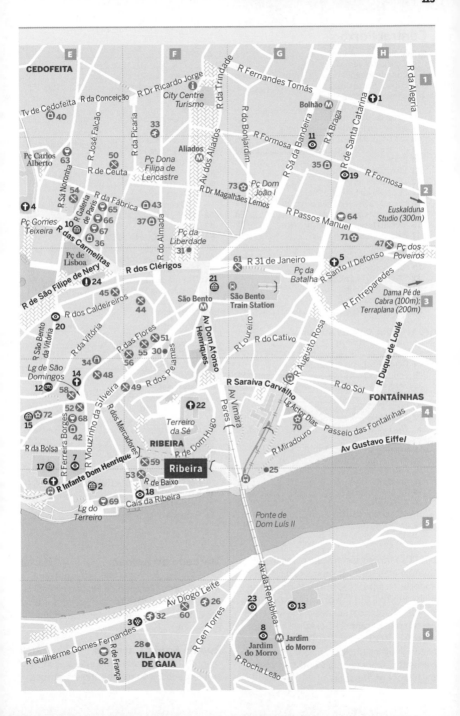

115

CEDOFEITA

Tv de Cedofeita
40

R da Conceição
R Dr Ricardo Jorge
City Centre Turismo
R da Trindade
R Fernandes Tomás
R da Alegria

Pç Carlos Alberto
63
R José Falcão
R da Picaria
33
Aliados
Bolhão Ⓜ
1

50
R de Ceuta
Pç Dona Filipa de Lencastre
Av dos Aliados
R do Bonjardim
R Formosa
R Sá da Bandeira
R A Braga
R de Santa Catarina
11

4
R Sá Noronha
54
R Galeria de Paris
R da Fábrica
65
43
73
Pç Dom João I
R Dr Magalhães Lemos
35
19
R Formosa
Euskalduna Studio (300m)

Pç Gomes Teixeira
10
R das Carmelitas
66
67
36
37
R do Almada
Pç da Liberdade
31
R Passos Manuel
64
71
47
Pç dos Poveiros

Pç de Lisboa
R de São Filipe de Nery
24
R dos Clérigos
21
61
R 31 de Janeiro
Pç da Batalha
5
R Santo Il Defonso
R Entreparedes
Dama Pé de Cabra (100m); Terraplana (200m)

45
44
São Bento Ⓜ
São Bento Train Station
R Loureiro
R do Cativo
R Augusto Rosa
R Duque de Loulé

20
R São Bento da Vitória
R dos Caldeireiros
R da Vitória
P das Flores
51
55
30
56
Av Dom Afonso Henriques
FONTAÍNHAS

Lg de São Domingos
34
14
48
R dos Pelames
49
22
R do Sol

12
58
Terreiro da Sé
Av Vimara Peres
Lg Actor Dias
70
Passeio das Fontainhas

72
15
52
68
42
RIBEIRA
R Miradouro
Av Gustavo Eiffel

17
7
R Ferreira Borges
R Mouzinho da Silveira
R dos Mercadores
R Infante Dom Henrique
59
Ribeira
25

6
2
53
R de Baixo
18
Cais da Ribeira
Ponte de Dom Luís II

Lg do Terreiro
69

Av Diogo Leite
26
23
13
Av da República

3
32
60
R Gen Torres
8
Jardim do Morro
Ⓜ Jardim do Morro

R Guilherme Gomes Fernandes
62
28
VILA NOVA DE GAIA
R de França
R Rocha Leão

Central Porto

back to a more graceful age of rail travel. Completed in 1903, it seems to have been imported from 19th-century Paris with its mansard roof. But the dramatic *azulejo* panels of historical scenes in the front hall are the real attraction. Designed by Jorge Colaço in 1930, some 20,000 tiles depict historic battles (including Henry the Navigator's conquest of Ceuta), as well as the history of transport.

Mercado do Bolhão   Market

(Map p114; Rua Formosa) The 19th-century, wrought-iron Mercado do Bolhão closed its doors in spring 2018 for a major restoration project. No fixed date has been given for its reopening.

Rua de Santa Catarina   Area

(Map p114) This street is absurdly stylish and romantic, with trim boutiques, striped stone footpaths and animated crowds. It's home to Porto's most ornate tearoom, the art nouveau **Café Majestic** (Map p114; www.cafemajestic.com; Rua de Santa Catarina 112; ◎9.30am-11.30pm Mon-Sat), and the extraordinary *azulejo*-bedecked **Capela das Almas** (Map p114; Rua de Santa Catarina 428; ◎7.30am-7pm Mon-Fri, 7.30am-1pm & 6-7pm Sat).

Torre dos Clérigos   Tower

(Map p114; www.torredosclerigos.pt; Rua de São Filipe de Nery; €5; ◎9am-7pm) Sticking out on Porto's skyline like a sore thumb – albeit a beautiful baroque one – this 76m-high tower was designed by Italian-born baroque master Nicolau Nasoni in the mid-1700s. Climb its 225-step spiral staircase for phenomenal views over Porto's tiled rooftops, spires and the curve of the Douro to the port-wine lodges in Gaia. It also harbours an exhibition that chronicles the history of the tower's architects and residents.

◎ Miragaia

Museu Nacional
Soares dos Reis   Museum

(Map p114; www.museusoaresdosreis.pt; Rua Dom Manuel II 44; adult/child €5/free; ◎10am-6pm Tue-Sun) Porto's best art museum presents a stellar collection ranging from neolithic carvings to Portugal's take on modernism, all housed in the formidable Palácio das Carrancas.

Miradouro da Vitória   Viewpoint

(Map p114; Rua São Bento da Vitória) Porto is reduced to postcard format at this *miradouro* (viewpoint), perched high and mighty above a mosaic of terracotta rooftops that tumble down to the Douro. It's a highly atmospheric spot at dusk when landmarks such as the Ponte Dom Luís I bridge are illuminated and the lights on Vila Nova de Gaia's wine lodges flick on one by one.

Rua de São Bento da Vitória   Area

(Map p114) With its cobblestones polished smooth by centuries of shoe leather and pretty tiled houses with little wrought-iron balconies and window boxes brimming with pot plants, this narrow, gently curving street was the beating heart of Jewish Porto in late medieval times. Keep your eyes peeled for telltale sights of Jewish heritage, such as bronze Hamsa (protective hand) door knockers.

Igreja das Carmelitas   Church

(Map p114; Rua do Carmo; ◎7.30am-7pm Mon-Fri, 9am-6.45pm Sat & Sun) Blink and you might miss that this is a church in its own right, snuggled as close as it is to the Igreja do Carmo. The twin churches are separated only by a 1m-wide house, once the dividing line between the monks of Carmo and the Carmelite nuns. Dating to the 17th century, its modest classical facade belies its lavishly gilded nave.

◎ Vila Nova de Gaia

Jardim do Morro   Gardens

(Map p114; Avenida da República) The cable car swings up to this hilltop park, which can also be reached by crossing the upper level of Ponte de Dom Luís I. Shaded by palms, these gardens are all about the view. From here, Porto is reduced to postcard format, with the pastel-hued houses of Ribeira on the opposite side of the Douro and the snaking river below.

Espaço Porto Cruz   Winery, Museum

(Map p114; www.myportocruz.com; Largo Miguel Bombarda 23; ◎11am-7pm Tue-Sun) This swank port-wine emporium inside a restored 18th-century riverside building celebrates all things port. In addition to a shop where tastings are held (by the glass starting at €3 or €9.50 for three ports), there's a rooftop terrace with panoramic views and 3rd-floor **De Castro Gaia** (Map p114; ☏910 553 559; petiscos €5-10, mains €10-16.50; ◎12.30-3pm & 7.30-11pm Tue-Sat, 12.30-3pm Sun) restaurant. The 1st and 2nd floors are given over to a small, free, port-related exhibition, the highlight of which is the 360-degree wine journey – a virtual flight over Porto and the Douro.

◉ Massarelos

Jardins do
Palácio de Cristal
Gardens

(Map p114; Rua Dom Manuel II; ⊙8am-9pm Apr-Sep, to 7pm Oct-Mar; 🚼) Sitting atop a bluff, this gorgeous botanical garden is one of Porto's best-loved escapes, with lawns interwoven with sun-dappled paths and dotted with fountains, sculptures, giant magnolias, camellias, cypress and olive trees. It's actually a mosaic of small gardens that open up little by little as you wander – as do the stunning views of the city and Rio Douro.

Museu do Carro Eléctrico
Museum

(Tram Museum; www.museudocarroelectrico. pt; Alameda Basílio Teles 51; adult/child €8/4; ⊙2-6pm Mon, 10am-6pm Tue-Sun) Housed in an antiquated switching-house, this museum is a tram-spotter's delight. It displays dozens of beautifully restored old trams – from early 1870s models once pulled by mules to streamlined, bee-yellow 1930s numbers.

◉ Boavista

Mercado Bom Sucesso
Market €

(www.mercadobomsucesso.pt; Praça Bom Sucesso; ⊙10am-11pm Sun-Thu, to midnight Fri & Sat) For a snapshot of local life and a bite to eat, nip into Boavista's revamped Mercado Bom Sucesso. A complete architectural overhaul has brought this late 1940s market hall bang up to date. Now bright, modern and flooded with daylight, the striking curved edifice harbours a fresh produce market, a food court, cafes and the slick design hotel, Hotel da Música.

◉ Foz do Douro & Serralves

Serralves
Museum

(www.serralves.pt; Rua Dom João de Castro 210; adult/child museums & park €10/free, park only €5/free, 10am-1pm 1st Sun of the month free; ⊙10am-7pm Mon-Fri, to 8pm Sat & Sun May-Sep, reduced hours Oct-Apr) This fabulous cultural institution combines a museum, a mansion and extensive gardens. Cutting-edge exhibitions, along with a fine permanent collection featuring works from the late 1960s to the present, are showcased in

Jardins do Palácio de Cristal

TRABANTOS/SHUTTERSTOCK ©

the **Museu de Arte Contemporânea**, an arrestingly minimalist, whitewashed space designed by the eminent Porto-based architect Álvaro Siza Vieira. The delightful, pink **Casa de Serralves** is a prime example of art deco, bearing the imprint of French architect Charles Siclis. One ticket gets you into both museums.

The museums sit within the marvellous 18-hectare **Parque de Serralves**. Lily ponds, rose gardens, formal fountains and whimsical touches – such as a bright-red sculpture of oversized pruning shears – make for a bucolic outing in the city. The estate is located 6km west of the city centre; take bus 201 from in front of Praça Dom João I, one block east of Avenida dos Aliados.

Jardim do Passeio Alegre   Gardens

(Rua Passeio Alegre; ⛟) A joy for the aimless ambler, this 19th-century garden is flanked by graceful old buildings and dotted with willowy palms, sculptures, fountains and a bandstand that occasionally stages concerts in summer. Listen to the crash of the ocean as you wander its tree-canopied avenues. There's also crazy golf for the kids.

Parque da Cidade   Park

(Avenida da Boavista; ⛟) The hum of traffic on the Avenida da Boavista soon fades as you enter the serene, green Parque da Cidade, Portugal's largest urban park. Laced with 10km of walking and cycling trails, this is where locals come to unplug and recharge, picnic (especially at weekends), play ball, jog, cycle, lounge in the sun and feed the ducks on the lake.

⊖ COURSES

Workshops Pop Up   Cooking

(Map p114; ⛟966 974 119; www.workshops-pop up.com; Rua do Almada 275; 3hr class incl lunch or dinner €35) This cool indie arts, crafts and interior design store hosts regular three-hour, hands-on cookery workshops, followed by lunch or dinner with wine pairing. Themes range from healthy snacks and Indian food to Cook and Taste Portugal, where you'll learn to cook Portuguese classics like

 Street Art in Porto

Porto's growing tribe of street artists have painted bold, eye-catching works across crumbling ancient walls, empty storefront glass and neglected stucco. A far cry from graffiti scrawls, the spray-paint wonders reveal artistic flair and creative expression that transcend the conventional and stop you dead in your tracks: a stencilled pilgrim here, a cloaked bodhisattva there.

Porto-born or -based artists include the startlingly prolific Hazul Luzah, whose works dance across dilapidated city walls in the shape of flowers, exotic birds or religious motifs. Other home-grown talent includes Costah, known for his playful, brightly coloured murals; Frederico Draw, master of striking black-and-white graffiti portraits; and the ever-inventive MrDheo.

To plug into the scene today, arrange your own self-guided tour of Porto's must-see street art. High on any list should be the **Travessa de Cedofeita** and **Escadas do Codeçal**, as well as the car park at Trindade, with its large-scale murals. Lapa, just one metro stop north, is another hot spot, as is the gallery-dotted **Rua Miguel Bombarda**. On **Rua das Flores**, clever graffiti sits side by side with beautifully restored historic buildings – look out for vibrantly patterned works by Hazul, glowing neon portraits by Costah and 15 electric boxes – each with its own burst of street-art colour.

Hazul Luzah art on the Rua das Flores
RAQUEL MARIA CARBONELL PAGOLA/LIGHTROCKET VIA GETTY IMAGES ©

Casa da Música

Grand and minimalist, sophisticated yet populist, Porto's cultural behemoth **Casa da Música** (☑220 120 220; www.casadamusica.com; Avenida da Boavista 604-610; guided tour €10; ☺English guided tours 11am & 4pm) boasts a shoebox-style concert hall at its heart, meticulously engineered to accommodate everything from jazz duets to Beethoven's Ninth.

The hall holds concerts most nights of the year, from classical and blues to fado and electronica, with occasional summer performances staged outdoors in the adjoining plaza. The top-floor bar and terrace command great views, with occasional Saturday night DJ sessions.

Casa da Música
ZACARIAS PEREIRA DA MATA/SHUTTERSTOCK ©
ARCHITECT: REM KOOLHAAS

bacalhau à lagareiro (codfish cooked in extra virgin olive oil) and *pastéis de nata* (Portuguese-style custard tarts).

⊙ TOURS
eFun GPS Tours   Tours
(Map p114; ☑914 173 671, 220 945 375; www.efungpstours.com; Rua Cândido dos Reis 55; ☺10am-7pm) Whether you want to explore Porto on foot or head further afield by minivan, eFun GPS Tours have got it nailed. Clued-up guides lead everything from three-hour walks of the historic centre (€19) to food-focused walking tours (€60) and Jewish heritage tours (€25), as well as excursions to Braga, Guimarães and deeper into the Douro Valley.

Other Side   Tours
(Map p114; ☑916 500 170; www.theotherside.pt; Rua Souto 67; ☺9am-8pm) Well-informed, congenial guides reveal their city on half-day walking tours of hidden Porto (€19), a walking and food tour (€49), and wine tours (€55). They also venture further afield with full-day trips to the Douro's vineyards (€95), and to Guimarães and Braga (€85).

Be My Guest   Walking
(☑938 417 850; www.bemyguestinporto.com; 3hr tours €20) To get better acquainted with Porto, sign up for one of Be My Guest's terrific themed walking tours of the city, skipping from an insider's peek at *azulejos* to belle époque architecture and urban art. Run by two incredibly passionate guides – Nuno and Fred – it also arranges four-hour cookery workshops (€35) and wine-tasting tours (€25). Meeting points vary. Check in advance.

Blue Dragon Tours   Tours
(Map p114; ☑222 022 375; www.bluedragon.pt; Avenida Gustavo Eiffel 280; tours from €18) This reputable outfit runs old town and riverside bike tours (€32.50), which make the link between the historic centre and the sea. It also offers several half-day walking tours, including the Best of Porto (€18) and a food and wine tour (€55), as well as two-hour Segway tours (€45) to tick off the highlights. Prices can depend on group sizes.

Taste Porto   Food & Drink
(☑920 503 302; www.tasteporto.com; Downtown Food Tour adult/child €65/42, Vintage Food Tour €70/42; ☺Downtown Food Tour 10.45am & 4pm Tue-Sat, Vintage Food Tour 10am & 4.15pm Mon-Sat, Photo Food Experience 9.45am daily) Loosen a belt notch for Taste Porto's superb downtown food tours, where you'll sample everything from Porto's best slow-roast-pork sandwich to éclairs, fine wines, cheese and coffee. Friendly, knowledgeable guide André and his team lead these indulgent and insightful 3½-hour walking tours, which take in viewpoints and historic

Museu do Carro Eléctrico (p118)

back lanes en route to restaurants, grocery stores and cafes.

Porto Walkers
Walking

(Map p114; 📞918 291 519; www.portowalkers. pt; Praça da Liberdade, Avenida dos Aliados) Peppered with anecdotes and personality, these young, fun, three-hour guided walking tours are a great intro to Porto, starting at 10.45am daily. The tours are free (well, the guides work for tips, so give what you can). Simply turn up at the meeting point on Praça da Liberdade and look out for the guide in the red T-shirt.

Douro Azul
Boating

(Map p114; 📞223 402 500; www.douroazul.com; Cais de Gaia; 6-bridge cruise adult/child €12/6; ⏰9.30am-6pm) Douro Azul is the largest of several outfits that offer cruises in ersatz *barcos rabelos*, the colourful boats that were once used to transport port wine from the vineyards. Cruises last 45 to 55 minutes and depart at least hourly on summer days. Board at Cais de Gaia. Audio guides are available in 16 languages.

🔒 SHOPPING

Shopping in Porto is very much a local experience, whether you are tasting port before selecting the perfect take-home bottle, nattering to the friendly *senhora* at an old-school grocery about the merits of *tremoços* (lupin beans), or talking to resident artists and designers at pop-ups, galleries and concept stores.

Oliva & Co
Food

(Map p114; www.facebook.com/pg/OlivaeCo; Rua Ferreira Borges 60; ⏰10am-7pm Sun-Fri, to 8pm Sat) Everything you ever wanted to know about Portuguese olive oil becomes clear at this experiential store, which maps out the country's six Protected Designation of Origin (PDO) regions producing the extra-virgin stuff. Besides superb oils and olives, you'll find biscuits, chocolate and soaps made with olive oil. Try before you buy or join one of the in-depth tastings.

43 Branco
Arts & Crafts

(Map p114; Rua das Flores 43; ⏰11am-7pm Mon-Sat) One-of-a-kind Portuguese crafts, fashion and interior design take centre stage at this new concept store, which brings a breath of fresh creativity to Rua das Flores. Here you'll find everything from filigree, gem-studded Maria Branco jewellery to funky sardine pencil cases, Porto-inspired Lubo T-shirts and beautifully packaged Bonjardim soaps.

Workshops Pop Up   Arts & Crafts
(Map p114; ☑966 974 119; www.workshops-popup.com; Rua do Almada 275; ☺1-7.30pm Sun-Fri, 10am-7.30pm Sat) Bringing a new lease of life to a restored smithy, this store is the brainchild of Nuno and Rita. It harbours an eclectic mix of pop-ups selling everything from original ceramics to vintage fashion, accessories and prettily wrapped Bonjardim soaps. It also runs three-hour cookery workshops (p119), some of which are in English.

Touriga   Wine
(Map p114; ☑225 108 435; Rua da Fábrica 32; ☺11am-7pm Mon-Sat) Run with passion and precision by David Ferreira, this fabulous wine shop is a trove of well- and lesser-known ports and wines – many from small producers. Stop by for a wine or port-wine tasting (€5 to €20). Shipping can be arranged.

A Pérola do Bolhão   Food & Drinks
(Map p114; Rua Formosa 279; ☺9.30am-7.30pm Mon-Fri, 9am-1pm Sat) Founded in 1917, this delightfully old-school deli sports Porto's most striking art nouveau facade and is stacked to the rafters with smoked sausages and pungent mountain cheeses, olives, dried fruits and nuts, wine and port. The beautiful *azulejos* depict flowers and two goddess-like women bearing *café* (coffee) and *chá* (tea) plants.

Coração Alecrim   Arts & Crafts
(Map p114; www.coracaoalecrim.com; Travessa de Cedofeita 28; ☺11am-7pm Mon-Sat) 'Green, indie, vintage' is the strapline of this enticing store, accessed through a striking doorway painted with woodland animals (crickets chirrup a welcome as you enter). It stocks high-quality handmade Portuguese products, from pure-wool blankets and beanies to one-off *azulejos,* shell coasters and beautiful ceramics.

A Vida Portuguesa

Serralves (p118)

A Vida Portuguesa
Gifts & Souvenirs

(Map p114; www.avidaportuguesa.com; Rua Galeria de Paris 20; ☺10am-8pm Mon-Sat, 11am-7pm Sun) This lovely store in an old fabric shop showcases a medley of stylishly repackaged vintage Portuguese products – classic toys, old-fashioned soaps and retro journals, plus those emblematic ceramic Bordallo Pinheiro *andorinhas* (swallows).

Águas Furtadas
Art, Fashion

(Map p114; www.facebook.com/aguasfurtadas; Rua do Almada 13; ☺10am-8pm Mon-Sat, 1-7pm Sun) This boutique is a treasure trove of funky Portuguese fashion, design, crafts and accessories, including born-again Barcelos cockerels in candy-bright colours and exquisitely illustrated pieces by influential Porto-based graphic designer Benedita Feijó.

CC Bombarda
Mall

(Map p114; Rua Miguel Bombarda 285; ☺noon-8pm Mon-Sat) Amid the galleries along Rua Miguel Bombarda, this small, unique shopping mall is a highlight. Inside you'll find stores selling locally designed urban wear, gourmet teas, organic cosmetics, jewellery, vinyl, bonsai trees, stylish home knickknacks and other hipster-pleasing delights. There's a cafe serving light bites in an internal courtyard.

Armazém
Arts & Crafts

(Map p114; Rua da Miragaia 93; ☺11.30am-8pm) Bang on trend with Porto's current thirst for creative spaces is the hipsterish Armazém, located in a converted warehouse down by the river. A gallery, cafe and store all under one roof, with an open fire burning at its centre, it sells a pinch of everything – vintage garb, antiques, vinyl, artwork, ceramics and funky Portuguese-designed bags and fashion.

CRU
Arts & Crafts

(Map p114; www.cru-cowork.com; Rua do Rosário 211; ☺9.30am-8.30pm Mon-Fri, 10am-8pm Sat) Allowing Portuguese designers to give flight to their fantasy, this unique gallery space crackles with creativity. What's on offer changes frequently, but at any one time you might find understated fashion, ceramics, accessories, art and beautifully handcrafted jewellery.

Jimão

EATING

Porto's food scene has gone through the roof in recent years. Hot at the moment are *petiscos* (small Portuguese plates, ideal for sharing), lazy weekend brunches, creative vegetarian buffet-style restaurants with bags of charm and imaginative riffs on hand-me-down recipes, and old-school taverns championing slow food. And don't forget the temptation of local cafes and patisseries around nearly every corner.

Ribeira

Taberna do Largo Portuguese €

(Map p114; ☏222 082 154; Largo de São Domingos 69; petiscos €2-14; ⊙5pm-midnight Tue-Thu, to 1am Fri, noon-1am Sat, to midnight Sun; ☎) Lit by wine-bottle lights, this sweet grocery store, deli and tavern is run with passion by Joana and Sofia. Tour Portugal with your taste buds with their superb array of hand-picked wines, which go brilliantly with tasting platters of smoked tuna, Alentejo *salpicão* sausage, Azores São Jorge cheese, Beira *morcela* (blood sausage), *tremoços* and more.

Da Terra Vegetarian €

(Map p114; ☏223 199 257; www.daterra.pt; Rua Mouzinho da Silveira 249; buffet €9.95; ⊙noon-11pm Wed, Thu, Sun & Mon, to 11.30pm Fri & Sat; ☎⚘) Porto's shift towards lighter, super-healthy food is reflected in the buffet served at Da Terra. This popular, contemporary bistro puts its own spin on vegetarian and vegan food – from creative salads to Thai-style veggies and tagines. It also does a fine line in fresh-pressed juices and desserts. The website posts details of upcoming workshops and cookery courses.

Mercador Café Cafe €

(Map p114; ☏223 323 041; www.facebook.com/mercadorcafe; Rua das Flores 180; snacks €3-6; ⊙9am-8pm Mon-Sat; ☎) Mercador is a cute and cosy pit stop smack bang in the middle of one of Porto's prettiest streets, Rua das Flores. Browse the sweets cabinet for homemade cakes and pastries, settle for a simple toastie or order a traditional cooked lunch from the daily menu.

Cantina 32   Portuguese €€

(Map p114; ☎222 039 069; www.cantina32.com; Rua das Flores 32; petiscos €3.50-20; ⏱12.30-3pm & 6.30-10.30pm Mon-Sat; 🛜) Industrial-chic meets boho at this delightfully laid-back haunt, with its walls of polished concrete, mismatched crockery, verdant plants, and vintage knick-knacks ranging from a bicycle to an old typewriter. The menu is just as informal – *petiscos* such as *pica-pau* steak (bite-sized pieces of steak in a garlic-white-wine sauce), quail egg croquettes, and cheesecake served in a flower pot reveal a pinch of creativity.

Taberna dos Mercadores   Portuguese €€

(Map p114; ☎222 010 510; Rua dos Mercadores 36; mains €14-22; ⏱12.30-3.30pm & 7-11pm Tue-Sun) The chefs run a tight ship in the open kitchen at this curvaceous, softly lit, bottle-lined tavern, sizzling, stirring and delivering superb Portuguese grub with a smile from noon to night. On the menu are spot-on dishes as simple as *polvo com arroz no forno* (octopus rice baked in the oven), *feijoada* (black bean one-pot), grilled fish and meats.

Jimão   Tapas €€

(Map p114; ☎220 924 660; www.jimao.pt; Praça da Ribeira 11; tapas €4.50-8.50; ⏱noon-10pm Wed-Mon) Many of the restaurants on **Praça da Ribeira** (Map p114) are tourist central, Jimão being the exception. Service is genuinely friendly, the upstairs dining room has a cracking view of Ribeira, and the tapas – garlicky *gambas* (prawns), codfish and octopus salad, sardine toasts and the like – are prepared with care and served with great wines.

Cantinho do Avillez   Gastronomy €€

(Map p114; ☎223 227 879; www.cantinhodo avillez.pt; Rua Mouzinho da Silveira 166; mains €18-40; ⏱12.30-3pm & 7pm-midnight Mon-Fri, 12.30pm-midnight Sat & Sun) Rock star chef José Avillez' latest venture is a welcome fixture on Porto's gastro scene. A bright, con-temporary bistro with a retro spin, Cantinho keeps the mood casual and buzzy. On the

 Festa de São João

In the sweet heat of midsummer, Porto pulls out all the stops for one of Europe's wildest street parties – the Festa de São João, celebrated in riotous style on 23 and 24 June. If ever the full force of love is going to hit you when you least expect it, it's going to be here – one of the festival's unique traditions is to thwack whomever you fancy over the head with a squeaky plastic hammer *(martelo)*.

Though the exact origins of the *festa* are veiled in mystery, *tripeiros* (Porto residents) will tell you that it is rooted in pagan festivals to celebrate the summer solstice and bountiful harvests. Expect hammer-wielding locals of all ages scoffing grilled sardines, drinking *vinho* and dancing like there is no tomorrow.

Fireworks at Festa de São João
LUSOSTOCK/ALAMY STOCK PHOTO ©

menu are seasonal Portuguese dishes with a dash of imagination: from flaked *bacalhau* (dried salt-cod) with melt-in-the-mouth 'exploding' olives to giant red shrimps from the Algarve with Thai spices.

DOP   Gastronomy €€€

(Map p114; ☎222 014 313; www.dop restaurante.pt; Palácio das Artes, Largo de São Domingos 18; mains €25-28, tasting menus €80-90; ⏱7.30-11pm Mon, 12.30-3pm & 7.30-11pm Tue-Sat; 🛜) Housed in a grand edifice, DOP is one of Porto's most stylish addresses, with its high ceilings and slick, monochrome interior. Much-feted chef Rui Paula puts a creative, seasonal twist on outstand-ing ingredients, with dish after delicate, flavour-packed dish skipping from octopus carpaccio to cod with lobster rice.

⊗ Aliados & Bolhão

Cafe Santiago Portuguese €

(Map p114; ☑222 055 797; www.caferestaurante santiago.com.pt; Rua Passos Manuel 226; mains €8-12; ⊘noon-11pm Mon-Sat) This is hands down one of the best places to try Porto's classic gut-busting treat, the *francesinha* – a thick, open-faced sandwich piled with cheese, sausage, egg and/or assorted meats, plus a tasty, rich beer sauce. This classic will set you back €9.75, which might seem pricey for a sandwich, but trust us: it's a meal in itself.

Cultura dos Sabores Vegetarian €

(Map p114; ☑222 010 556; Rua de Ceuta 80; buffet €12; ⊘noon-3.30pm & 6-11pm Tue-Sun; ☜🖋) A hip, healthy addition to central Porto, this vegetarian and vegan restaurant can easily be spotted by the swings in its window. You can help yourself to the lunch and dinner buffet, which often includes hearty soups,

salads, wild rice or pasta dishes. Herbal teas and detox juices are available.

Leitaria da Quinta do Paço Bakery, Cafe €

(Map p114; www.leitariadaquintadopaco.com; Praça Guilherme Gomes Fernandes 47; éclairs €1.40; ⊘9am-8pm Mon-Thu, to 9pm Fri & Sat) Since 1920 this cafe-patisserie has given a pinch of Paris to Porto with its delectable sweet and savoury éclairs, which are now justifiably famous. Sit in the slick interior or on the plaza terrace for a *cimbalinho* (espresso) and feather-light, cream-filled éclairs in flavours from classic lemon to the more unusual blue cheese, apple and fennel or chocolate and port wine.

Euskalduna Studio Gastronomy €€€

(☑935 335 301; www.euskaldunastudio.pt; Rua de Santo Ildefonso 404; 10-course tasting menu €95-110; ⊘7-10pm Wed-Sat) Everyone loves surprises, especially edible ones prepared with flawless execution, experimental finesse and a nod to the seasons. Just 16 lucky diners (eight at the green marble counter peeking into the kitchen and eight

Vinum (p128)

at oak tables) get to sample Vasco Coelho Santos' stunning 10-course menus that allow flavours and textures to shine.

All In Porto
Portuguese €€

(Map p114; ☑220 993 829; www.facebook.com/allinporto; Rua Arquitecto Nicolau Nasoni 17; petiscos €8-22, tasting boards €12-16; ⊙noon-11pm) Wine-barrel tables, lanterns and funky Porto murals create a hip, laid-back space for sampling a stellar selection of Portuguese wines and nicely prepared *petiscos*. These range from flame-grilled *chouriço* (spicy sausage) to spicy sardine roe, cheeses and *conservas* (canned fish). Quiet enough for conversing, it's also a chilled spot to begin or end an evening over drinks.

Tapabento
Tapas €€

(Map p114; ☑222 034 115, 912 881 272; www.tapabento.com; Rua da Madeira 222; tapas & sharing plates €3-20, mains €14-27.50; ⊙7-10.30pm Tue, noon-4pm & 7-10pm Wed-Sun) There's a good buzz at split-level Tapabento, discreetly tucked behind São Bento train station. Stone walls, bright prints and cheek-by-jowl tables set the scene for outstanding tapas and Douro wines. Sharing is the way to go – be it fresh oysters with shallot vinaigrette, razor clams with garlic and coriander or Azores cheese with rocket and walnuts.

Dama Pé de Cabra
Cafe €€

(☑223 196 776; Passeio de São Lázaro 5; light bites & petiscos €2-7.50; ⊙9.30am-3.30pm Tue-Thu, 9.30am-3.30pm & 7.30-10pm Fri & Sat) The *bemvindo* is heartfelt at this cute, bottle-lined grocery store turned cafe. It's a cheerful spot for breakfast, brunch, coffee and cake, or a laid-back lunch of homemade breads with Portuguese hams and tangy cheeses.

⊗ Miragaia

A Sandeira
Sandwiches €

(Map p114; ☑223 216 471; www.asandeira.pt; Rua dos Caldeireiros 85; sandwiches €4.90, lunch menu €6; ⊙9am-midnight Mon-Sat; 🛜) Charming, boho-flavoured and lit by fairy lights, A Sandeira is a great bolthole for an

MEO Marés Vivas

Over a weekend in mid-July, Afurada dusts off its party clothes to host the Marés Vivas (Living Tides), welcoming big rock and pop names to the stage. Headliners have included Elton John, Jamiroquai, Beth Orton and Joss Stone.

Elton John performing at MEO Marés Vivas
DIOGO BAPTISTA/ALAMY STOCK PHOTO ©

inexpensive lunch. Chipper staff bring to the table creative salads such as smoked ham, rocket, avocado and walnuts, and Porto's best sandwiches (olive, feta, tomato and basil, for instance). The lunch menu, including soup, a salad or sandwich and a drink, is a steal.

Taberna de Santo António
Portuguese €

(Map p114; ☑222 055 306; Rua das Virtudes 32; mains €8.50-12; ⊙noon-3pm & 7-10pm Tue-Sun) This family-run tavern prides itself on serving up honest Portuguese grub with a smile. It dishes up generous helpings of codfish, grilled sardines and *cozido* (meat and vegetable stew) to the lunchtime crowds. It's a friendly TV-and-tiles place in the traditional Portuguese mould, with pavement seating on warm days.

Belos Aires
Argentine €€

(Map p114; ☑223 195 661; www.facebook.com/belosairesrestaurante; Rua de Belomonte 104; mains €17-25; ⊙8-11.30am & 7pm-midnight Mon-Sat; 🛜) At the heart of this intimate part-Argentine, part-Portuguese restaurant is Mauricio, a chef with a big personality and an insatiable passion for

Football in Porto

The flashy 52,000-seat Estádio do Dragão is home to heroes-of-the-moment FC Porto. It's northeast of the centre, just off the VCI ring road. Boavista FC is FC Porto's worthy cross-town rival. Its home turf is the Estádio do Bessa, which lies west of the centre just off Avenida da Boavista (take bus 3 from Praça da Liberdade). Check the local editions of *Jornal de Notícias* for upcoming matches.

FRANCISCO LEONG/AFP/GETTY IMAGES ©

his homeland, revealed as you watch him dashing around in the open kitchen. The market-fresh menu changes frequently, but you'll always find superb steaks and to-die-for *empanadas* (savoury turnovers). Save an inch for the chocolate brownie with *dulce de leche*.

🍽 Vila Nova de Gaia

Taberninha Do Manel Portuguese €€
(Map p114; 📞223 753 549; www.taberninhado manel.com; Avenida Diogo Leite 308; mains €11-18; ⏱11am-midnight Tue-Sun) Super-friendly service, big views across the Douro to Ribeira, and a menu crammed with well-executed Portuguese classics – Iberian pork, *petiscos* (tapas), *bacalhau* in different guises – reel folk into Taberninha Do Manel. There's pavement seating for warm days and a rustic interior jam-packed with what looks like the contents of your grandmother's attic.

Vinum Portuguese €€€
(Map p114; 📞220 930 417; www.vinumat grahams.com; Graham's Port Lodge, Rua do Agro 141; mains €24-29, menus €50-100; ⏱12.30-11pm) Vinum manages the delicate act of combining 19th-century port-lodge charm with contemporary edge. Peer through to the barrel-lined cellar from the pine-beamed restaurant, or out across the Douro and Porto's rooftops from the conservatory and terrace. Portuguese menu stunners include green ceviche fresh from Matasinhos fish market and dry-aged Trás-os-Montes beef, complemented by a stellar selection of wines and ports.

🍽 Massarelos

O Antigo Carteiro Portuguese €€
(📞937 317 523; www.facebook.com/oantigo carteiro; Rua Senhor da Boa Morte 55; mains €14-19; ⏱noon-3pm & 7-11pm Tue-Sat, noon-3pm Sun; 🚻) Coyly tucked away on a lane back from the river, O Antigo Carteiro is as close as you'll get to eating in a Portuguese family home. Attentive, clued-up staff pair regional wines with well-executed classics – garlicky octopus, pork tenderloin, *bacalhau com broa* (codfish with cornbread crust) and the like.

🍽 Boavista

Essência Vegetarian €€
(📞228 301 813; www.essenciarestaurante vegetariano.com; Rua de Pedro Hispano 1190; mains €10.50-15; ⏱12.30-3pm & 8-10.30pm Mon-Thu, to midnight Fri & Sat; 🍴) This bright, modern brasserie is famous Porto-wide for its generous vegetarian (and non-vegetarian!) dishes, stretching from wholesome soups and salads to curries, pasta dishes, risotto and *feijoada* (pork and bean casserole). There's a terrace for warm-weather dining.

🍽 Foz do Douro

Cafeína Modern European €€
(📞226 108 059; www.cafeina.pt; Rua do Padrão 100; 3-course lunch €18, mains €17-21; ⏱12.30-6pm & 7.30pm-12.30am Sun-Thu, to 1.30am

IGOR MARKOV/ALAMY STOCK PHOTO ©

Cafe on the Rio Douro

Fri & Sat; 🍴) Hidden coyly away from the seafront, Cafeína has a touch of class, with soft light casting a flattering glow across its moss-green walls, crisp tablecloths, lustrous wood floors and bookcases. The food is best described as modern European, simple as stuffed squid with saffron purée or rack of lamb in a herb and lemon crust, expertly matched with Portuguese wines.

🍷 DRINKING & NIGHTLIFE

While Porto isn't going to steal the clubbing crown any time soon, *tripeiros* (Porto residents) love to get their groove on, especially in the Galerias, with its speakeasy-style bars and the party spilling out onto the streets. There's just enough urban edge to keep the scene fresh-faced: a night out here can easily jump from indie clubs to refined rooftop bars.

🍷 Ribeira

Prova   Wine Bar

(Map p114; www.prova.com.pt; Rua Ferreira Borges 86; ⏰5pm-1am Wed-Sun; 🛜) Diogo,

the passionate owner, explains the finer nuances of Portuguese wine at this chic, stone-walled bar, where relaxed jazz plays. Stop by for a two-glass tasting (€5), or sample wines by the glass – including beefy Douros, full-bodied Dãos and crisp Alentejo whites. These marry well with sharing plates of local hams and cheeses (€14). Diogo's port tonics are legendary.

Wine Quay Bar   Wine Bar

(Map p114; www.winequaybar.com; Cais da Estiva 111; ⏰4-11pm Mon-Sat; 🛜) Sunset is prime-time viewing on the terrace of this terrific wine bar by the Rio Douro. As you gaze across to the graceful arc of the Ponte Dom Luís I and over to the port cellars of Vila Nova de Gaia, you can sample some cracking Portuguese wines and appetisers (cured ham, cheese, olives and the like).

🍷 Aliados & Bolhão

Era uma Vez em Paris   Bar

(Map p114; Rua Galeria de Paris 106; ⏰11am-2am Mon-Wed, to 4am Thu-Sat) A little flicker of bohemian Parisian flair in the heart of Porto, Era uma Vez em Paris time warps you back to the more decadent 1920s. Its ruby-red walls, retro furnishings and frilly lampshades spin a warm, intimate cocoon for coffee by day and drinks by night. DJs keep the mood mellow with indie rock and funk beats.

Aduela   Bar
(Map p114; Rua das Oliveiras 36; ⊕3pm-2am Mon, 10am-2am Tue-Thu, to 4am Fri & Sat, 3pm-midnight Sun) Retro and hip but not self-consciously so, chilled Aduela bathes in the nostalgic orange glow of its glass lights, which illuminate the green walls and mishmash of vintage furnishings. Once a sewing machine warehouse, today it's where friends gather to converse over wine and appetising *petiscos* (€3 to €8).

Terraplana   Cafe
(www.terraplanacafe.com; Avenida Rodrigues de Freitas 287; ⊕6pm-midnight Sun-Thu, to 3am Fri & Sat) Totally relaxed and boho-cool without trying, Terraplana is the bar of the moment in this neck of Porto. Murals adorn the artsy, stone-walled interior, and there's a pretty patio for summer imbibing. Besides inventive cocktails (around €10 a pop), they also have a solid selection of wines, gins and beers. These marry well with super-tasty pizzas (€8.50 to €9.50).

La Bohème   Wine Bar
(Map p114; www.facebook.com/laboheme.baixa; Rua Galeria de Paris 40; ⊕6pm-2am Tue-Thu, to 4am Fri & Sat, 7pm-2am Sun) With a high-ceilinged, Scandi-style pine interior, La Bohème is one of the most stylish, intimate bars on Rua Galeria de Paris. It's a nicely chilled choice for pairing fine wines with *petiscos*. DJs spin as the evening wears on.

Galeria de Paris   Bar
(Map p114; www.facebook.com/restaurante galeriadeparis; Rua Galeria de Paris 56; ⊕8.30am-3am Sun-Thu, to 4am Fri & Sat) The original on the strip that's now synonymous with the Porto party scene, this whimsically decorated spot has toys, thermos flasks, old phones and other assorted memorabilia

lining the walls. In addition to cocktails and draught beer, you'll find tapas at night.

⊜ Miragaia
Pinguim Café   Bar
(Map p114; www.facebook.com/PinguimCafe; Rua de Belomonte 65; ⊕9pm-4am Mon-Fri, 10pm-4am Sat & Sun) A little bubble of bohemian warmth in the heart of Porto, Pinguim attracts an alternative crowd. Stone walls and dim lighting create a cosy, intimate backdrop for plays, film screenings, poetry readings, rotating exhibitions of local art and G&T sipping. It's full to the rafters at weekends.

⊜ Vila Nova de Gaia
360° Terrace Lounge   Wine Bar
(Map p114; www.myportocruz.com; Espaço Porto Cruz, Largo Miguel Bombarda 23; ⊕12.30pm-12.30am Tue-Thu, to 1.30am Fri & Sat, to 7pm Sun) From its perch atop the Espaço Porto Cruz, this decked terrace affords expansive views over both sides of the Douro and the city, fading into a hazy distance where the river meets the sea. As day softens into dusk, this is a prime sunset spot for sipping a glass of port or a cocktail while drinking in the incredible vista.

7G Roaster   Coffee
(Map p114; www.facebook.com/7groaster; Rua de França 26; ⊕10am-6pm Mon-Thu, to 7pm Fri-Sun) The baristas really know their stuff at this speciality coffee roasters. In the cool, monochrome, wood-floored space, you can sip a perfectly made espresso or go for brunch (€12), which includes everything from sheep's cheese to homemade granola, pastries and fresh-pressed juice. Sit on the terrace to gaze up at the vertical garden.

⊜ Foz do Douro
Praia da Luz   Bar
(www.praiadaluz.pt; Avenida do Brasil; ⊕9am-2am) Praia da Luz is a worthwhile stop when out exploring Porto's coastline. It rambles over tiered wooden decks to its own private rocky cove, and while you could probably skip the food, you should definitely kick back and enjoy the view over a coffee or cocktail.

Aduela

⭐ ENTERTAINMENT

Hot Five Jazz & Blues Club — Jazz

(Map p114; ☎934 328 583; www.hotfive.pt; Largo Actor Dias 51; ⊙10pm-3am Wed-Thu, to 4am Fri & Sat, to 2am Sun) True to its name, this spot hosts live jazz and blues as well as the occasional acoustic, folk or all-out jam session. It's a modern but intimate space, with seating at small round tables, both fronting the stage and on an upper balcony. Concerts often start later than scheduled.

Teatro Municipal Rivoli — Theatre

(Map p114; ☎223 392 200; www.teatro municipaldoporto.pt; Praça Dom João I; 👬) This art deco theatre is one of the linchpins of Porto's evolving cultural scene. It traverses the whole spectrum from theatre to music, contemporary circus, cinema, dance and marionette productions.

Maus Hábitos — Performing Arts

(Map p114; www.maushabitos.com; 4th fl, Rua Passos Manuel 178; ⊙noon-midnight Tue, to 2am Wed & Thu, to 4am Fri & Sat, noon-5pm Sun) Maus Hábitos or 'Bad Habits' is an arty, nicely chilled haunt hosting a culturally ambitious agenda. Changing exhibitions and imaginative installations adorn the walls, while live bands and DJs work the small stage.

ℹ INFORMATION

City Centre Turismo (Map p114; ☎300 501 920; www.visitporto.travel; Rua Clube dos Fenianos 25; ⊙9am-8pm May-Jul & Sep-Oct, to 9pm Aug, to 7pm Nov-Apr) The main city *turismo* has a detailed city map, a transport map and the *Agenda do Porto* cultural calendar, among other printed materials.

ℹ GETTING THERE & AWAY

AIR

Situated around 16km northwest of the city centre, the gleaming, ultra-modern **Francisco de Sá Carneiro Airport** (☎229 432 400; www. aeroportoporto.pt; 4470-558 Maia) operates direct flights to major international hubs including London, Brussels, Madrid, Frankfurt and Toronto.

BUS

As in many Portuguese cities, bus services in Porto are regrettably dispersed, with no central bus terminal. The good news is that there are frequent services to just about everywhere in northern Portugal, as well as express services to Coimbra, Lisbon and points south.

Renex-Rede Expressos (www.rede-expressos. pt; Campo 24 de Agosto) is the choice for Lisbon (€19, 3½ hours), with the most direct routes and eight to 12 departures daily, including one continuing on to the Algarve. They also have frequent services to Braga (€6, one hour). Buses depart from Campo 24 de Agosto.

There are Eurolines (www.eurolines.com) departures from Interface Casa da Música (Rua Capitão Henrique Calvão). Northern Portugal's own international carrier, **Internorte** (www. internorte.pt; Interface Casa da Música), departs from the same place. Most travel agencies can book outbound buses with either operator.

TRAIN

Porto is the principal rail hub for northern Portugal. Long-distance services start at **Campanhã** (Rua Monte da Estação) station, 3km east of the centre.

Direct IC destinations from Porto include Lisbon (2nd class €24.70 to €30.80, 2½ to three hours, hourly).

Most *urbano*, *regional* and *interregional* (IR) trains depart from the stunning indoor-outdoor **São Bento** (Praça Almeida Garrett) station, though all of these lines also pass through Campanhã.

For destinations on the Braga, Guimarães and Aveiro lines, or up the Douro Valley as far as Marco de Canaveses, take one of the frequent *urbano* trains.

GETTING AROUND

Metro Porto's compact, six-line metro network runs from 6am to 1am daily. It's handy for zipping between neighbourhoods and getting to/ from the airport and beaches north of the city.

Tram Porto's vintage trams are transport at its atmospheric best. There are three lines: tram 1 running along the river from the historic centre to Foz, tram 18 between Massarelos and Carmo, and tram 22 doing a loop through the centre from Carmo to Batalha/Guindais.

Bus Central hubs of Porto's extensive bus system include the Jardim da Cordoaria, Praça da Liberdade and São Bento station.

Taxi Expect to pay between €5 and €8 to cross town. There's a 20% surcharge at night. There are taxi ranks throughout the centre.

TRANSPORT CARDS

○ For maximum convenience, Porto's transport system offers the rechargeable Andante Card (www.linhandante.com), allowing smooth movement between tram, metro, funicular and many bus lines.

○ The card itself costs only €0.60 and can be charged with travel credit at metro ticket machines, funicular stations and other locations.

Where to Stay

Porto's sleeping scene has experienced a renaissance in recent years, with the arrival of hipsterish hostels, retro-cool guesthouses, swanky five-star hotels, and slickly modern apartments. Book well in advance during peak season and major festivals.

Neighbourhood	For	Against
Aliados & Bolhão	Near sights, nightlife, shops, restaurants... everything. Great transport links.	Can be crowded and pricey.
Boavista	Good for off-the-beaten track exploring. Close to Casa da Música.	Far from main sights. More residential/corporate.
Foz do Douro	Located on the Atlantic, with beaches and a waterfront promenade, plus numerous shops, cafes and restaurants.	Less appealing in the cooler months.
Massarelos	Low-key and authentic/untouristy neighbourhood with a handful of sights and restaurants, plus the lovely Jardins do Palácio de Cristal.	Limited sleeping options, and far from Porto's centre.
Miragaia	Charismatic hilltop neighbourhood, spilling down to the river, with pretty gardens and viewpoints, plus inexpensive, artsy guest houses and restaurants.	Steep streets to climb. Limited transport links.
Ribeira	Historic Porto at its best, packed with sights, restaurants and bars. Good transport links.	Can be touristy. Book early!
Vila Nova de Gaia	Close to the port-wine lodges for tours and tastings. Fine views of Ribeira.	Not well connected by public transport.

THE ALGARVE

The Algarve at a Glance...

The alluring coast of the Algarve receives much exposure for its breathtaking cliffs, golden beaches, scalloped bays and sandy islands. But 'S' (for sun, surf and sand) is only one letter in the Algarvian alphabet; other initials stand for activities, beach bars, castles (both sand and real), diving, entertainment, fun...

Portugal's premier holiday destination sold its soul to tourism in the '60s and never really looked back. Behind sections of the south coast's beachscape loom brash resorts. However, the west coast is another story – one that's more about nature. The enchanting inner Algarve boasts pretty castle towns and historic villages and the wonderful Via Algarviana hiking trail.

Two Days in the Algarve

On day one take a boat trip through the scenic **Parque Natural da Ria Formosa** (p142), followed by window shopping and dining in Faro's pedestrianised centre. On the second day, head to Tavira for a wander through the historic old town, and beach fun on the **Ilha de Tavira** (p144).

Four Days in the Algarve

Spend the third day in Lagos (p149), indulging in aquatic activities followed by dining and drinking in the lively cobble-stone centre. On day four, head west to Aljezur. Explore the wild beaches beyond town, go surfing (or take a lesson) and treat yourself to a seafood feast at the spectacularly sited **O Paulo** (p161).

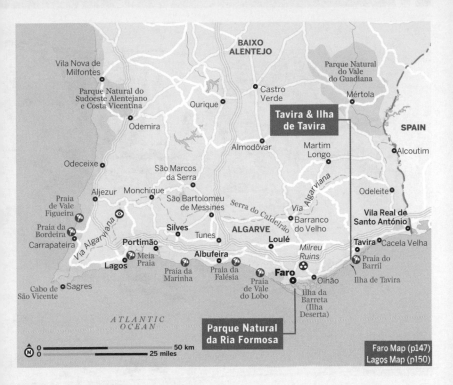

BAIXO ALENTEJO

Vila Nova de Milfontes

Parque Natural do Sudoeste Alentejano e Costa Vicentina

Ourique

Castro Verde

Parque Natural do Vale do Guadiana

Mértola

Odemira

Tavira & Ilha de Tavira

SPAIN

Almodôvar

Martim Longo

Alcoutim

Odeceixe

São Marcos da Serra

Aljezur   Monchique

Praia de Vale Figueira

São Bartolomeu de Messines

Serra do Caldeirão

Via

Odeleite

Via Algarviana

Vila Real de Santo António

Praia da Bordeira

Silves

ALGARVE

Tunes

Barranco do Velho

Carrapateira

Via Algarviana

Portimão

Loulé

Tavira   Cacela Velha

Lagos   Meia Praia

Albufeira

Milreu Ruins

Praia do Barril

Praia da Marinha

Praia da Falésia

Faro

Cabo de São Vicente   Sagres

Praia de Vale do Lobo

Olhão

Ilha de Tavira

ATLANTIC OCEAN

Ilha da Barreta (Ilha Deserta)

Parque Natural da Ria Formosa

0 — 50 km
0 — 25 miles

Faro Map (p147)
Lagos Map (p150)

Arriving in the Algarve

With national bus and train connections, as well as an international airport, Faro has excellent connections to both Portugal and major cities in Europe.

Other major towns of the Algarve, including Lagos, Portimão, Olhão and Tavira have decent bus and train connections to Lisbon.

Where to Stay

The Algarve has the full range of accommodation options you would expect to find in a resort-packed region, from five-star hotels to backpacker hostels.

Rates can almost double or even triple in July and especially August, and a bed can be almost impossible to come by in the busiest resorts. From September to June there are some amazing deals to be had.

Praia da Marinha

WIESDIE/SHUTTERSTOCK ©

Beaches of the Algarve

The top reason the vast majority of tourists visit the Algarve is the 150km of enticing golden sands. Photogenic beach strolls, surfing and frolicking in the waves are all essential parts of the Algarve experience.

Great For...

☑ Don't Miss

There are many less-frequented beaches on the Algarve's underrated west coast.

Geography of the Coast

The Algarve's coastline has everything from small, secluded coves to wide stretches of rugged, dune-backed shores, and from simple rock-backed nooks with calm waters (great for kids) to jagged coasts with huge swells.

The coast's varied geography changes dramatically along its length and makes for some quirky beachscapes. From Vila Real de Santo António to the tiny village of Cacela Velha, the beaches are a dune system. The central coast sees kilometres of limestone cliffs – think eroded rock towers and plenty of crevices and caves.

The increasingly rocky coast from Lagos to Sagres culminates in the wind-scoured grandeur of the Cabo de São Vicente. Here, dramatic black cliffs, bordered by beautiful sandy stretches, head north along the

Odeceixe

Parque Natural do Sudoeste Alentejano e Costa Vicentina (Costa Vicentina Natural Park). This stretch is made for serious surfers.

Top 10 Beaches

Our (highly subjective) picks include the following stretches of sand.

Odeceixe Only just in the Algarve, this Atlantic beach has a river on one side and the ocean on the other.

Praia da Falésia A posh 'resort' beach between Quarteira and Albufeira backed by high ochre-hued cliffs.

Praia da Marinha Great snorkelling, with a novel entry via a long staircase – just east of Carvoeiro.

Meia Praia Lagos' beach is a vast, popular and scenic place, with options for water sports.

ⓘ Need to Know

All of the Algarve's beaches are public and therefore free to access.

✕ Take a Break

A seafood stew for two called a *cataplana* is the culinary highlight across the region.

★ Top Tip

Water sports are big on the Algarve – countless agencies can help you get out on the water.

Praia do Barril Crown jewel of Ilha de Tavira, with an anchor cemetery.

Ilha da Barreta (Ilha Deserta) South of Faro, this beach island is accessed by boat through nature-filled lagoons.

Praia de Vale Figueira Near Salema, this is a long stretch of wild, little-frequented coast.

Praia da Bordeira Untamed beauty (with surfing) – near Carrapateira on the west coast.

Praia de Dona Ana & Camilo Enchanting, golden rock formations near Lagos

Praia de Vale do Lobo West of Faro, this beach has all the tourist services within reach and on tap.

Water Sports

Getting into, onto and occasionally above the water is what it's all about along the coast of the Algarve, whether that be surfing, diving, boat trips, kayaking or wildlife spotting. And have no fear – there are plenty of outfits in every resort waiting to help you do it.

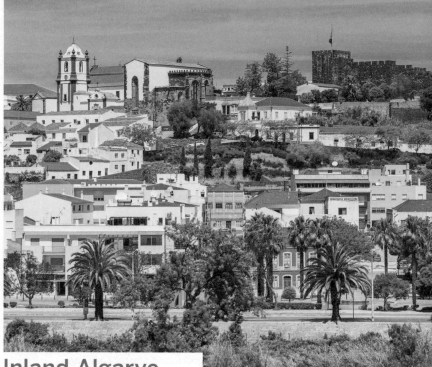

Inland Algarve

The Algarve isn't all about the coast – head inland to discover historic towns, spas and a superb hiking trail. Explore by car to reveal the Algarve's more remote, less-inhabited side.

Via Algarviana

Covering some of the most beautiful scenery in the Algarve, the 300km-long Via Algarviana walking trail crosses the breadth of Portugal from Alcoutim to Cabo de São Vicente, taking in the wooded hillsides of the Serra do Caldeirão and Monchique.

The Via Algarviana is fairly well marked. It's divided into 14 sections, covering up to 30km per day over two weeks. At the start of each stage is an information panel; starting point GPS coordinates are provided in the route guide, available as a free download at www.viaalgarviana.org (run by environmental group Almargem) and at tourist offices throughout the region.

The best time to walk the trail is between March and May. Be sure to carry enough water at all times as water often isn't available en route.

Great For...

☑ **Don't Miss**

Unwinding at the spa in Monchique after hiking in the surrounding hills.

Silves

PAWEL KAZMIERCZAK/SHUTTERSTOCK ©

displaying fascinating finds from the town and around. It's built around an 18m-deep Moorish well with a spiral staircase heading into its depths.

Roman Ruins at Milreu

Set in beautiful countryside north of Faro are the impressive ruins of a Roman **villa** (📞289 997 823; www.monumentosdoalgarve. pt; Rua de Faro; adult/child €2/free; ⏱10.30am-1pm & 2-6.30pm May-Sep, 9.30am-1pm & 2-5pm Oct-Apr). The villa, inhabited from the 1st century AD, has the characteristic peristyle form, with a gallery of columns around a courtyard. Highlights include the temple, the fish mosaics and former central pool, which suggest that it was devoted to a water cult.

Loulé

One of the Algarve's largest inland towns, and only 16km northwest of Faro, Loulé has an attractive old quarter and Moorish castle ruins, and its history goes back to the Romans. A few of Loulé's artisan traditions still survive; crafty folk toil away making wicker baskets and at copperworks and embroidery in hole-in-the-wall workshops about town. The town's most impressive piece of architectural heritage is its art nouveau market, a 1908 revivalist neo-Moorish confection with four oriental-looking cupolas at the four corners and Moorish features picked out in raspberry red against cream walls.

Silves

Some 15km north of Portimão, Silves is an attractive town of jumbling orange rooftops and winding streets scattered over a hillside above the Rio Arade. It boasts one of the best-preserved castles in the Algarve, a russet-coloured, Lego-like structure affording enjoyable views over the town. Just below the castle is the **Sé** (Rua da Sé; by donation; ⏱9am-12.30pm & 2-5.30pm Mon-Fri year-round, plus 9am-1pm Sat Jun-Aug), built in 1189 on the site of an earlier mosque. In many ways, this is the Algarve's most impressive cathedral, with a substantially unaltered Gothic interior. The town's other unmissable is the **Museu Municipal de Arqueologia** (📞282 444 838; www.cm-silves.pt; Rua das Portas de Loulé 14; adult/child €2.10/1.05, joint ticket with Castelo €3.90; ⏱10am-6pm), a modern museum

SABINE LUBENOW/GETTY IMAGES ©

Parque Natural da Ria Formosa

The eastern Algarve coast between Faro and Tavira consists of offshore islands backed by estuaries, with glorious ocean beaches and a wetland reserve that's an important habitat for birds and shellfish.

Great For...

☑ Don't Miss

Birdwatching on a boat tour operated from Faro (don't forget to bring binoculars).

Coastal Habitats

The **Parque Natural da Ria Formosa** (www.icnf.pt) is mostly a lagoon system stretching for 60km along the Algarve coastline and encompassing 18,000 hectares, from west of Faro to the tiny village of Cacela Velha. It encloses a vast area of *sapal* (marsh), *salinas* (salt pans), creeks and dune islands. To the west there are several freshwater lakes, including those at Ludo and Quinta do Lago; the marshes are an important area for migrating birds. The park provides some of the most stunning natural vistas in the Algarve and is a must for anyone staying in the area. Birdwatchers are drawn to the park due to the huge variety of wetland birds here, along with ducks, shorebirds, gulls and terns. This is a favourite nesting place of the little tern and a rare purple gallinule.

Chameleon

TONY MILLS/SHUTTERSTOCK ©

São João da Venda · Olhão · Fuseta · Faro · **Parque Natural da Ria Formosa**

ℹ Need to Know

Boat trips out into the Parque Natural da Ria Formosa run year-round and cost around €28.

✕ Take a Break

The only place to eat in the Parque Natural da Ria Formosa is Estaminé (p148).

★ Top Tip

Take a picnic, water, binoculars and swimwear, plus a waterproof jacket if the weather looks iffy.

Getting into the Park

Boats leave from Faro waterfront with several tour companies offering trips. **Animaris** (Map p147; ☑918 779 155; www.ilha-deserta.com; Rua Comandante Francisco Manuel; return ferry/speedboat €5/10, 1hr boat trip from €27.50; ☉10am-4.45pm) ✔ runs trips to Ilha da Barreta (Ilha Deserta). Ferries take 45 minutes, while speedboats zip across in 15 minutes. It also runs year-round guided boat trips through Parque Natural da Ria Formosa, dropping you at the island to return by ferry or speedboat at your own pace. Boats leave from the pier next to Arco da Porta Nova. The company operates the ecofriendly restaurant Estaminé (p148) on the Ilha da Barreta.

The recommended **Formosamar** (Map p147; ☑918 720 002; www.formosamar.com; Avenida da República, Stand 1, Faro Marina) ✔

promotes environmentally responsible tourism. Among its excellent tours are two-hour birdwatching trips around the Parque Natural da Ria Formosa (€25), dolphin watching (€45), cycling (€37) and a two-hour kayak tour negotiating some of the narrower lagoon channels (€35). All trips have a minimum number of participants (usually two to four). It has departures from Olhão and Tavira, too, and various ticket offices around the Faro waterfront.

Exploring on Your Own

You don't have to go with a group to explore the Ria Formosa Natural Park. The **Lands** (Map p147; ☑914 539 511; www.lands. pt; Avenida da República, Stand 3, Faro Marina) ✔ agency rents out kayaks (€35 per half day) for you to explore Ria Formosa on your own. Staff can give advice on where you should head and the rest is up to you. Some previous kayaking experience is a good idea, but it's not essential.

Rio Gilão, Tavira

JUAMPITER/GETTY IMAGES ©

Tavira & Ilha de Tavira

Sitting pretty on either side of the meandering Rio Gilão, Tavira is arguably the Algarve's most charming town. A hilltop castle and an old Roman bridge are the main draws.

Great For...

☑ Don't Miss

The elaborate, Islamic-era Tavira vase found in the Núcleo Islâmico.

Tavira

Tavira's ruined **castelo** (Largo Abu-Otmane; ⊘8am-5pm Mon-Fri, 9am-7pm Sat & Sun, to 5pm winter) **FREE** rises high and mighty above the town. Possibly dating back to Neolithic times, the structure was rebuilt by Phoenicians and later taken over by the Moors. The interior holds a pleasantly exotic botanic garden, and the octagonal tower offers fine views over Tavira. Near the castle rises the Torre da Tavira, formerly the town's water tower (100m), which now houses a camera obscura, revealing a 360-degree panoramic view of Tavira. Down from the castle, the **Igreja da Misericórdia** (www.diocese-algarve.pt; Largo da Misericórdia; church incl museum €2, fado performances €8; ⊘10am-12.30pm & 3-6.30pm Tue-Sat Jul & Aug, 9.30am-12.30pm & 2-5.30pm Tue-Sat Sep-Jun, fado performances 3.15pm Sat year-round) is the Algarve's most important

Ilha de Tavira

CARLOS NETO/SHUTTERSTOCK ©

Santo
Estevão

Tavira

⊙ **Tavira
Island**

ℹ️ Need to Know

Regular buses and trains run to Faro.

✖️ Take a Break

O Tonel (📞963 427 612; Rua Dr Augo Silva Carvalho 6; tapas €3.50-7.50; mains €9-16; ⊘6.30-10pm Mon-Sat) serves outstanding contemporary Portuguese cuisine; reserve well ahead.

⭐ Top Tip

Sample some daytime fado at the excellent **Fado Com História** (www.fadocom historia.com; Rua Damião Augo de Brito Vasconcelos 4; adult/child €8/free; ⊘shows 12.15pm, 3.15pm & 5.15pm Mon-Fri, 12.15pm & 5.15pm Sat) near the castle.

Renaissance monument, with a magnificent carved doorway. Down by the river on Praça da República, be sure to pop into the **Núcleo Islâmico** (📞281 320 570; www.cm-tavira.pt; Praça da República 5; adult/child €2/1, with Palácio da Galeria €3/1.50; ⊘9.15-12.30pm & 1.30-4.30pm Tue-Sun), a 21st-century museum exhibiting impressive Islamic pieces discovered in various excavations around the old town.

Ilha de Tavira

Sandy islands stretch along the coast from Cacela Velha to just west of Faro, and this is one of the finest. Made up of dunes, gently shelving sand and a strip of woodland, this is the Algarve at its best: a real hideaway only reachable by boat. You can even enjoy a camping holiday on the island. The huge beach at Ilha de Tavira's eastern end, opposite Tavira, has water sports, a campground and cafe-restaurants. Reached by ferry from Quatro Águas, 2km from Tavira, the island usually feels wonderfully remote and empty, but gest busy during July and August.

Getting to Ilha de Tavira

Silnido (📞918 278 934; www.silnido.com; Estrada das Quatro Águas; return €1.50; ⊘8am-midnight Jul & Aug, 8am-7pm Mar-Jun, Sep & Oct, 9am-4.45pm Nov-Feb) ferries make the five-minute hop to the island from Quatro Águas, 2km southeast of Tavira. From June to September, it also runs a direct service from Rua Dr José Pires Padinha in central Tavira (€2 return, 20 minutes one way, 10am to 5.30pm). Sequa Tours runs a water taxi (around €18 one way) 24 hours a day from July to mid-September, and until midnight from May to June. A bus goes to Quatro Águas from the Tavira bus station from July to mid-September (eight daily). A taxi costs around €6.

Faro

The Algarve's capital has a more distinctly Portuguese feel than most resort towns. Many visitors only pass through this underrated city, which is a pity; it makes for an enjoyable stopover. It has an attractive marina, well-maintained parks and plazas, and a picturesque *cidade velha* (old town) ringed by medieval walls. The old town's winding, cobbled pedestrian streets, squares and buildings were reconstructed in a melange of styles following successive batterings – first by marauding British and then by two big earthquakes – and are home to museums, churches, a bone chapel and alfresco cafes.

SIGHTS

Sé
Cathedral

(Map p147; www.paroquiasedefaro.org; Largo da Sé; adult/child €3/free; ☺10am-6pm Mon-Fri, 10am-1pm Sat Jun-Sep, 10am-5.30pm Mon-Fri, 10am-1pm Sat Oct-May) The centrepiece of the Cidade Velha, the *sé* was completed in 1251 but heavily damaged in the 1755 earthquake. What you see now is a variety of Renaissance, Gothic and baroque features. Climb the tower for lovely views across the walled town and estuary islands. The cathedral also houses the **Museu Capitular**, with an assortment of chalices, priestly vestments and grisly relics (including both forearms of St Boniface), and a small 18th-century shrine built of bones.

Igreja de Nossa Senhora do Carmo & Capela dos Ossos
Church

(Map p147; www.diocese-algarve.pt; Largo do Carmo; €2; ☺church 9am-6pm Mon-Fri, 9am-1pm Sat Jun-Sep, 9am-5pm Mon-Fri, 9am-1pm Sat Oct-May, chapel 10am-1pm & 3-5.30pm Mon-Fri, 10am-1pm Sat year-round) One of the Algarve's most dazzling churches, this twin-towered baroque masterpiece was completed in 1719 under João V. After the 1755 earthquake, its spectacular facade was paid for with Brazilian gold, and the interior is gilded to the extreme, with numerous cherubs.

Accessed through the church at the back, the 19th-century **Capela dos Ossos** is built from the bones and skulls of over 1000 monks as a reminder of earthly impermanence. It's quite a sight.

Museu Regional do Algarve
Museum

(Map p147; ☎289 870 893; www.cm-faro.pt; Praça da Liberdade 2; adult/child €1.50/free; ☺10am-1.30pm & 2.30-6pm Mon-Fri) Three of the four halls at this worthwhile museum house exhibitions on rural life in the Algarve, including mock-ups of 19th-century shops and rooms, a real fishing boat, some impressively woven creations in wicker, bamboo and palm leaves, and lots of rag rugs and fishing nets. The fourth hall is always given over to a temporary show on a folksy local theme.

Praia de Faro
Beach

(Ilha de Faro) On the Ilha de Faro, 9km west of the centre, the town's beach has sweeping sand, windsurfing and kitesurfing operators, and a handful of cafes. It's crammed in high summer. Take bus 14 or 16 (p149) from the bus station (€2.30, 20 minutes, up to two per hour daily July to September, hourly Monday to Friday only October to June).

🔒 SHOPPING

Chocolates de Beatriz
Chocolate

(Map p147; ☎289 820 358; www.chocolatesde beatriz.com; Rua Veríssimo de Almeida 5; ☺10am-1pm & 3-7pm Tue-Sat) 🍫 Chocolates made in Odemira in the neighbouring Alentejo region are enticingly displayed in glass cabinets at this little shop. Dark, milk and white chocolates have fillings such as Portuguese-harvested sea salt, fig paste, *medronho* (strawberry-tree liqueur) or Algarve oranges. Walk through and you'll find a tiny cafe where you can sit down for a hot chocolate and treats on site.

EATING

A Venda
Portuguese €

(Map p147; Rua Do Compromisso 60; dishes €4-9; ☺1-3pm & 7.30-11pm Tue-Sat) Homestyle

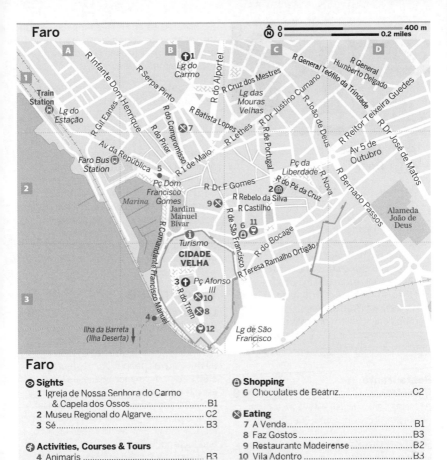

Faro

◎ **Sights**

  1 Igreja de Nossa Senhora do Carmo
    & Capela dos Ossos.............................B1
  2 Museu Regional do Algarve...................C2
  3 Sé B3

◆ **Activities, Courses & Tours**

  4 Animaris B3
  5 Formosamar...B2
    Lands ....(see 5)

◉ **Shopping**

  6 Chocolates de Beatriz...........................C2

✖ **Eating**

  7 A Venda B1
  8 Faz Gostos B3
  9 Restaurante Madeirense B2
  10 Vila Adentro B3

◉ **Drinking & Nightlife**

  11 Epicur...C2
  12 O Castelo...B3

Portuguese food at bargain prices –
Monchique blood sausage stew, fava bean
fritters with smoked paprika sauce – and
a retro interior with an ancient tiled floor,
mismatched furniture and antique glass
display cases make this backstreet place a
red-hot favourite with local students. DJs
often spin on summer nights.

Vila Adentro   Portuguese €€
(Map p147; ☎933 052 173; www.vilaadentro.pt;
Praça Dom Afonso III 17; mains €9-17.50,

cataplanas €39-49; ☺9am-midnight; 🖶) With
tables on the square in Faro's old town and
a dining room decorated with floor-to-
ceiling *azulejos*, this Moorish 15th-century
building is a romantic spot for elevated
Portuguese cuisine: pork, clam and lobster
cataplanas (stew) for two, chargrilled
octopus with fig and carob sauce, and
tangerine-stuffed pork filet. Wines hail from
around the country.

 Algarve Rock

The Algarve's first **craft brewery** (📞289 815 203; www.algarverock.com; Unidade B, Parq Vale da Venda; ⊙9am-5pm Mon-Fri) 🥢 opened in 2018, producing organic, preservative-free, vegan brews inspired by the region, such as piri-piri pilsner and carob stout. It's located in an industrial estate 6.5km northwest of Faro. At the time of writing, tours and tastings (€25 per person) were for groups only (call to confirm), but you can buy direct from the brewery.

RADIOKAFKA/SHUTTERSTOCK ©

Restaurante Madeirense
Madeiran €€

(Map p147; 📞967 168 140; www.facebook.com/restaurantemadeirensefamilia; Rua 1 Dezembro 28; mains €8-17; ⊙noon-10.30pm Tue-Sun) For an exotic take on Portuguese cuisine, this small Madeiran restaurant bangs down plates loaded with specialities you'll only get on the Island of Eternal Spring. *Espada* (scabbard fish), *bolo de caco* (potato bread) and *pudim de maracuja* (maracuja pudding) are just some of the treats on offer; round things off with a *poncha* (sugar-cane liqueur) or sweet Madeira wine.

Estaminé
Seafood €€€

(📞917 811 856; www.estamine.deserta.pt; Ilha da Barreta; mains €18-28; ⊙10am-6pm) 🥢 Built to look like a crab when viewed from above, this remote restaurant rises up on boardwalks from the Ilha da Barreta as its sole building. It's an entirely self-sufficient operation, using 100% solar power and desalinated water. Fresh-as-it-gets seafood dishes span Ria Formosa oysters, cracked crab and lobster to char-grilled prawns and fish, and aromatic stews.

Faz Gostos
Portuguese €€€

(Map p147; 📞914 133 668; www.fazgostos.com; Rua do Castelo 13; mains €12-25; ⊙noon-3pm & 6.30-10pm Sun-Fri, 6.30-10pm Sat; 🛜) Sophisticated twists on Portuguese classics at this stylish restaurant in the old town might include *xarém* (maize porridge) with Ria Formosa clams, steamed sea bass with olive-oil-poached potatoes, cornbread-topped cod, or chorizo-stuffed pork loin with fig sauce, depending on what's in season. Presentation is exquisite. The cellar has more than 250 Portuguese wines.

🍷 DRINKING

O Castelo
Bar

(Map p147; www.facebook.com/OCasteloBar. CidadeVelha.Faro; Rua do Castelo 11; ⊙10.30am-4am Wed-Mon; 🛜) O Castelo is all things to all people: bar, restaurant, club and performance space. Its location atop the old town walls provides stunning Ria Formosa views, especially at sunset. Beers, wine and cocktails are accompanied by tapas such as flambéed chorizo and local cheeses.

In summer the terrace morphs into a party space and there are regular fado (traditional song) nights.

Epicur
Wine Bar

(Map p147; 📞914 614 612; www.epicur.wine; Rua Alexandre Herculano 22; ⊙5pm-midnight Tue-Sat) More than 250 Portuguese wines are stocked at this stylish new wine bar, 30 of them by the glass. All of the country's major wine regions are represented, including the Algarve. Pair them with *presunto* (charcuterie), tinned fish, local cheeses and Ria Formosa oysters. There are regular meet-the-winemakers events; you can also buy bottles to take home.

Igreja de Nossa Senhora do Carmo & Capela dos Ossos (p146)

🛈 INFORMATION

Turismo (Map p147; www.visitalgarve.pt; Rua da Misericórdia 8; ⊗9.30am-1pm & 2-5.30pm; 🛜) Efficient office at the edge of the old town.

🛈 GETTING THERE & AWAY

AIR

Faro Airport (ΓAO; ☏289 800 800; www.aeroportofaro.pt; 🛜) is 7km west of the centre.
TAP (Air Portugal; ☏202 015 051; www.flytap.com) has multiple daily Lisbon–Faro flights (40 minutes).

BUS

Buses arrive at and depart from the **bus station** (Map p147; ☏289 899 760; Avenida da República 5), on the northern side of the marina. Most services are run by **Eva** (☏289 899 760; www.eva-bus.com; Avenida da República 5). Key destinations include Lisbon (€20, 3¼ hours, six per day), Spain's Seville (€20, 3½ hours, two daily) via Huelva (€16, 2½ hours) and Tavira (€4.45, one hour, nine daily).

TRAIN

From Faro's train station, 500m northwest of the centre, there are direct trains to Lisbon daily (€22.90, four hours), as well as Albufeira (€3.35, 30 minutes, every two hours) and Lagos (€7.30, 1¾ hours, every two hours).

🛈 GETTING AROUND

From the airport, **Próximo** (☏289 899 700; www.proximo.pt; Avenida da República 5) city buses 14 and 16 run to the bus station (€2.25, 20 minutes, half-hourly). From here it's an easy stroll to the centre.

A taxi into town costs around €20 (20% more after 10pm and on weekends), plus around €2 for each luggage item.

Lagos

As tourist towns go, Lagos (*lah*-goosh) has got the lot. The port town that launched many naval excursions during Portugal's extraordinary Age of Discovery lies along the bank of the Rio Bensafrim. Its old

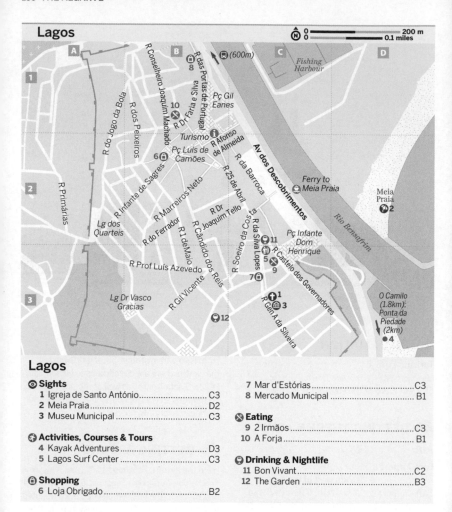

Lagos

⊙ Sights

town's pretty, cobbled lanes and picturesque squares and churches are enclosed by 16th-century walls. Beyond the walls is a modern but not overly unattractive sprawl and some truly fabulous beaches.

It's not surprising that people of all ages are drawn to Lagos, with its huge range of activities including water sports, boat trips and horse riding, and excellent restaurants and a pumping nightlife.

⊙ SIGHTS

Museu Municipal Museum

(Map p150; ☑282 762 301; www.cm-lagos.com; Rua General Alberto da Silveira; adult/child €3/1.50; ☉9.30am-12.30pm & 2-5pm Tue-Sun) The town museum holds a bit of everything: swords and pistols, landscapes and portraits, minerals and crystals, coins, Moorish pottery, miniature furniture, Roman mosaics, African artefacts, stone tools, model boats, the original 1504 town charter and an intriguing model of an imaginary Portuguese town. Exhibits are scattered randomly through the museum, with limited explanations, making it unwittingly like a treasure hunt. The museum is also the entry point for the baroque Igreja de Santo António.

✪ ACTIVITIES

Meia Praia   Beach

(Map p150) Arcing in a 4km-long crescent, this vast expanse of golden sand has water-sports outlets, and laid-back restaurants and beach bars.

An informal seasonal **boat service** (Map p150; one way €1; ☼sunrise-sunset Jun-Oct) shuttles back and forth from the waterfront in Lagos.

Lagos Surf Center   Surfing

(Map p150; ☑282 764 734; www.lagossurfcenter. com; Rua da Silva Lopes 31; 1-/3-/5-day courses €60/165/250) This surf school travels along the Algarve to locations with suitable swells. Private lessons per day cost €120. It also rents out wetsuits (€5 per day) and boards (€10 to €25) and offers beach kayaking and stand-up paddleboarding (half/full day €30/50). Children must be accompanied by a family member over 14 years of age.

Kayak Adventures   Kayaking

(Map p150; ☑917 716 202; www.kayakadventures lagos.com; Cais da Solara, Avenida dos Descobrimentos; 2½hr kayaking trip €30; ☼Mar-Oct) Kayaking trips from Praia da Batata give you an up-close perspective of the caves and fissures in the cliffs along the Ponta da Piedade. Advance online bookings are essential.

Blue Ocean   Diving

(☑964 665 667; www.blue-ocean-divers.de; Hotel Âncora Park, Estrada de Porto de Mós 837; 1/10 dives €35/270, with gear €55/450) Blue Ocean runs out to eight different dive sites, including reefs, wrecks and caves. Night dives are possible by request; beginners can take a half-day discovery experience (€30). It also organises snorkelling trips (half-day €30) and kayak safaris (half/full day €30/45). Lessons take place in the pool at the Hotel Âncora Park.

 Ponta da Piedade

Protruding 2.5km south of Lagos, **Ponta da Piedade** (Point of Piety) is a dramatic wedge of headland with contorted, polychrome sandstone cliffs and towers, complete with a lighthouse and, in spring, hundreds of nesting egrets, with crystal-clear turquoise water below. The surrounding area blazes with wild orchids in spring. On a clear day you can see east to Carvoeiro and west to Sagres. The only way to reach it is by car or on foot.

Tours

Algarve Water World   Wildlife, Cruise

(☑938 305 000; www.algarvewaterworld. com; Marina de Lagos; adult/child 90min tour €40/25, 75min grotto tour €15/7.50; ☼Mar-Oct) This small outfit offers excellent dolphin spotting trips on a 7.4m rigid inflatable named *Dizzy Dolphin*. Along with three species of dolphins (common, bottlenose and risso), you'll often spot sharks, turtles, orcas and fin whales. Grotto trips aboard the *Captain Nemo* take you to caves, cliffs and beaches.

🛍 SHOPPING

Mar d'Estórias   Concept Store

(Map p150; www.mardestorias.com; Rua Silva Lopes 30; ☼10am-7pm Mon, 10am-10pm Wed-Sat) ✐ Portuguese handicrafts at this artisan emporium include ceramics, blankets, scarves and bags, along with stationery, cookbooks and music, while gourmet

Gate to the old town, Lagos

LUCKY TEAM STUDIO/SHUTTERSTOCK ©

goods include olive oils, honey, cheeses, preserves, tinned fish, sweets, beers, wines and liqueurs. On the mezzanine, the in-house cafe serves *petiscos* and platters, as well as full meals; you can also dine on its panoramic roof terrace.

Loja Obrigado   Arts & Crafts

(Map p150; www.facebook.com/loja.obrigado; Praça Luís de Camões 3; ◷10am-7pm Mon-Sat) ✐ Inside a landmark building covered in textured palm-green tiles, this little shop sells local crafts including ceramic bowls, vases, tiles, wall hangings and adorable wooden toys and games made by the **Fábrica de Brinquedos** (www.projectotasa.com/project/ artisans/da-torre; Rua de Torre, Torre, Fonte Santa; ◷9am-1pm Mon-Fri) ✐ workshop in the Serra do Caldeirão hills.

Mercado Municipal   Market

(Map p150; www.cm-lagos.pt; Avenida dos Descobrimentos; ◷8am-2pm Mon-Sat) Lagos' covered market is an intriguing place to wander, and a great spot to stock up on fresh produce and super-fresh seafood.

🗙 EATING

O Camilo   Seafood €€

(☏282 763 845; www.restaurantecamilo.pt; Praia do Camilo; mains €11.50-23.50; ◷noon-4pm & 6-10pm Jun-Sep, to 9pm Oct-May; 🛜) Perched above pretty Praia do Camilo, this sophisticated restaurant is renowned for its high-quality seafood dishes. Specialities include razor clams, fried squid, lobster and oysters in season, along with grilled fish. The 40-seat dining room is light, bright and airy, and the large 28-seat terrace overlooks the ocean. Bookings are a good idea any time and essential in high season.

2 Irmãos   Tapas €€

(Map p150; Travessa do Mar 2; mains €14-24, tapas €7-9, cataplanas €31-34.50; ◷11am-midnight; 🛜) Housed in a quaint old building on Praça Infante Dom Henrique, 2 Irmãos has lovely outdoor seating overlooking the Igreja de Santa Maria and the statue of Prince Henry the Navigator. The sublime selection of *petiscos* (tapas) spans everything from pipis to pigs ears. *Cataplanas* (seafood stew) for two and grilled fish are available, too.

A Forja
Portuguese €€

(Map p150; ☑282 768 588; Rua dos Ferreiros 17; mains €8.50-22.50, cataplanas €30-35; ☺noon-3pm & 6.30-10pm Mon-Sat) Hearty, top-quality traditional food served in a bustling environment at great prices sees this buzzing *adega tipica* (wine bar) pull in the crowds. Daily specials are always reliable, as are simply prepared fish dishes such as grilled sole, turbot and mackerel on stainless steel plates, and two-person *cataplanas*.

 DRINKING

The Garden
Beer Garden

(Map p150; www.facebook.com/thegardenlagos; Rua Lançarote de Freitas 48; ☺bar 1pm-midnight, kitchen to 10pm May-Nov; ☎) Filled with flowering hibiscus, bougainvillea and citrus trees, with a mural of a barrelling wave, this fabulous beer garden is a brilliant spot for lounging with a beer or cocktail on a sunny afternoon. The aromas of barbecuing meat and seafood will make you want to stay for a meal. Look for the kissing snails painted on the outside wall.

Bon Vivant
Bar

(Map p150; www.bonvivantbarinlagos.com; Rua 25 de Abril 105; ☺4pm-3.30am Mon-Thu, to 4am Fri-Sun; ☎) Spread across five levels, including two underground rooms and a roof terrace, each with its own bar, cherry-red-painted Bon Vivant shakes up great house cocktails including the signature Mr Bonvivant (jenever, absinthe, strawberry-infused Aperol and bitters). Happy hour runs from 5pm to 9pm; DJs spin nightly downstairs.

Bahia Beach Bar
Bar

(www.bahiabar.pt; Estrada de São Roque, Meia Praia; ☺10.30am-11pm daily Jul & Aug, 10.30am-7pm Tue-Sun May, Jun, Sep & Oct; ☎) An essential hang-out on the sand at Meia Praia, busy Bahia has homemade sangria, fruit-based cocktails, Algarve and Alentejo wines, gourmet dining (poultry pie with foie gras; lobster and cod terrine) and live music at weekends.

 Praia da Rocha

Just 3km south of Portimão, Praia da Rocha has one of the Algarve's best beaches, backed by ochre-red cliffs and the small 16th-century Fortaleza da Santa Catarina.

Behind the beach looms the town; it has long known the hand of development, with high-rise condos and luxury hotels sprouting along the cliffside, and a row of restaurants, bars and clubs packed along the main thoroughfare.

If you look hard beyond the concrete facade, Praia da Rocha has several vestiges of an elegant past, including some 19th-century mansions, which are now atmospheric guest houses. The sleek Marina de Portimão, painted autumnal colours (to match the cliffs), is at the beach's eastern end, just inside the river mouth.

LUCYNAKOCH/GETTY IMAGES ©

 INFORMATION

Turismo (Map p150; ☑282 763 031; www.visit algarve.pt; Praça Gil Eanes 17; ☺9.30am-1pm & 2-5.30pm) Helpful office on the main square.

 GETTING THERE & AWAY

BUS

Buses run by Eva (www.eva-bus.com) and Rede Expressos (www.rede-expressos.pt) use the **bus station** (Rua Mercado de Levante). Aside from Lisbon and many Algarve destinations, there's also service to Seville, Spain (€21, 5½ hours, two daily).

TRAIN

Lagos is at the western end of the Algarve line. Trains to Lisbon require a change at Tunes (€22.15, four hours, five daily).

Portimão

Dating back to the time of the Phoenicians, Portimão is the Algarve's second-most-populous city. Most visitors only pass through the city en route to Praia da Rocha, but while it's rough around the edges, it does have a long waterfront promenade and an excellent museum in a former fish cannery. You can also take a boat trip up the Rio Arade.

◎ SIGHTS & ACTIVITIES

Museu de Portimão   Museum
(☎282 405 230; www.museudeportimao.pt; Rua Dom Carlos I; adult/child €3/free; ☷2.30-6pm Tue, 10am-6pm Wed-Sun Sep-Jul, 7.30-11pm Tue, 3-11pm Wed-Sun Aug) Housed in a 19th-century fish cannery, the ultramodern, award-winning Museu de Portimão is the city's number-one

draw. The museum focuses on three areas: archaeology, underwater finds and, the most fascinating, a re-creation of the fish cannery (mackerel and sardines). You can see former production lines, complete with sound effects – clanking and grinding and the like. An excellent video (in Portuguese) of the fishing industry reveals each step in the process, from netting the shoals to packaging.

Santa Bernarda   Cruise
(☎967 023 840; www.santa-bernarda.com; Ribeirinha; adult/child from €35/20) Santa Bernarda runs trips along the river and out to sea, visiting the caves and coastal cliffs, on a 23m pirate-themed wooden sailing ship with wheelchair access. The full-day trip includes a beach barbecue and time to swim. Trips to Cabo de São Vicente are also available.

Eating & Drinking
**Clube Naval
de Portimão**   Seafood €€
(☎282 417 529; www.clubenavaldeportimao.com; Zona Ribeirinha; mains €14-24; ☷noon-3pm & 7-11pm Tue-Sun; ☎) On the waterfront near

Museu de Portimão

Carvoeiro beach

the Museu de Portimão, the Naval Club has fancy Restaurante do Cais upstairs, which has unsurpassed views over the river from its terrace. Choose from the day's catch or go for monkfish skewers, prawns sautéed in garlic and chilli or oysters in season. The downstairs snack bar is great for a waterside coffee or beer.

ℹ️ INFORMATION

Turismo Municipal (☎ 282 402 487; www. visitalgarve.pt; Largo 1 de Dezembro 3; ⏱ 9.30am-12.30pm & 1.30-5.30pm Mon-Fri) Housed in the city's theatre, Teatro Municipal de Portimão ('Tempo').

ℹ️ GETTING THERE & AWAY

BUS

Buses run by Frota Azul (www.frotazul-algarve. pt) and Eva buses (www.eva-bus.com) depart from the **bus station** (Avenida Guanaré).

Services include Cabo São Vicente (€6.55, 1½ hours, one daily), Faro (€5.70, 1¾ hours, seven daily), Lagos (€4, 35 minutes, up to two per hour) and Lisbon (€20, 3¼ hours, six daily).

TRAIN

The train station is on Rua do Moinho, 700m north of the centre. Trains to/from Lisbon (€28.85, 4½ hours, five daily) require a change in Tunes. Direct services go to Silves (€1.55, 15 minutes, nine daily) and Lagos (€2.05, 20 minutes, 10 daily).

Carvoeiro

Carvoeiro is a cluster of whitewashed buildings atop gold-tinged cliffs and backed by gentle hills. Shops, bars and restaurants rise steeply from the small arc of beach that is the focus of the town, with holiday villas sprawling across the hillsides beyond. It's prettier and more laid-back than many of the Algarve's bigger resorts, but Carvoeiro's diminutive size means that it gets full-to-bursting in summer.

◉ SIGHTS

The town's handkerchief-sized sandy beach, **Praia do Carvoeiro**, is surrounded by the steeply mounting town. On the coastal road 800m east is the bay of **Algar Seco**, a favourite stop on the tour-bus itinerary thanks to its dramatic rock formations.

If you're looking for a stunning swimming spot, continue 2.2km further east along the main road, Estrada do Farol, to **Praia de Centianes**, where the secluded cliff-wrapped beach is almost as dramatic as Algar Seco.

Benagil Caves   Cave

(Algar de Benagil; Praia de Benagil) One of the Algarve's – and Portugal's – most emblematic sights, this huge natural seaside cave has a hole in its ceiling through which streaming sunlight illuminates the sandstone and beach below. The only way to access the interior is via the water. Numerous companies along the coast, such as Taruga Tours, run boat trips, and hire kayaks and stand-up paddleboards to paddle here yourself. Swimming to the caves is discouraged due to strong tides and currents, and high watercraft traffic.

From the cliffs above, you can look down to see the hole in the cave's roof.

Praia da Marinha   Beach

One of a few nearby beaches with karst rock stacks, Praia da Marinha is among the most beautiful. It's 7.5km east of Carvoeiro; the nicest way to reach it is via **Percurso dos Sete Vales Suspensos**.

🛍 SHOPPING

Porches Pottery   Ceramics

(☏282 352 858; www.porchespottery.com; N125, Porches; ☺9am-6pm Mon-Fri, 10am-2pm Sat) 🍴 Watch artists hand-painting traditional *azulejo* tiles at this pottery stocking a vast array of ceramics, from fridge magnets to plates, bowls, vases, lamps and pots. International shipping is available. Opening to a bougainvillea-draped front terrace, its enchanting on-site cafe is clad in classic blue-and-white tiles, and serves light dishes (sandwiches, quiches, salads,

Benagil Caves

MARCO BOTTIGELLI/GETTY IMAGES ©

cakes) on its own crockery at tile-topped tables.

It's 9km northeast of Carvoeiro.

 ACTIVITIES

Taruga Tours   Cruise, Kayaking

(☑969 617 828; www.tarugatoursbenagilcaves. pt; Praia de Benagil; 30/75min boat tours €15/25, 90min kayak/SUP hire €30/60; ⊙9.30am-6.30pm May-Sep, 10.30am-4.30pm Oct-Apr) Taruga's boat trips visit the extraordinary Benagil Caves; longer tours take you past other cliff-side caves and through natural arches. It also rents kayaks and stand-up paddleboards to reach the caves under your own steam. Book well ahead in summer. It's 6km east of Carvoeiro; park at the top of the hill on the eastern side of the beach.

Divers Cove   Diving

(☑282 356 594; www.divers-cove.com; Quinta do Paraíso; 1-day discovery course €135, 1 dive with/ without gear €50/35, 6 dives €250/175; ⊙9am-7pm Mon-Sat, 10am-7pm Sun) This multilingual, family-run diving centre provides equipment, dives and PADI certification.

Slide & Splash   Water Park

(☑282 340 800; www.slidesplash.com; Vale de Deus 125, Estômbar; adult/child €27/20; ⊙10am-6.30pm Aug, to 6pm Jul & early–mid-Sep, to 5.30pm Jun, to 5pm Apr, May & mid–late Sep) Set over 7 hectares, 8km north of Carvoeiro, this water park is widely considered Portugal's best, thanks to the sheer quantity of slides, toboggans and pools, along with reptile and birds-of-prey shows, and multiple restaurants. There's enough here to keep kids and adults entertained for most of a day, though with no family ticket available it can be an expensive outing.

 EATING

A Marisqueira   Seafood €€

(☑282 358 695; www.facebook.com/a marisqueira.carvoeiro; Estrada do Farol 95; mains €7-20.50; ⊙noon-2.30pm & 6.30-10pm Mon-Sat) You'll smell the smoky aromas of this well-established seafood restaurant before you see it, as almost everything is cooked over a flaming charcoal grill – sardines, sole, sea bream, squid and prawns included. It's 600m up the main road east of Praia do Carvoeiro.

Le Crô Portugal   Tapas €€

(☑910 983 443; Estrada do Farol 77; tapas €4.50-7.50, mains €8-13.50; ⊙12.30-3pm & 6.30-10pm Thu-Tue; ☑) Run by husband-and-wife team Hugo and Marina, this tiny wine-bar-style place turns out terrific *petiscos* such as sea bass ceviche, chorizo and squid, and marinated anchovies. Plentiful vegetarian options include local cheeses and olives, and aubergine-stuffed figs. It stocks a connoisseur's selection of wines, most from the surrounding area. Cash only.

 DRINKING

Restaurante Boneca Bar   Bar

(☑282 358 391; www.facebook.com/Restaurante BonecaBar; Estrada do Algar Seco; ⊙10am-midnight) Hidden in the rock formations at Algar Seco, 750m east of the beach in Carvoeiro (just below the cliff-side car park and reached by a steep staircase), this long-standing place is a glorious spot for a cocktail, beer or wine, particularly at sunset.

Portuguese dishes include grilled sardines and pork steaks.

ℹ INFORMATION

Turismo (☑282 357 728; www.visitalgarve. pt; Largo da Paia; ⊙9.30am-1pm & 2-5.30pm Tue-Sat) Just back from the beach in the centre of town.

ℹ GETTING THERE & AWAY

Buses run on weekdays between Carvoeiro and Portimão (€3.35, 35 minutes, eight daily).

Parking is difficult in summer – it's best to head to Estrada do Farol and walk.

Aerial view of Olhão

Olhão

Olhão (ol-*yowng*) is the Algarve's biggest fishing port, with an active waterfront and pretty, bustling lanes in its old quarters. There aren't many sights, but the flat-roofed, Moorish-influenced neighbourhoods and North African feel make it a charming place to wander. The town's fish restaurants draw the crowds, as does the morning fish and vegetable market, best visited on Saturday.

Olhão is also a springboard for Parque Natural da Ria Formosa's sandy islands, Culatra and Armona, and the park's environmental centre at Quinta de Marim.

◎ SIGHTS & ACTIVITIES

Starting from Rua da Fábrica Velha, an interesting 300m walking route winds its way through Olhão's knot of alleyways just back from the seafront, connecting five tiny idyllic squares. Information boards relate myths and legends associated with the area.

Quinta de Marim   Nature Reserve

(www.natural.pt; Quelfes; ⊘8am-8pm Mon-Fri, 10am-8pm Sat & Sun Jun-Sep 9am-noon & 2-5pm daily Oct-May) Situated 2.5km east of Olhão is the beautiful 60-hectare Centro Educação Ambiental de Marim (commonly known as Quinta de Marim). A 3km trail takes you through various ecosystems – dunes, salt marshes, pine woodlands – as well as to a wildlife rescue centre and a historic water mill. Chameleons and purple gallinule birds are among the rare local species. The Parque Natural da Ria Formosa headquarters and environmental centre are also here.

Mercados Municipais   Market

(Avenida 5 de Outubro; ⊘7am-2pm Mon-Sat) By the water, these two noble centenarian red-brick buildings are excellent examples of industrial architecture and house picturesque traditional fruit and fish markets that are worth a look at any time but are especially appealing on a Saturday morning. A string of simple seafood stalls and cafes makes them an atmospheric spot for a bite with water views.

S-STUDIO/SHUTTERSTOCK ©

EATING

The seafront Avenida 5 de Outubro has a market and is lined with touristy seafood restaurants serving *cataplanas* and *xerém* (cornflour mash similar to polenta with clams, sardines and bacon); more local options hide in the old town's tangle of lanes.

Tacho à Mesa
Portuguese €€

(☎961 624 577; www.facebook.com/tachoamesa olhao; Rua dos Lavadouros 46; mains €7-15, cataplanas €28-34; ⏰11am-3pm Mon, 11am-3pm & 7.30-10.30pm Tue-Sat, closed Jan; 🐾) A white, modern interior is the stylish setting for first-rate traditional cooking using fresh produce purchased twice daily from the markets. Menu highlights include aromatic *cataplanas*, super-juicy *bochechas de porco* (pork cheeks) and other Algarvian-Alentejan dishes. Wines come from all over Portugal, with a few from Spain. Book ahead in summer.

Tasca o Galo
Portuguese €€

(☎964 709 746; Rua a Gazeta de Olhão 7; mains €8-18; ⏰6pm-midnight Mon-Sat, closed Jan & Feb) Just back from the seafront, this converted merchant's store has just 22 seats, so booking well in advance is a good idea. Begin with award-winning olive oil and bread before dining on homemade dishes like *cataplanas*, piri-piri prawns, roast rabbit loin with cherry jus, and charred Algarve orange with pepper honey and rosemary brittle for dessert.

DRINKING

Snack-Bar A Velha
Cafe

(Avenida da República 16; ⏰10am-10pm Mon-Sat) A real slice of historic Portugal, this no-frills old-timers bar in the centre of town has a nicotine-stained interior and is so authentic you can forgive the gruff welcome. Drinks are limited to coffee, beer and house wine. Look for the vintage tiled Schweppes sign out front. Hours can fluctuate.

Island Beaches

Olhão is separated from the ocean by the islands and estuaries of the Parque Natural da Ria Formosa. **Ferries** (Avenida 5 de Outubro) to the islands depart year-round from the pier just east of Jardim Patrão Joaquim Lopes to the island beaches of Armona, Culatra and Farol. Zip across to soak up some sun or explore the little fishing hamlets.

Ferry schedule:

Ilha da Armona (€6 return, 20 minutes) Hourly July and August, every two hours September to June.

Ilha da Culatra (€6 return, 30 minutes) Hourly July and August, every two hours September to June.

Ilha do Farol (€7 return, one hour) Hourly June to August, four daily September to May.

HEMIS/ALAMY STOCK PHOTO ®

ℹ️ INFORMATION

Turismo (☎289 713 936; www.visitalgarve.pt; Largo Sebastião Martins Mestre 6; ⏰9am-5pm Tue-Thu, 9am-1pm & 2-5.30pm Fri-Mon) In the centre of the pedestrian zone.

ℹ️ GETTING THERE & AWAY

BUS

Eva (www.eva-bus.com) buses run to Faro (€3.35, 20 minutes, up to two per hour), Lisbon (€20, 3¾ hours, four daily) and Tavira (€4.25, 40 minutes, every two hours).

TRAIN

Regular trains run to Faro (€1.45, 10 minutes, 10 daily) and east to Fuseta (€1.45, 10 minutes, hourly) and Tavira (€2.35, 25 minutes, hourly).

Aljezur

Spectacular beaches along the Algarve's western coast are backed by beautiful wild vegetation and are wonderfully undeveloped thanks to building restrictions imposed to protect the Parque Natural do Sudoeste Alentejano e Costa Vicentina.

Straddling a narrow river, Aljezur makes an appealing base for exploring the area. Nearby beaches, edged by black rocks that reach into the white-tipped, bracing sea, are surfing hotspots. The surrounding countryside, which is part of the natural park, is a tangle of yellow, mauve and green wiry gorse and heather.

◉ SIGHTS

Wonderful, unspoilt beaches near Aljezur include **Praia da Arrifana** (10km southwest, near a tourist development called Vale da Telha), a dramatic, curved black-cliff-backed bay with one restaurant, balmy pale sands and some big northwest swells (a surfer's delight); and **Praia do Monte Clérigo**, 8.5km northwest. **Praia da Amoreira**, 6km away, is a wonderful beach where the river meets the sea. More difficult to reach but worth the effort is the remote **Praia de Vale Figueira**, 15km southwest of Aljezur via rugged dirt roads.

➕ ACTIVITIES

Algarve Adventure   Outdoors
(☑913 533 363; www.algarve-adventure. com; Praia do Monte Clérigo; 4hr rock-climbing course beginner/advanced from €60/120) The energetic team at Algarve Adventure can take you rock climbing along the coast and in the Algarve's hilly interior. Prices include transport and gear. The company also runs a local surf school (half-/full-day lesson

with gear €35/60) and rents equipment (surfboard/wetsuit per day €25/10) and mountain bikes (half/full day from €15/20).

Burros e Artes   Tours
(☑967 145 306, 282 995 068; www.burros-artes. blogspot.com; Vale das Amoreiras; self-guided donkey trek per day from €60, 1-/3-/7-day guided tours from €85/490/895) Fans of slow travel will enjoy covering 10km to 15km per day on foot through stunning landscapes, accompanied by your *burro* (donkey), which carries your luggage. This company coordinates trips including accommodation, food and optional multilingual guides; alternatively, go it alone, in which case the added fun is tending to the donkey (there are strict rules regarding its care).

Prices depend on a number of factors, including your standard of accommodation.

Burro e Artes is located 4km northeast of Aljezur.

Arrifana Surf School   Surfing
(☑961 690 249; www.arrifanasurfschool. com; Praia da Arrifana; 1-/3-/5-day course €55/150/225, surfboard/wetsuit hire per half day €20/10; ⊘closed Feb) Based at Praia da Arrifana, this surf school offers a complete range of hire and lessons, as well as packages with accommodation.

✴ EATING

Mó Veggie Bistro   Vegetarian, Vegan €
(☑925 289 246; www.facebook.com/MoVeggie Bistro; Rua João Dias Mendes 13; dishes €5.50-11; ⊘12.30-4pm & 6.30-10pm Tue-Sat Apr-Nov; 🛜🌱) 🌿 A former wheat mill now houses this brilliant split-level bistro with raw timbers, comfy sofas and suspended lighting. All dishes are vegetarian and many are vegan. Menu highlights include Vietnamese spring rolls, sweet-potato hummus with beetroot, basil, mango and chia-seed salad, towering bean-patty burgers and open-faced toasties, plus cakes (some gluten-free). Yoga workshops and live music gigs regularly take place.

Praia de Vale Figueira

O Paulo
Seafood €€

(📞934 975 250; www.restauranteopaulo.com; Rua Serpa Pinto 32, Arrifana; mains €9-25; ⏰kitchen 9.30am-10pm, bar to midnight Apr-Nov, hours vary Nov-Mar; 🛜) Adjacent to the ruined fortress of Arrifana, O Paulo has a romantic covered terrace with majestic clifftop views as far as Cabo de São Vicente. The vistas are hard to live up to, but it does, with tanks of live lobsters and crabs, superfresh fish and delicacies such as razor clams and traditional brine-boiled goose barnacles (a local speciality).

🍷 DRINKING

O Sargo
Bar

(📞912 995 839; Praia do Monte Clerigo; ⏰9am-10pm Thu-Tue Mar–mid-Nov) Directly across the beach, with glass walls buffering the wind and sand, O Sargo is a great place to slake your postsurf thirst, with cold-pressed juices, craft beers, ciders, local wines, and white and red sangrias. Live music – everything from fado to Spanish flamenco and funk – plays on weekends from June to September; the bar also hosts regular full-moon parties.

ℹ️ GETTING THERE & AWAY

Eva (www.eva-bus.com) buses run between Aljezur and Lagos (€4, 50 minutes, four on weekdays, one on Saturday). Rede Expressos (www.rede-expressos.pt) buses run north to Lisbon (€17.60, 3¾ hours, two daily) and south to Lagos (€7.60, 35 minutes, two daily) and Portimão (€8.70, 55 minutes, two daily).

If you're driving, there's a free car park opposite the *turismo*.

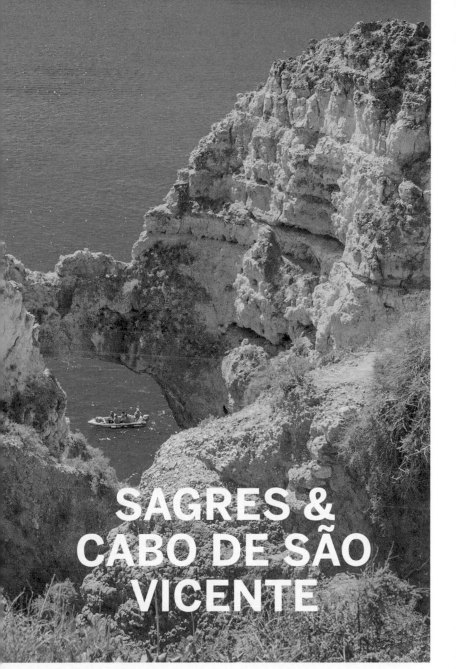

SAGRES &
CABO DE SÃO
VICENTE

Sagres & Cabo de São Vicente at a Glance...

Overlooking some of the Algarve's most dramatic scenery, the small, elongated village of Sagres has an end-of-the-world feel with its sea-carved cliffs and empty, wind-whipped fortress high above the frothing ocean. Its appeal lies in its sense of isolation, plus access to some fine beaches. The village has a laid-back vibe and simple, cheery cafes and bars; it's become particularly popular in recent years with a surfing crowd.

Outside town, the striking cliffs of Cabo de São Vicente make for an enchanting visit. This is Europe's southwesternmost point, the last land America-bound sailors see as they head out into the Atlantic.

Two Days in Sagres & Cabo de São Vicente

The vast majority of visitors stay in Sagres, a place boasting some fine beaches. Spend your first day enjoying the **beach** (p169), followed by a seafood feast in the evening. On day two take a trip to **Cabo do São Vicente** (p166) to view one of the edges of the ancient world.

Four Days in Sagres & Cabo de São Vicente

Contact one of the local surfing companies, hire some gear and get out onto those rollers on day three (or take a lesson if you're new to surfing). Spend day four exploring Sagres' huge **Fortaleza de Sagres** (p168) and hitting the surfer bars in the evening.

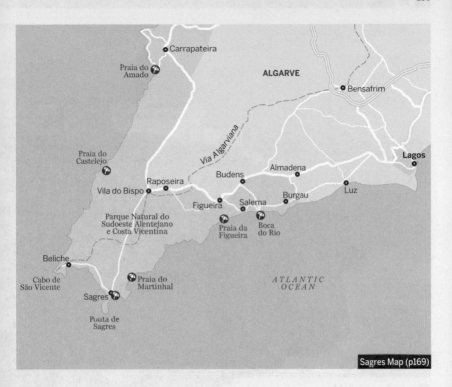

Sagres Map (p169)

Arriving in Sagres & Cabo de São Vicente

In Sagres, the main bus stop for services to Cabo de São Vicente and Lagos is next to the tourist office. You can buy tickets on the bus.

Buses travel to/from Lagos (€4, one hour, hourly Monday to Friday, fewer on weekends). There are weekday services to Cabo de São Vicente (€2.10, 10 minutes, two daily Monday to Friday).

Where to Stay

Sagres fills up in summer, though it's marginally easier to find accommodation here than in the rest of the Algarve during high season, thanks in part to the number of informal 'hostels' and the private houses that advertise rooms or apartments. Prices can halve outside high season, including top-end options.

Cabo de São Vicente

TOMASZ WOZNIAK/500PX ©

Portugal's Southwest Tip

There's an end-of-the-world feel at the southwesternmost extremity of the Portuguese mainland. Beyond the high cliffs and pounding surf stretches the vast Atlântico.

Great For...

☑ Don't Miss

The walk from Sagres to Cabo de São Vicente along a clifftop path.

Sagres

Surfers and tourists pack out tiny Sagres when the sun is shining, the former to catch some of the shimmering waves tumbling off the seething Atlantic, the latter using the place as a base to explore this far-flung chunk of the Algarve. The beaches around the town are superb and draw big crowds from May to September. Other than that, Sagres has some good eating options and a row of funky surfer cafe-bars, characterful places to hang out in the evenings, even if you've never set foot on a board.

Cabo de São Vicente

Five kilometres from Sagres, Europe's southwesternmost point is a barren headland, the last piece of home that Portuguese sailors once saw as they launched

Beach at Sagres

VALENTINA MANCINI/GETTY IMAGES ©

History of the Cape

The cape – a revered place even in the time of the Phoenicians and known to the Romans as Promontorium Sacrum – takes its present name from a Spanish priest martyred by the Romans. It was here that Henry the Navigator, the monarch who launched Portugal's expansion into the Atlantic and the New World, is said to have founded a school of navigation, though the exact site is unknown. Many famous sea battles have taken place off the cape.

Surfing

Surfing is the reason many head down to Portugal's far southwest, most hoping to catch some of the curling waves that pound angrily against the beaches and cliffs. There's a great surfer vibe around the village, especially at night when weary, salt-encrusted surfers head out for some food and a few beers after a day of riding the tide. There are several surfing schools and equipment hire centres in Sagres offering lessons for beginners and you can book lodging and lesson packages at Free Ride Sagres (p170), one of several surf camps in Sagres. Other waterborn activities on offer include paddleboarding and off-shore wildlife-spotting trips.

into the unknown. It's a spectacular spot: al sunset you can almost hear the hissing as the sun hits the sea. The **Farol de São Vicente** (☎282 624 606; www.faros.pt; N268; adult/child €1.50/1; ☉10am-6pm Apr-Oct, to 5pm Oct-Mar) contains a small but excellent museum that has a good overview of Portugal's maritime-navigation history, displays replica folios of a 1561 atlas and gives information on the history of the lighthouse.

A kilometre before reaching the lighthouse, you'll pass the Fortaleza do Beliche, built in 1632 on the site of an older fortress. The interior, once a hotel, is off limits, but you can descend a pretty pathway to near the water. The sheltering walls here make for a more appealing picnic spot than the wind-whipped cape.

⊙ SIGHTS

Fortaleza de Sagres — Fortress

(Map p169; ☎282 620 142; www.monumento
sdoalgarve.pt; adult/child €3/1.50; ⊙9.30am-
8pm May-Sep, to 5.30pm Oct-Apr) Blank, hulking and forbidding, Sagres' fortress offers
breathtaking views over the sheer cliffs,
and all along the coast to Cabo de São
Vicente. Legend has it that this is where
Prince Henry the Navigator established his
navigation school. It's quite a large site, so
allow at least an hour to see everything.

Inside the gate is a huge, curious stone
pattern that measures 43m in diameter.
Named the *rosa dos vento*s (literally, a
pictorial representation of a compass), this
strange configuration is believed to be a
mariner's compass or a sundial of sorts.
Excavated in 1921, the paving may date
from Prince Henry's time but is more likely
to be from the 16th century.

The precinct's oldest buildings include
a cistern tower to the east, a house and
the small, whitewashed, 16th-century
Igreja de Nossa Senhora da Graça (Map
p169; www.promontoriodesagres.pt; Fortaleza
de Sagres; ⊙9.30-8pm May-Sep, to 5.30pm
Oct-Apr), a simple barrel-vaulted structure
with a gilded 17th-century altarpiece. Take
a closer look at the tiled altar panels, which
feature elephants and antelopes.

Many of the gaps you see between
buildings are the result of a 1960s spring
clean of 17th- and 18th-century ruins
that was organised to make way for a
reconstruction (later abandoned) that was
to coincide with the 500th anniversary of
Henry's death.

Its visitors centre contains a gift shop, an
exhibition centre and a cafe.

It's a great walk around the perimeter
of the promontory; information boards
(in English and Portuguese) shed light on
the rich flora and fauna of the area. Don't
miss the limestone crevices descending
to the sea, or the labyrinth art installation
by Portugal's famous sculptor-architect
Pancho Guedes.

Near the southern end of the promontory is a lighthouse. Death-defying anglers
balance on the cliffs below the walls, hoping
to land bream or sea bass.

Igreja de Nossa Senhora da Graça

Sagres

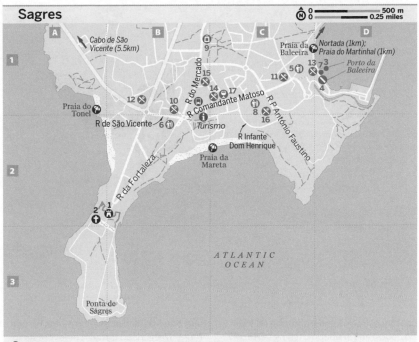

Sagres

⊙ **Sights**

1 Fortaleza de Sagres	B2
2 Igreja de Nossa Senhora da Graça	A2

✪ **Activities, Courses & Tours**

3 Cape Cruiser	D1
4 DiversCape	D1
5 Free Ride Sagres Surfcamp	C1
Mar Ilimitado	(see 3)
6 Sagres Natura	B2
7 Sea Xplorer Sagres	D1
8 Wave Sensations	C1

🛍 **Shopping**

9 Mercado Municipal 25 de Abril	B1

✕ **Eating**

10 A Casínha	B1
11 A Grelha	C1
12 A Sagres	B1
13 A Tasca	C1
14 Mum's	C1
15 Three Little Birds	B1
16 Vila Velha	C1

🍸 **Drinking & Nightlife**

17 Agua Salgada	C1
Dromedário	(see 17)
Pau de Pita	(see 17)

🏃 ACTIVITIES

There are four good beaches a short drive or long walk from Sagres: **Praia da Mareta**, just below the town; lovely **Praia do Martinhal** to the east; **Praia do Tonel** on the other side of the Ponta de Sagres, which is especially good for surfing; and isolated **Praia de Beliche**, on the way to Cabo de São Vicente.

Mar Ilimitado   Wildlife, Cruise
(Map p169; 📞916 832 625; www.marilimitado. com; Porto da Baleeira) 🐾 Mar Ilimitado's team of marine biologists lead a variety of highly recommended, ecologically sound

Praia de Beliche (p169)

boat trips, from dolphin spotting (€35, 1½ hours) and seabird watching (€45, 2½ hours) to excursions up to Cabo de São Vicente (€25, one hour). Incredible marine life you may spot includes loggerhead turtles, basking sharks, common and bottlenose dolphins, orcas and minke and fin whales.

Sagres Natura   Surfing

(Map p169; ☑282 624 072; www.sagres-surf camp.com; Rua São Vicente; ☉Mar–mid-Dec) This highly recommended surf school runs full-day group lessons (€55 including gear) and also hires bodyboards (€15 per day), surfboards (€20) and wetsuits (€10). It has bikes for hire (€10), and the same company also runs a surf-equipment shop and hostel (dorms from €17.50). A one-week surf camp including lessons, equipment, accommodation, breakfast and a barbecue party starts at €410.

Walkin'Sagres   Walking

(☑925 545 515; www.walkinsagres.com) Multilingual Ana Carla explains the history and other details of the surrounds on her tours. Walks head through pine forests to the cape's cliffs, and vary from shorter 7.7km options (€25, three hours) to a longer 15km walk (€40, four hours). There's also a 2.5km weekend walk for parents with young children (adult/child €15/free, 1½ hours).

Free Ride Sagres Surfcamp   Surfing

(Map p169; ☑916 089 005; www.frsurf.com; Hotel Memmo Baleeira, Sítio da Baleeira; 1-/3-/5-day lessons €60/165/255, board or wetsuit hire per day €15) One of several surf schools in the area, this set-up offers lessons, packages and hire, as well as free transport from Sagres and Lagos to wherever the surf's good that day. It also runs stand-up paddleboard tours around the cliffs and beaches (€35, 1½ hours).

DiversCape   Diving

(Map p169; ☑965 559 073; www.diverscape. com; Porto da Baleeira) The PADI-certified DiversCape organises dives of between 12m and 30m around shipwrecks, caves and canyons. A dive and equipment costs

€50/250/400 for one/six/10 dives, while the four-day PADI open-water course is €400. Beginners' courses (from €80) are available, and there are even sessions for children aged over eight years (€60).

Sea Xplorer Sagres   Wildlife, Cruise

(Map p169; ☑918 940 128; www.seaxplorer sagres.com; Porto da Baleeira; ☺tours Jun-Aug, fishing year-round) Leaving from the harbour in Sagres, Sea Xplorer boat trips include dolphin watching (€35, two hours), the cliffs of Cabo São Vicente from the sea (€35, one hour) and fishing (€50 including equipment, four hours).

Cape Cruiser   Wildlife, Cruise

(Map p169; ☑919 751 175; www.capecruiser. org; Porto da Baleeira) Boat trips run by Cape Cruiser include dolphin watching (€35, 1½ hours), seabird watching (€45, 2½ hours), trips to Cabo São Vicente (€25, 1½ hours) and various fishing excursions.

Wave Sensations   Surfing

(Map p169; ☑282 624 856; www.wave sensations.com; Rua Comandante Matoso) Wave Sensations runs a range of lessons in surfing and stand-up paddleboarding (€55 per day), hires equipment (surfboards/wetsuits €20/10) and can arrange packages including accommodation at **Casa Azul** (☑282 624 856; www.casaazulsagres.com; Rua Dom Sebastião; d/apt from €110/176; ❄🐱).

🔒 SHOPPING

Mercado Municipal
25 de Abril   Market

(Map p169; www.cm-viladobispo.pt; Rua do Mercado; ☺8am-2pm Mon-Sat) Sagres' municipal market has stalls selling seafood along with fruit, vegetables and meat.

❌ EATING

There are cafes and restaurants on Praça de República and a couple on the sands of Praia do Martinhal. Good value, more typically Portuguese restaurants popular with locals cluster on and around Rua

 Walking the Rota Vicentina

The **Rota Vicentina** comprises two walking trails – one coastal and one inland – and runs along the southwest coast to Cabo de São Vincente. The coastal walk (referred to as 'the fishermen's trail') begins in Porto Côvo. It uses paths forged by beachgoers and fisherfolk and passes through some of the harsher, yet stunning, coastal scenery and wilderness. The inland route (dubbed the 'historical way') is equally appealing. It runs through the Parque Natural do Sudoeste Alentejano e Costa Vicentina, plus rural towns and villages, cork-tree forests and valleys.

Both trails are made up of sections, and it's never more than 25km between villages, where you can lodge for the night (thus no need to bring camping gear).

Private companies have cottoned on to the route, providing luggage transfer between each night's lodging, but there's nothing to stop you from doing it alone If you're prepared to carry your things. Numerous accommodation options are along both routes. For further information see www.rotavicentina.com.

Porto Covo

Comandante Matoso just before it reaches the harbour.

A Grelha   Portuguese €

(Map p169; ☑282 624 193; Rua Comandante Matoso; mains €8-13.50; ☺noon-3pm & 7-10pm

 Prince Henry the Navigator

Somewhere near Sagres once stood Henry the Navigator's semimonastic school of navigation, a place that specialised in cartography, astronomy and ship design. As governor of the Algarve, Henry had ships built and crewed, launching Portugal towards the Age of Discoveries.

The expeditions commissioned by Henry advanced further into the Atlantic and down the African coast. The sea route to west Africa brought much wealth to Portugal and the Algarve; trade with this region had previously been a monopoly of the trans-Saharan caravans. Unhappily, Henry's expeditions also marked the beginning of what would now be called colonialism, as well as the European slave trade in Africa. It's also likely that Henry's expeditions discovered, or at least suspected the existence of, the South American continent that was not officially reached by Portuguese until the 'discovery' of what is now Brazil by Pedro Álvares Cabral in 1500.

Prince Henry the Navigator statue, Lagos
CHRISDORNEY/SHUTTERSTOCK ©

Mon-Fri Apr-Oct) More appealing on the inside than out, with bright paper tablecloths and terrazzo floors, this simple spot is a decent bet for budget-priced grilled chicken and local fish.

Three Little Birds
Cafe €€

(Map p169; ☑282 624 432; www.three-little-birds.org; Rua do Mercado; dishes €9-14; ◔5-11pm Feb-Nov; 🛜🅿) Sagres' coolest cafe makes everything from scratch – tortillas, corn chips and brioche buns included – for its tacos, nachos and burgers (eg piri-piri chicken with bacon jam and grilled pineapple, or cod with lime aioli, avocado and cucumber salsa), all with veggie options. Drinks include 20 craft beers and gin-based cocktails. Live reggae, funk and soul plays on Saturdays in summer.

A Casínha
Portuguese €€

(Map p169; ☑917 768 917; www.facebook.com/acasinhasagres; Rua São Vicente; mains €14-22, cataplanas €28-40; ◔12.30-3pm & 7-10.30pm Mon-Sat Mar-Oct) Built on the site of the owner's grandparents' house, this cosy terracotta-and-white spot serves wonderfully authentic Portuguese cuisine, including stand-out barbecued fish, a variety of *cataplanas* (seafood stews) for two people, and *arroz de polvo* (octopus rice). It's popularity means service can be slow in high summer, but the wait is invariably worth it.

A Eira do Mel
Portuguese €€

(☑282 639 016; Estrada do Castelejo, Vila do Bispo; mains €11-22, cataplanas €27-35; ◔noon-2.30pm & 7.30-10pm Tue-Sat) A rustic former farmhouse 9km north of Sagres is the atmospheric setting for José Pinheiro's lauded slow-food cooking. Seafood is landed in Sagres, with meats, vegetables and fruit sourced from local farms. Dishes such as octopus *cataplana* with sweet potatoes, spicy piri-piri Atlantic wild shrimp, rabbit in red wine, and *javali* are accompanied by regional wines.

A Tasca
Seafood €€

(Map p169; ☑282 624 177; Porto da Baleeira; mains €13-30, tapas €3.50-16, seafood platters €60-115; ◔12.30-3pm & 6.30-10pm Thu-Tue) Seafood doesn't come fresher than at this converted fish warehouse, with a timber-decked terrace overlooking the marina and Ilhotes do Martinhal offshore. Inside, the vaulted interior's walls are inlaid with glass bottles, ceramic plates, shells and pebbles. A live tank sits alongside the bar strung with strands of dried garlic

A Tasca

and chillies. Daily-changing platters and *cataplanas* are specialities.

Mum's
International €€

(Map p169; 📞968 210 411; www.mums-sagres.com; Rua Comandante Matoso; mains €15-23; 🕒kitchen 7pm-midnight, bar to 2am Wed-Mon; 🛜💢) 🍴 Eclectically decorated with retro TVs and radios, toasters, bottles, books and framed photos, this cosy spot on the main drag serves mostly vegetarian dishes (such as marinated tofu with chestnut purée, roasted beetroot and wild berry sauce) and some seafood (eg cornbread-crusted cod with Parmesan foam). Staff are happy to recommend wine pairings. Cash only.

A Sagres
Portuguese €€

(Map p169; 📞282 624 171; www.a-sagres.com; Ecovia do Litoral; mains €7.50-16; 🕒noon-3pm & 7-10pm Thu-Tue) A Sagres' interior of beamed ceilings, *azulejos* (hand-painted tiles) and heavy timber furniture opens to a sunny dining terrace. Char-grilled fish and meats come with simple sides like boiled potatoes and tomato salads.

Nortada
Cafe €€

(📞918 613 410; www.facebook.com/Nortada beachbar; Praia do Martinhal; dishes €5-18.50; 🕒10am-10pm Apr-Oct; 🛜👪) Set on the white-sand, resort-backed Martinhal beach, this cute cobalt-blue wooden shack is a relaxing spot in the summer months, with indoor and outdoor seating. Salads, sandwiches, burgers and pastas feature on the menu alongside grilled seafood.

Vila Velha
International €€€

(Map p169; 📞282 624 788; www.vilavelha-sagres.com; Rua Patrão António Faustino; mains €12.50-29.50; 🕒6.30pm-midnight Tue-Sun) In an elegant old house accessed by a lovely, mature front garden, upmarket Vila Velha offers consistently good seafood mains (go for the catch of the day), plus meat dishes such as wine-stewed rabbit, garlic- and herb-crusted lamb cutlets, and sirloin steak with wild mushroom sauce. Book ahead in high season.

🍷 DRINKING & NIGHTLIFE

The centre of Sagres' postsurfing scene is Rua Comandante Matoso, which has a closely packed string of places where you can get everything from a coffee to a caipirinha. Cafes by day, they're also good dining options and lively bars by night.

Agua Salgada   Bar
(Map p169; ☑282 624 297; Rua Comandante Matoso; ☺10am-2am Sun-Wed, to 3am Thu-Sat; 🛜) One of Sagres' liveliest bars, sky-lit Agua Salgada has a party vibe thanks to DJs and occasional live gigs. Fresh fruit forms the basis of its extensive range of cocktails (eg a 'kiwi colada').

Dromedário   Bar
(Map p169; ☑282 624 219; Rua Comandante Matoso; ☺10am-2am Sun-Wed, to 3am Thu-Sat; 🛜) Founded in 1985, Sagres' original cafe-bar is still its best, and a cool spot to hang out in after a day on the waves. Spot its namesake *dromedário* (camel) painted on its facade and tiled in mosaics on its bar. Creative cocktails include watermelon-and-ginger martinis; DJs spin regularly and gourmet burgers come in veggie varieties.

Pau de Pita   Cafe
(Map p169; Rua Comandante Matoso; ☺10am-3am; 🛜) Natural timber features throughout the rustic-chic interior of this lively cafe-bar, which has a great postsurf vibe. The upper level has a sun-drenched terrace overlooking the sea, while the ground floor has a toasty wood-burning stove and opens out to a laneway with picnic tables. Coffees, juices and smoothies are available, along with cocktails and beers.

ℹ️ INFORMATION

Turismo (Map p169; ☑282 624 873; www.visitalgarve.pt; Rua Comandante Matoso 75; ☺9.30am-1pm & 2-7pm daily Jul & Aug, 9.30am-1pm & 2-5.30pm Tue-Sat Sep-Jun) On a patch of green lawn, 100m east of Praça da República.

Praia do Tonel (p169)

Dolphins swimming off the coast of Sagres

PETER LLEWELLYN/GETTY IMAGES ©

🛈 GETTING THERE & AWAY

The **bus stop** (Map p169; Rua Comandante Matoso) is by the *turismo*. You can buy tickets on the bus.

Buses travel to/from Lagos (€4, one hour, hourly Monday to Friday, fewer on weekends) via Vila do Bispo (€2.20, 20 minutes) and Salema (€2.55, 30 minutes). There are weekday services to Cabo de São Vicente (€2.10, 10 minutes, two daily Monday to Friday).

🛈 GETTING AROUND

Hire bicycles from Sagres Natura (p170) or **Maretta Shop** (☑282 624 535; www.marettashop. com; Rua Comandante Matoso; per day bike hire €8-25, scooter hire €29; ⊙10am-8pm).

ÉVORA

Évora at a Glance...

One of Portugal's most beautifully preserved medieval towns, Évora is an enchanting place to delve into the past. Inside the 14th-century walls, Évora's narrow, winding lanes lead to striking architectural works: an elaborate medieval cathedral and cloisters; the cinematic columns of the Templo Romano; and a picturesque town square, once the site of some rather gruesome episodes courtesy of the Inquisition. Aside from its historic and aesthetic virtues, Évora is also a lively university town, and its many attractive restaurants serve up hearty Alentejan cuisine. Outside town, Neolithic monuments and rustic wineries make for fine day trips.

Two Days in Évora

Your first day in Évora should be spent taking in the town's architectural gems such as the **Igreja de São Francisco** (p180) and the **Templo Romano** (p181). Spend day two exploring the **Sé** (p180) and the **Museu do Évora** (p182). Round off both days with some delicious Alentejan fare in one of the town's celebrated restaurants.

Four Days in Évora

On day three get out of town to see the **megaliths** (p186) that dot the surrounding landscapes west of Évora. These Neolithic remains date back 5000 to 7500 years but you'll need a car to find them. You could spend day four seeking out local wineries or seeing some of the town's less well-known sites such as the **Museu do Évora** (p182).

Previous page: Medieval cathedral Sé (p180)
MANUEL HURTADO/GETTY IMAGES ©

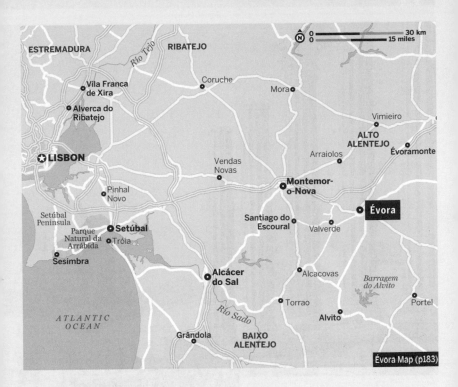

Arriving in Évora

The bus station, located 600m west of the walled centre, handles long-distance coach services to towns and cities across southern Portugal and beyond.

Évora train station is outside the walls, 600m south of the **Jardim Público** (p182). There are daily trains to/from Lisbon (€13.70, two hours), Lagos (€25 to €28, five hours) and Faro (€26.20, 4½ hours).

Where to Stay

Évora has the best assortment of accommodation in the Alentejo, and makes a good base for exploring the region. It has hostels, charming midrange guest houses and plush boutique hotels. Most of Évora's best accommodation is within the town walls where about a fifth of the population also lives. From outside the walls it can be a trek to the sights of the city centre.

Roman Ruins

BRUNOMILL/GETTY IMAGES ©

Évora's Architectural Treasures

Few cities in Portugal boast the wealth and diversity of architecture that Évora does. An almost uninterrupted ring of defensive town walls contains Roman and medieval sites aplenty.

Great For...

☑ Don't Miss

You can take a walk in the countryside along Évora's 16th-century aqueduct – ask the tourist office for details.

Medieval Gems

Évora's best-known church is the **Igreja de São Francisco** (Map p183; www.igrejade saofrancisco.pt; Praça 1 de Maio; ⊙9am-6.30pm Jun-Sep, to 5pm Oct-May), a tall and huge Manueline-Gothic structure, completed around 1510 and dedicated to St Francis. Legend has it that the Portuguese playwright Gil Vicente is buried here.

Guarded by a pair of rose granite towers, Évora's fortress-like medieval cathedral, the **Sé** (Map p183; Largo do Marquês de Marialva; €2.50 cathedral & cloister, with towers €3.50, with museum €4.50; ⊙9am-5pm), has fabulous cloisters and a museum jam-packed with ecclesiastical treasures. It was begun around 1186, during the reign of Sancho I, Afonso Henriques' son, and was completed about 60 years later; there was probably a

Capela dos Ossos

MARIANO VILLAFAÑE/SHUTTERSTOCK ©

mosque here before. The flags of Vasco da Gama's ships were blessed here in 1497.

The small, fabulous **Igreja de São João** (Church of St John the Evangelist; Map p183; ☑967 979 763; www.palaciocadaval.com; Rua Augo Filipe Simões; church €4, church & palace €8; ⊘10am-12.30pm & 2-5pm Tue-Fri & Sun, 2-5pm Sat), which faces the Templo Romano, was founded in 1485 by one Rodrigo Afonso de Melo, count of Olivença and the first governor of Portuguese Tangier, to serve as his family's pantheon. It is still privately owned, by the Duques de Cadaval, and notably well kept.

Roman Ruins

Once part of the Roman Forum, the remains of **Templo Romano** (Temple of Diana; Map p183; Largo do Conde de Vila Flor), dating from the 2nd or early 3rd century,

are a heady slice of drama right in town. It's among the best-preserved Roman monuments in Portugal, and probably on the Iberian Peninsula. Though it's commonly referred to as the Temple of Diana, there's no consensus about the deity to which it was dedicated, and some archaeologists believe it may have been dedicated to Julius Caesar.

Inside the entrance hall of the *câmara municipal* are more Roman vestiges, only discovered in 1987. These impressive **Roman baths** (Map p183; Praça do Sertório; ⊘9am-5.30pm Mon-Fri) **FREE**, which include a laconicum (heated room for steam baths) with a superbly preserved 9m-diameter circular pool, would have been the largest public building in Roman Évora. The complex also includes an open-air swimming pool, discovered in 1994.

Capela dos Ossos

One of Évora's most popular sights is also one of its most chilling. The walls and columns of this mesmerising *memento mori* (reminder of death) are lined with the bones and skulls of some 5000 people. This was the solution found by three 17th-century Franciscan monks for the overflowing graveyards of churches and monasteries.

◎ SIGHTS

Praça do Giraldo   Plaza
(Map p183) The city's main square has seen some potent moments in Portuguese history, including the 1483 execution of Fernando, Duke of Bragança; the public burning of victims of the Inquisition in the 16th century; and fiery debates on agrarian reform in the 1970s. Nowadays it's still the city's focus, host to less dramatic activities such as sitting in the sun and drinking coffee.

The narrow lanes to the southwest were once Évora's *judiaria* (Jewish quarter). To the northeast, Rua 5 de Outubro, climbing to the sé (cathedral), is lined with handsome townhouses wearing wrought-iron balconies, while side alleys pass beneath Moorish-style arches.

Museu do Évora   Museum
(Map p183; ☑266 730 480; Largo do Conde de Vila Flor; adult/child €3/free; ☺9.30am-5.30pm Tue-Sun) Adjacent to the cathedral (p180), in what used to be the archbishop's palace (built in the 16th century), is this elegant museum. The cloistered courtyard reveals Islamic, Roman and medieval remains. In polished rooms upstairs are former Episcopal furnishings and a gallery of Flemish paintings. Most memorable is *Life of the Virgin,* a 13-panel series originally part of the cathedral's altarpiece, created by anonymous Flemish artists working in Portugal around 1500.

Jardim Público   Gardens
(Map p183; ☺8am-9pm May-Aug, to 7pm Mar, Apr, Sep & Oct, to 5.30pm Nov-Feb) For a lovely tranquil stroll, head to the light-dappled public gardens (with a small outdoor cafe) south of the Igreja de São Francisco. Inside the walls of the 15th-century Palácio de Dom Manuel is the **Galeria das Damas** (Ladies' Gallery; Map p183; Palácio de Dom Manuel; ☺10am-noon & 2-6pm Mon-Fri, 2-6pm Sat) **FREE**, an indecisive hybrid of Gothic, Manueline, neo-Moorish and Renaissance styles. It's open when there are temporary art exhibitions.

Fórum Eugénio de Almeida   Museum
(Map p183; ☑266 748 300; www.fea.pt; Largo do Conde de Vila Flor; adult/child €2/free, Sun free; ☺10am-6pm Tue-Sun) In a building that once housed the Holy Office of Inquisition, this centre of arts and culture hosts some of Évora's most thought-provoking art exhibitions throughout the year. Also part of the foundation is the **Casas Pintadas** (Map p183; €1; ☺10am-6pm Tue-Sun), a small collection of outdoor murals facing a little garden.

Palácio Cadaval   Palace
(Palace of Cadaval; Map p183; www.palacio cadaval.com; incl Igreja de São João €8; ☺10am-12.30pm & 2-5pm Tue-Fri & Sun, 2-5pm Sat) Just northwest of the Igreja de São João (p181) is the 17th-century facade of a much older palace and castle, as revealed by the two powerful square towers that bracket it. The Palácio Cadaval was given to Martim Afonso de Melo, the governor of Évora, by Dom João I, and it also served from time to time as a royal residence. Today the rooms contain a collection of illuminated manuscripts, Arraiolos carpets and 18th-century paintings of Portuguese royals.

A section of the palace is still in use as the private quarters of the de Melo family.

Coleção de Carruagens   Museum
(Carriage Collection; Map p183; Largo Dr Mário Chicò 4; €1, Sun free; ☺10am-1pm & 3-7pm Tue-Sun Jun-Sep, 10am-12.30pm & 1.30-6pm Tue-Sun Oct-May) Part of the Eugénio de Almeida Foundation, this pint-sized museum houses an intriguing collection of old carriages. It's hidden away behind the Sé (p180) and is largely overlooked by most visitors.

Universidade de Évora   University
(Map p183; ☑266 740 800; Rua do Cardeal Rei; €3; ☺main building 9am-8pm Mon-Fri, to 6pm Sat) Just outside the walls to the northeast is the university's main building (Colégio do Espírito Santo), a descendent (reopened in 1973) of the original Jesuit institution founded in 1559 (which closed when the Jesuits got shooed out by Marquês de

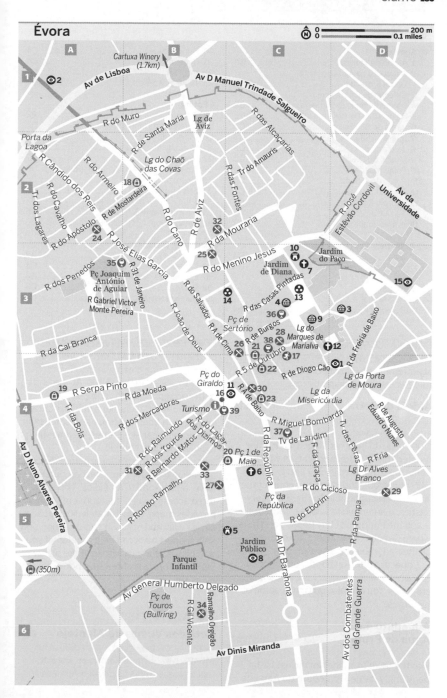

Évora

Cartuxa Winery
(1.7km)

Av de Lisboa

Av D Manuel Trindade Salgueiro

R do Muro

R de Santa Maria

Lg de
Aviz

R das Alcáçarias

Porta da
Lagoa

R Cândido dos Reis

R do Armeiro

Lg do Chaõ
das Covas

Tr do Amauris

Tr dos Lagares

R do Cavalho

R de Mostardeira

18

R das Fontes

R José Estêvão Cordovil

Av da
Universidade

R do Apóstolo

24

R José Elias Garcia

R do Cano

R de Aviz

R da Mouraria

32

25

R do Menino Jesus

10
7

Jardim
do Paço

R dos Penedos

35

Pç Joaquim
António
de Aguiar

R 31 de Janeiro

Jardim
de Diana

15

R Gabriel Victor
Monte Pereira

14

R das Casas Pintadas

13

4

R da Cal Branca

R João de Deus

R do Salvador

36

3

9

R A de Cima

Pç de
Sertório

R de Burgos

28

Lg do
Marques de
Marialva

12

R da Freiria de Baixo

19

R Serpa Pinto

26

21

38

17

1

R da Moeda

Pç do
Giraldo

11
16

R 5 de Outubro

22

R de Diogo Cão

Lg da Porta
de Moura

Tr da Bola

Av D Nuno Álvares Pereira

R dos Mercadores

Turismo

39

30
23

R A de Baixo

Lg da
Misericórdia

R de Augusto
Eduardo Nunes

R do Raimundo

R do Lagar
dos Dragos

R Miguel Bombarda

37

Tv das Feras

R Fria

R dos Touros

Tv de Landim

R da Graça

Lg Dr Alves
Branco

31

R Bernardo Matos

20

Pç 1 de
Maio

6

R da República

29

(350m)

33

27

R Romão Ramalho

Pç da
República

R do Cicioso

R do Eborim

R da Pampa

5

Jardim
Público

8

Av Dr Barahona

Parque
Infantil

Av General Humberto Delgado

Pç de
Touros
(Bullring)

R Gil Vicente

34

Ramalho Orgrigao

Av Dinis Miranda

Av dos Combatentes
da Grande Guerra

Évora

Pombal in 1759). Inside are arched, Italian Renaissance–style cloisters, the Mannerist-style Templo do Espírito Santo and beautiful *azulejos* (hand-painted tiles).

Aldeia da Terra   Art Studio

(Map p183; ☑266 746 049; www.aldeiadaterra. pt; Rua de São Manços 19; adult/child €2/1; ☺10am-6pm) The artist Tiago Cabeça has created this wondrous miniature world of Portugal moulded in clay and peopled with humorous and irreverent characters. You'll find recognisable Alentejo imagery – castles, painted-white villages, cathedrals – and the interiors of tiny houses and lanes where Cabeça's characters are captured in all their adorable, big-eyed whimsy.

Cabeça is often on hand, and is happy to explain the vision behind his eye-catching creations. You can also purchase some of his works.

Aqueduto da Água de Prata   Landmark

(Aqueduct of Silver Water; Map p183) Jutting into the town from the northwest is the beguilingly named Aqueduto da Água de Prata, designed by Francisco de Arruda (better known for Lisbon's Tower of Belém) to bring clean water to Évora. It was completed in the 1530s. At the end of the aqueduct, on Rua do Cano, the neighbourhood feels like a self-contained village, with houses, shops and cafes built right into its perfect arches, as if nestling against the base of a hill.

It's possible to walk for around 8.5km alongside the aqueduct, starting outside town, on the road to Arraiolos. There are three access points; the tourist office provides maps. Unfortunately, it's not a circuit walk and heads in one direction only, so transport back can be a problem if you don't have your own wheels. Take plenty of liquids – ironically, there's no potable water along the way.

◎ ACTIVITIES

Rota dos Vinhos do Alentejo   Wine

(Wine Route of the Alentejo; Map p183; ☑266 746 498; www.vinhosdoalentejo.pt; Rua 5 de Outubro; wine tasting €3; ☺11am-7pm Mon-Fri, to 1pm Sat) Head here to sample some of the great wines of the Alentejo. Every week new wines are on offer, with more than 70 wineries represented. You can taste six or so varieties on hand for a minimal fee. Bottles will set you back anything from €4.50 to €65.

Cartuxa Winery   Wine

(☑266 748 383; www.cartuxa.pt; Estrada da Soeira; from €5; ⊙tours 10.30am, 11.30am, 3pm & 4.30pm) For a taste of history, Cartuxa is one of the oldest wineries in the Alentejo. Run by local philanthropic foundation Eugénio de Almeida, it produces good wines at all prices, plus olive oils and other products. You must reserve a tour (strictly at times given); prices start at €5 and then depend on how many wines you want to taste.

The winery is about 2km northwest of the old city walls.

⊙ TOURS

Ebora Megalithica   Tours

(☑964 808 337; www.eboramegalithica.com; per person €25, maximum 7 people; ⊙tours 10am & 2.30pm Mon-Sat) If you're interested in the megaliths – Almendres, Zambujeiro and the Menir dos Almendres – this three-hour tour is a must. Young archaeologist enthusiast Mário Carvalho makes the megalithic sites accessible in every sense, providing the where, what, why and how. He succeeds in making the experience an educational yet relaxed one.

Agia   Walking

(Map p183; ☑963 702 392; www.alentejo guides.com; adult/child €15/free, minimum 2 people; ⊙10am) Agia offers daily two-hour guided walking tours of Évora, departing from outside the *turismo* (tourist office) on Praça do Giraldo.

Évora Local Tours   Cultural

(☑961 792 740; www.facebook.com/evoralocal tours; per person €30) The highly knowledge-able Andreia Sousa runs fascinating three-hour tours that take visitors by 4WD out to

 Wine Route of the Alentejo

Wines here, particularly the reds, are fat, rich and fruity. But tasting them is much more fun than reading about them, so drop in on some wineries. The Rota dos Vinhos do Alentejo (Wine Route of the Alentejo) splits the region into three separate areas – the Serra de São Mamede (dark reds, full bodied, red fruit hints); Historic (smooth reds, fruity whites) around Évora, Estremoz, Borba and Monsaraz; and the Rio Guadiana (scented whites, spicy reds). Some wineries also have accommodation options.

You'll see brown signs all over the Alentejo announcing that you are on the wine trail, and you can pick up a map and get info on wineries open to visitors at the helpful Rota dos Vinhos do Alentejo headquarters.

MAGDALENA PALUCHOWSKA/SHUTTERSTOCK ©

a cork farm outside town. There you'll get a close-up look at this age-old sustainable industry, and its relation to traditional agri-culture, wildlife and regional gastronomy.

🔘 SHOPPING

Gente da Minha Terra   Food, Gifts & Souvenirs

(Map p183; ☑964 956 259; www.facebook.com/ gentedaminhaterraevora; Rua 5 de Outubro 39; ⊙10am-7pm) On a boutique-lined street leading off the main plaza, this is a great one-stop shop for gifts. The shelves are packed with quality olive oils, *azulejos*,

📖🍴 Megaliths

Megaliths, built around 5000 to 7500 years ago, dot the European Atlantic coast, but here in the Alentejo there is an astounding number of prehistoric structures. Dolmens (Neolithic stone tombs; *antas* in Portuguese) were probably temples and/or collective tombs, covered with a large flat stone and usually built on hilltops or valleys, near water lines. Menhirs (individual standing stones) point to fertility rites – as phallic as skyscrapers, if on a smaller scale; and cromlechs *(cromeleques)*, organised sets of standing stones, seem to incorporate basic astronomic orientations related to seasonal transitions (equinoxes and solstices).

Set within a beautiful landscape of olive and cork trees stands the **Cromeleque dos Almendres**. This huge, spectacular oval of standing stones, 15km west of Évora, is the Iberian Peninsula's most important megalithic group. Some 95 rounded granite monoliths – some of which are engraved with symbolic markings – spread down a rough slope.

The **Anta Grande do Zambujeiro** (Great Dolmen of Zambujeiro), 13km southwest of Évora, is Europe's largest dolmen. Under a huge sheet-metal protective shelter in a field of wildflowers and yellow broom, stand seven stones and a 'closing slab' that connects the chamber with the corridor.

Cromeleque dos Almendres
INACIO PIRES/SHUTTERSTOCK ©

textiles, ceramics and pretty packages of tinned sardines and other preserves.

Feiras no Largo — Market
(Map p183; Praça 1 de Maio; ⊗8am-2pm Sat & Sun) Each weekend sees the Feiras no Largo, one of four different markets held in the city. Expect antiquities, used books and collectables, art and *artesenato* (craft items).

Bookmark Évora — Books
(Map p183; www.thebookmarkevora.com; Rua Serpa Pinto 94; ⊗10am-7pm; 🛜📶) When you need a break from sightseeing, retreat to this delightful bookshop, owned by expat and author Julie Hodgson. You'll find a good selection of affordable books in various languages, a special room for Harry Potter fans and steaming cups of tea.

Montsobro — Homewares
(Map p183; www.montsobro.com; Rua 5 de Outubro 66; ⊗10am-7pm Mon-Sat) One of many shops along Rua 5 de Outubro, this was the first – and is still one of the best – that sells cork products.

Tou c'os Azeites — Food
(Map p183; 📱969 525 817; www.facebook.com/toucosazeites; Rua Alcárcova de Baixo 51; ⊗11am-3pm Mon, to 7pm Tue-Sat) The Alentejo produces outstanding olive oil, though it has little name recognition outside Portugal. At this tiny shop, you can buy high-quality olive oils. There's also a small selection of tapenade, chocolates, soaps and other locally produced items.

❌ EATING

Fábrica dos Pasteis — Portuguese €
(Map p183; 📱266 098 424; Rua Alcárcova de Cima 10; pastries €1-1.50; ⊗10am-8pm Tue-Sun) Take a stroll along the narrowest lane in town to find this gem of a bakery, which fires up the best *pastéis de nata* (custard tarts) for miles around, as well as good *salgados* (savoury meat, cheese, or chicken pasties). Thick stone walls and a

fado soundtrack add atmosphere to the cavernous low-lit space.

Pastelaria Conventual Pão de Rala
Bakery €

(Map p183; Rua do Cicioso 47; pastries €1.50-3; ⏲7.30am-8pm; 🛜) The *azulejo*-covered walls (complete with a bakery scene) and low-playing fado create a fine setting for nibbling on heavenly pastries and convent cakes, all made on the premises. Don't miss the *pão de rala* (a cake made with egg yolk, sugar, lemon zest and almonds) – it's sweet stuff and wonderfully sinful.

Vinarium Wine & Tapas
Tapas €

(Map p183; 📋968 217 574; www.facebook.com/vinariumevora; Praça Primeiro de Maio 27; tapas €3.50-5; ⏲noon-10pm Thu-Tue) In a thoughtfully designed space across from the **municipal market** (Municipal Market; Map p183; Praça 1 de Maio; ⏲7am-6pm Tue-Sat, to 2pm Sun), Vinarium is a must for wine lovers. Here you can sample fine quaffs from the Alentejo, which pair nicely with baked cheese and oregano, baked octopus, chickpeas with cod and other small sharing plates. *Provas* (tastings) of three to six wines (for €5 and €7) offer excellent value.

Salsa Verde
Vegetarian €

(Map p183; 📋266 743 210; www.salsa-verde.org; Rua do Raimundo 93A; small plate €5, per kg €15; ⏲noon-3pm & 7-9.30pm Mon-Fri, noon-3pm Sat; 🛜🍴) Vegetarians (and Portuguese livestock) will be thankful for this veggie-popping paradise. Pedro, the owner, gives a wonderful twist to traditional Alentejan dishes such as the famous bread dish, *migas,* prepared with mushrooms. Low-playing bossa nova and a cheerful airy design make a fine complement to the dishes – all made from fresh, locally sourced products (organic when possible).

Bistro Barão
Portuguese €€

(Map p183; 📋266 706 180; Rua da Zanguela 8; mains €15-25; ⏲6.30-10pm Mon, 12.30-3pm & 6.30-10pm Tue-Sat; 🍴) This tiny family-run restaurant serves exquisitely prepared Portuguese dishes using high-quality products. Start with sauté shrimp with garlic or stuffed

Igreja de São Francisco (p180)

🍴 Food of the Alentejo

Warning to vegetarians: pork will confront you at every repast in the Alentejo. Bread also figures heavily; you'll find it in gazpacho or *açorda*. During hunting season, *perdiz* (partridge), *lebre* (hare) and *javali* (wild boar) are the go. The Alentejo also has surf-and-turf blends such as *carne de porco à alentejana* (braised pork with baby clams).

Carne de porco à alentejana
STUDIO F22 RICARDO ROCHA/SHUTTERSTOCK ©

mushrooms, before moving on to black-pork tenderloin, lightly breaded octopus, grilled ribs and other hearty main courses.

With just a handful of tables, this place fills up quickly. Reserve ahead.

Momentos
Portuguese €€

(Map p183; 📞925 161 423; Rua Cinco de Outubro 61; mains €18-22; ⊗7-10.30pm Mon & Wed-Fri, 12.30-3pm & 7-10.30pm Sat & Sun; 🖉)
Jorge, the affable proprietor of Momentos, takes great pride in the bounty of the Alentejo, which he showcases each night on his changing blackboard menus. He works with small farmers, and you'll find flavour-packed organic vegetables accompanying black pork, oven-baked lamb and other delicacies. The chef can also whip up special dishes for vegetarians and vegans.

Botequim da Mouraria
Portuguese €€

(Map p183; 📞266 746 775; Rua da Mouraria 16A; mains €15-18; ⊗12.30-3pm & 7-10pm Mon-Sat)
Poke around the old Moorish quarter to find some of Évora's finest food and

Casas Pintadas, Fórum Eugénio de Almeida (p182)

GEOGPHOTOS/ALAMY STOCK PHOTO ©

Botequim da Mouraria

wine – gastronomes believe this is Évora's culinary shrine. Owner Domingos will guide you through the menu, which also features an excellent variety of wines from the Alentejo. There are no reservations and just nine stools at a counter.

It is extremely popular, and lines are long. To have any chance of getting a seat, arrive before it opens.

Piparoza · Portuguese €€

(Map p183; ☑ 266 709 517; www.facebook. com/piparoza; Alcarcova de Baixo 23; tapas €5-9, mains €15-18; ⊗ noon-midnight) Along the pedestrian lane of restaurant-lined Alcarcova de Baixo, the cavernous Piparoza is a standout for its huge menu and lively ambience. Open from noon to midnight, it's a good place for tapas and wines by the glass outside regular meal times. There's outdoor seating on warm days.

Vinho e Noz · Portuguese €€

(Map p183; ☑ 266 747 310; Ramalho Orgigão 12; mains €12-17; ⊗ noon-10pm Mon-Sat) This unpretentious place is run by a delightful family and offers professional service, a large wine list and good-quality cuisine. It's been going for over 30 years and is one of the best-value places in town.

Standout dishes include *secreto de porco alentejano* (grilled Alentejan pork loin), lamb chops with mint and the celebrated wild boar with chestnuts.

Taberna Típica Quarta Feira · Portuguese €€€

(Map p183; ☑ 266 707 530; Rua do Inverno 16; dinner per person incl starters, house wine & dessert €30; ⊗ 7.30-10pm Mon, 12.30-3pm & 7.30-10pm Tue-Sat) Don't bother asking for the menu since there's just one option on offer at this jovial eatery tucked away in the Moorish quarter. Luckily it's a stunner: slow-cooked black pork so tender it falls off the bone, plus freshly baked bread, grilled mushrooms (and other starters), dessert and ever-flowing glasses of wine – all served for one set price. Reserve ahead.

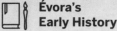

Évora's Early History

The Celtic settlement of Ebora had been established here before the Romans arrived in 59 BC and made it a military outpost, and eventually an important centre of Roman Iberia, when it was known as 'Ebora Liberalitas Julia'.

After a depressing spell under the Visigoths, the town got its groove back as a centre of trade under the Moors. In AD 1165 Évora's Muslim rulers were hoodwinked by a rogue Portuguese Christian knight known as Giraldo Sem Pavor (Gerald the Fearless). The well-embellished story goes like this: Giraldo single-handedly stormed one of the town's watchtowers by climbing up a ladder of spears driven into the walls. From there he distracted (some say killed) municipal sentries while his companions took the town with hardly a fight.

Évora's golden age was from the 14th to 16th centuries, when it was favoured by the Alentejo's own House of Avis, as well as by scholars and artists. Declared an archbishopric in 1540, it got its own Jesuit university in 1559.

When Cardinal-King Dom Henrique, last of the Avis line, died in 1580 and Spain seized the throne, the royal court left Évora and the town began wasting away. The Marquês de Pombal's closure of the university in 1759 was the last straw. French forces plundered the town and massacred its defenders in July 1808.

Universidade de Évora (p182)

🍸 DRINKING & NIGHTLIFE

Sociedade Harmonia Eborense   Bar

(Map p183; ☎266 746 874; Praça do Giraldo 72, 2nd fl; €3; ⊙4-7pm & 10pm-2am Mon-Sat) Join the bohemian crowd in the vintage drawing rooms of this cultural space, which hosts occasional concerts, art exhibtions and film screenings. At other times, you can play billiards, or hang out on the spacious terrace enjoying the views over the plaza.

Estrela d'Ouro   Bar

(Map p183; Largo de São Vicente 59; ⊙10am-2am; 🖥) This multilevel space has a striking cafe on the lower level decked out with chequered floors and pink walls, while its entrance around the corner leads to a low-lit bar with tall ceilings and vintage paintings on the walls. It gathers a cross-section of young imbibers, with the action spilling onto the small plaza out front on weekend nights.

Enoteca Cartuxa   Wine Bar

(Map p183; www.cartuxa.pt; Rua Vasco da Gama 15; ⊙10am-10pm Mon-Sat, noon-3pm Sun) Around the corner from the Templo Romano (p181), this bright, modern wine bar serves up quality pours from the well-known Cartuxa (p185) vineyard. You can pair those wines with a wide range of sharing plates – sauté shrimp, grilled mushrooms, cheese boards or heartier plates of roast meats or seafood.

Culpa Tua   Bar

(Map p183; Praça Joaquim António de Aguiar 6; ⊙5pm-2am Tue-Sat, to midnight Sun) Gin lovers from near and far gather over refreshing, goblet-sized gin and tonics at this friendly, easy-going spot north of Praça Giraldo. There's a small terrace in front.

Páteo   Wine Bar

(Map p183; ☎919 549 745; Beco da Espinhosa 53; ⊙noon-11pm; 🖥) Right in Évora's medieval heart, this bar has a pretty tree-shaded patio for nursing a glass of Alentejo wine. The food is pretty good too.

Look for the entrance off Rua 5 de Outubro.

Praça do Giraldo (p182)

ℹ️ INFORMATION

Turismo (Map p183; 📞266 777 071; www.cm-evora.pt; Praça do Giraldo 73; 🕐9am-7pm Apr-Oct, 9am-6pm Mon-Fri, 10am-2pm & 3-6pm Sat & Sun Nov-Mar) This central tourist office offers a great town map. Staff are more helpful if you have specific questions.

ℹ️ GETTING THERE & AWAY

If coming by car, leave your vehicle in one of the free car parks outside of the walled centre, such as the enormous car park south of the Jardim Público, off Av Humberto Delgado and Rua da República.

BUS

The **bus station** (Terminal Rodoviário; 📞266 738 120; Avenida São Sebastião) is 600m west of the walled centre. Major destinations include Lisbon (€12, two hours, hourly), Faro (€17, four hours, three to four daily) and Coimbra (€18, 4½ hours, two to five daily).

TRAIN

There are daily trains to/from Lisbon as well as Lagos and Faro.

ℹ️ GETTING AROUND

Taxis (📞266 735 735; www.radiotaxisevora.pt) congregate near Praça do Giraldo. On a weekday you can expect to pay about €6 from the train station to Praça do Giraldo. For a fun overview of town, book a ride on a tuk-tuk with **Tuk 2 You** (📞962 804 959; www.facebook.com/tuk2you; 15/60/90min tour €15/30/45).

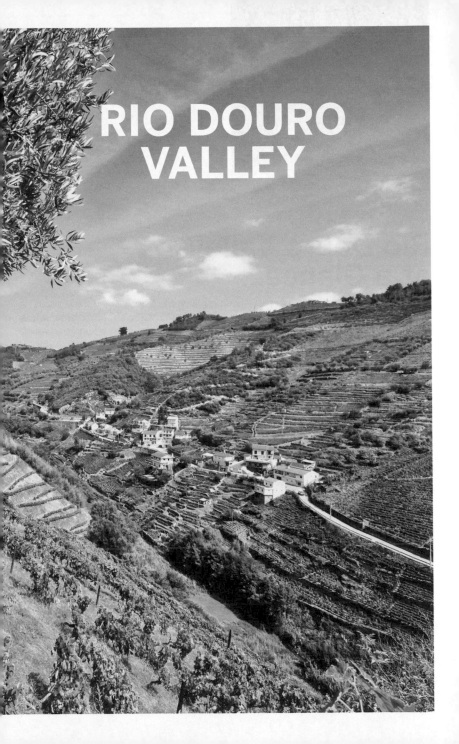

RIO DOURO VALLEY

Rio Douro Valley at a Glance...

One of the world's oldest demarcated wine regions, the Douro Valley showcases steep terrace vineyards carved into mountains, granite bluffs, whitewashed quintas (estates) and 18th-century wine cellars that draw in visitors from around the world. Come for the ports and wines, winding scenic roads, postcard-pretty villages and excellent regional restaurants.

The valley also hosts Portugal's most scenic train ride, the Linha do Douro running from Porto to Pocinho, a distance of 160km. The Douro can also be seen from cruise ships that ply its waters, stopping off along the way for wine-tasting sessions at the many producers en route.

Two Days in the Rio Douro Valley

Spend the first two days visiting wineries and taking in the scenery near Pinhão and Peso da Régua. Learn about great Douro vintages at the **Quinta do Crasto** (p197), admire the view from the **Miradouro São Leonardo de Galafura** (p201), walk the nature trails of Quinta Nova, and have a memorable meal at **DOC** (p201).

Four Days in the Rio Douro Valley

On day three, head to Lamego to discover its dazzling, *azulejo*-covered **staircase** (p204) and sample its famous *fumeiro* (smoked meat) – a fine match for the region's good wines. Spend the fourth day in Amarante. Visit the town's atmospheric, art-filled **Mosteiro de São Gonçalo** (p206) and stroll (or boat) along the **Rio Tâmega** (p206).

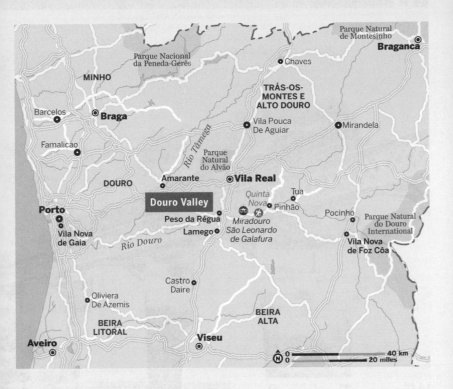

Arriving in the Rio Douro Valley

São Bento/Campanhã train station
Trains leave these stations for Peso da Régua where you change for the Douro Valley. At least five trains run all the way from Porto to Pocinho.

N108/222 These two roads follow the valley and offer some fantastic views along the way.

Where to Stay

From historic wine estates converted into rural hotels to swish five-star resorts and cosy family-run inns, the Rio Douro Valley offers a full spectrum of overnight experiences for just about every budget.

Book well ahead in summer and in early autumn. The Douro can be also be visited as a day trip from Porto, so consider options there, too.

Steam train, Rio Douro Valley

RICHARD SEMIK/SHUTTERSTOCK ©

GRAHA

Wines, Trains & the River Douro

One of the most attractive routes in Iberia, the road and rail journey through the Douro Valley is unmissable for fans of wine, trains and stunning landscapes.

Great For...

☑ **Don't Miss**

A tour and wine-tasting session at Quinta do Bomfim (p197), a historic winery in Pinhão.

Wines of the Douro

The Douro has been a demarcated wine region since 1756, and the reds and whites that emerge every autumn from the stunning valley in which they are produced holds Portugal's highest wine classification – Denominação de Origem Controlada (DOC). The Douro is best known for its port, but its table wines are equally as celebrated. It's thought grapes have been grown here since Roman times. Port made an appearance in the mid-18th century but it wasn't until the late 20th century that serious table wines were made for export. Countless lodges offer tastings. In 2001 the valley was declared a Unesco World Cultural Heritage Site, not only recognising the valley as a great wine producing region, but also placing it firmly on the tourist map.

Quinta do Bomfim

CHARLES O'REAR/CORBIS/VCG/GETTY IMAGES ©

❶ Need to Know

Trains from Porto run five times daily (from €13.50 each way, 3½ hours).

✕ Take a Break

Highly recommended DOC (p201) serves outstanding cuisine.

★ Top Tip

An excellent website to consult before heading into the Douro Valley is www. dourovalley.eu. It gives the low-down on wineries, the railway, cruises and many other aspects of touring in the region.

Great Train Journey

Without doubt Portugal's greatest rail journey, the 160km long line from Porto to Pocinho is a wonder of 19th-century engineering. The line opened in 1887 and once ran all the way from the Atlantic to the Spanish border. Branch lines once wriggled their way up side valleys to remote villages, but these were closed with the arrival of the petrol engine. This left just the main route with its 20 tunnels, 34 stations and 30 bridges. For a real 19th-century experience, try to catch one of the special steam services that run between Régua and Tua on summer weekends.

Cruise & Cycle

In addition to the train, cruise ships are another popular way of seeing the valley. Cruises leave from Porto and terminate at the Spanish border. Cycling is also a memorable way to travel. Some of the old railway lines in the valley have been converted into cycle trails.

Winery Visits

Conveniently located in downtown Pinhão, the **Quinta do Bomfim** (☑254 730 370; www.symington.com/visit-us; tours incl tasting from €17; ⊙10.30am-7pm daily Mar-Oct, 9.30am-6.30pm Tue-Sun Nov-Feb) showcases a small museum inside a restored historic winery. Multilingual guided tours (reservation required) offer views of the vineyards' ancient dry stone terraces and visit the 19th-century lodge where young wine is still aged in old wooden vats. Tours end in the gorgeous tasting room with its terrace overlooking the Douro.

Perched on a promontory above the Rio Douro, the **Quinta do Crasto** (☑254 920 020; www.quintadocrasto.pt; Gouvinhas, Sabrosa; tours incl tasting €20; ⊙by appointment) quite literally takes your breath away. The winery produces some of the country's best drops – reds that are complex, spicy and smooth, with wild berry aromas, and whites that are fresh, with a mineral nose and tang of citrus and apples. Stop by for a tour and tasting (of four wines) or lunch (€65 with wine).

Wines of the Douro Valley

Wine lovers have their work cut out for them on a leisurely journey through the Douro Valley, Portugal's premier wine country; not only is it one of the world's oldest demarcated wine regions, it's also dazzling – steep terraced vineyards rise sharply from the banks of the Douro River and whitewashed *quintas* (estates) perch high up in the hills. Visitors are just as wowed by these dramatic vistas as they are by the area's viticulture, which has been turning out some of Portugal's premier wines for centuries.

Start Porto
Distance 325km
Duration One week

Parque Nacional
da Peneda-Gerês

MINHO

3 Riverside **Peso da Régua** is set in the heart of vineyard country. Take in the lovely scenery on a river cruise to Pinhão offered by Tomaz do Douro.

1 Any self-respecting wine tour will begin in Porto (p101), gateway to the world's most famous port-wine region.

START **1**
2

*ATLANTIC
OCEAN*

Serra da Gralheira

2 Across the river is **Vila Nova de Gaia** (p110), where you can sample countless varieties at its many port-wine lodges. Graham's has a small museum.

4 A short detour south of the river, **Lamego** (p204) is known for its fine sparkling wine.

6 **Quinta Nova** (p200) and **Quinta do Crasto** are two of the best wineries in the Alto Douro. The Quinta do Crasto has been around since 1615.

Classic Photo
The Douro at Pinhão

5 **Pinhão** (p200), a quaint riverside village, is a great base for a few nights. From here you can explore the wineries of the Alto Douro.

Parque
Natural do
Alvão
▲
Valqueiro
(1315m)

▲ Marão
(1415m)
Serra do Marão

Río Douro

Río Douro

3

4

6

5

FINISH
7

BEIRA
ALTA

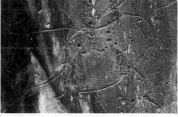

7 End your tour at **Vila Nova de Foz Côa** to view the thousands of examples of Palaeolithic art – mysterious rock engravings blanketing a valley.

N
0   20 km
0   10 miles

HEMIS/ALAMY STOCK PHOTO ©

Pinhão train station

Pinhão

Encircled by terraced hillsides, pretty little Pinhão sits on a particularly lovely bend of the Rio Douro, about 25km upriver from Peso da Régua. Wineries and their competing signs dominate the scene. Even the delightful train station has *azulejos* (hand-painted tiles) depicting the grape harvest.

In addition to drinking your fill, this is a good setting for country walks, and cruises along the river by boat or train.

🌀 ACTIVITIES

Quinta Nova   Hiking, Wine

(📞254 730 430; www.quintanova.com; Covas do Douro; guided tour €16, incl tasting €20-110; ⏰tours 10.45am, 12.15pm & 3.30pm year-round, plus 5pm Apr-Oct) Set on a stunning ridge, surrounded by luscious, ancient vineyards, overlooking the deep green Douro river with mountains layered in the distance, the Quinta Nova estate is well worth an in-depth exploration. The three hiking and

biking trails (the longest is three hours) are the best in the region.

Quinta do Portal   Wine

(📞259 937 000; www.quintadoportal.com; tours incl tasting €7.50; ⏰10am-1pm & 2-6pm) This award-winning vineyard produces ports, red and white table wines, and a little-known muscatel wine. The surrounding region is one of the only places in the country producing muscatel (the other is Setúbal). Tours include a visit to the cellar with a tasting of two wines.

Quinta das Carvalhas   Wine

(📞254 738 050; www.realcompanhiavelha.pt/pages/quintas/4; self-guided walk €10, bus/jeep tour €12.50/35, vintage tour incl premium wine tasting €90; ⏰10am-7.30pm Apr-Oct, to 6pm Nov-Mar) Just across the bridge from Pinhão, this *quinta* on the Douro's south bank welcomes visitors to its spiffy modern tasting room and wine shop and offers a variety of vineyard tours climbing to a ridgeline with gorgeous views. Choose from a self-guided walk, an open-top bus tour, a jeep tour or a personalised vintage tour guided by the in-house agronomist.

Quinta do Tedo
Wine

(☎254 789 165; www.quintadotedo.com; N222, Folgosa; tours incl 3-wine tasting €12, other tastings €22-60; ☉10am-7pm Apr-Oct, 9am-5.30pm Nov-Mar) Blessed with sublime real estate carved by two rivers, the Douro and Tedo, this American-French-Portuguese–owned, 14-hectare estate offers short tours of the certified organic winery, followed by a tasting of port, table wine and organic olive oil. There's a lovely self-guided 3km hiking trail on the property that's wonderful for birdwatching.

🍴 EATING

It's no gastronomic haven, but little Pinhão has a clutch of restaurants that will do the job of feeding you well. Some of the finest dining can be found in the *quintas* outside town, and one of the region's best restaurants is just a 15-minute drive out of town along the Douro.

🔭 Miradouro São Leonardo de Galafura

For jaw-dropping views of the Douro Valley, head for this magnificent **viewpoint** (Estrada São Leonardo, Galafura) between Régua and Pinhão. The N313-2 relentlessly switchbacks its way into the hills northeast from Régua, arriving a half-hour later at the overlook (640m), where the valley's full sweep spreads out before you, the Douro snaking off into the distance between kilometres of steeply terraced vineyards.

MAURICIO ABREU/GETTY IMAGES ©

Pinhão

HANS GEORG EIBEN/GETTY IMAGES ©

Vineyards in Peso da Régua

DOC — Portuguese €€€

(☏254 858 123; www.ruipaula.com; Estrada Nacional 222, Folgosa; mains €31-34; ☺12.30-3.30pm & 7.30-11pm) Architect Miguel Saraiva's ode to clean-lined, glass-walled minimalism, DOC is headed up by Portuguese star chef Rui Paula. Its terrace peering out across the river is a stunning backdrop. Dishes give a pinch of imagination to seasonal, regional flavours, from seafood *açordas* (shellfish stew) to game and wild mushrooms – all are paired with carefully selected wines from the cellar.

The restaurant is in Folgosa, midway between Peso da Régua and Pinhão, on the south side of the river.

Veladouro — Portuguese €€€

(☏254 738 166; Rua da Praia 3; mains €15-25; ☺10am-midnight) Wood-grilled meats and fish are the speciality at this schist-walled restaurant by the riverfront. On sunny days, the vine-shaded front terrace is the place to be, with views of local fishermen under their umbrellas on the adjacent dock. From the train station, follow the main road left for 150m, then turn left again under a railway bridge to the river.

GETTING THERE & AWAY

Regional trains travel between Pinhão and Peso da Régua (€2.80, 25 minutes, five daily), where you can catch an onward train to Porto.

Peso da Régua

Gateway to the Alto Douro, the sun-bleached town of Régua abuts the Rio Douro at the western edge of the demarcated port-wine region. Most tourists stick to the scenic riverfront, but the quaint old town one block uphill is an almost exclusively local scene, and well worth a wander.

◉ SIGHTS & ACTIVITIES

Museu do Douro — Museum

(www.museudodouro.pt; Rua Marquês de Pombal; adult/concession €6/3; ☺10am-6pm Mar-Oct, to

 Rock Art of the Ages

An astonishing collection of rock engravings – numbering in the thousands – lies in the Rio Côa valley. Discovered by chance in the late 1980s, today the area is known as **Parque Arqueológico do Vale do Côa** (☏279 768 260; www.arte-coa.pt; Rua do Museu; each park site adult/child €15/5, museum €6/3; ☺museum & park 9.30am-6pm Tue-Sun Mar-May, to 7pm Jun-Sep, to 5.30pm Oct-Feb), a Unesco World Heritage Site and renowned as one of Iberia's great archaeological treasures.

Because the entire valley is a working archaeological site, everyone must enter with a guided tour. Visitors gather at the various visitor centres, where they're taken, eight at a time, in the park's own 4WDs for a guided tour of one of the sites.

Visitor numbers are strictly regulated, so book a tour through the park office well in advance or you may miss out.

Five daily trains run to Pocinho, at the end of the Douro valley line, from Porto (€12.10, 4½ hours) and Peso da Régua (€6.50, 1½ hours), via Pinhão (€4.80, one hour). A taxi between Pocinho and Vila Nova de Foz Côa costs around €10.

Museum in the Parque Arqueológico do Vale do Côa
TAKASHI IMAGES/SHUTTERSTOCK ©
ARCHITECTS: CAMILO REBELO AND TIAGO PIMENTEL

5.30pm Nov-Feb) Bringing the Douro Valley's wine-producing history vividly to life, this wonderful museum has a wealth of artefacts and engaging displays, from a vast wall-size map of the river, annotated kilometre by kilometre, to old leather-bound texts, vintage port-wine posters and the remains of an old flat-bottomed port hauler. You'll find it all in a gorgeous converted riverside warehouse, with a restaurant and bar on-site. The gift shop, stocked with wine, handmade soaps, ceramics and jewelry, is also brilliant.

Tomaz do Douro   Cruise
(📞222 082 286; www.tomazdodouro.pt; Cais da Régua; cruises from €10) Tomaz do Douro offers different cruises along the Douro, including several that depart from Peso da Régua.

Comboio Histórico do Douro   Rail
(www.cp.pt; Estação CP, Largo da Estação; round-trip adult/child €42.50/19; ☺Sat & Sun Jun-Oct) This lovingly restored steam train runs once daily on summer and autumn weekends along the Douro from Régua to Tua, making a 20-minute stop in Pinhão. For identical views without the vintage train flavour, hop aboard one of the five regular daily trains along this same route (each way €4.05, 45 minutes).

🍴 EATING

A couple of traditional taverns that dish out good-value lunch menus and an inventive restaurant serving updated Portuguese classics make Régua a decent place to eat.

Castas e Pratos   Portuguese €€€
(📞254 323 290; www.castaspratos.com; Avenida José Vasques Osório; mains €20-35; ☺10.30am-11pm) The coolest dining room in town is set in a restored wood-and-stone railyard warehouse with exposed original timbers. You can order grilled *alheira* sausage or octopus salad from the tapas bar downstairs, or opt for green asparagus risotto or roasted kid goat and potatoes with turnip sprouts in the mezzanine.

Taberna do Jéréré   Portuguese €€
(📞254 323 299; Rua Marquês de Pombal 38; mains €8-18; ☺noon-3pm & 7.30-10.30pm Mon-Sat) Excellent Portuguese dishes, including the house speciality *bacalhau á Jéréré* (dried salt-cod with shrimp, mushroom and spinach), are served in a tastefully rustic

Museu de Lamego

HEMIS/ALAMY STOCK PHOTO ©

Igreja de Nossa Senhora dos Remédios

dining room with a beamed ceiling and granite floors. Great-value lunch specials.

ℹ INFORMATION

Loja Interativa de Turismo (☏254 318 152; www.cm-pesoregua.pt; Avenida do Douro; ⊙9.30am-12.30pm & 2-6pm) Régua's high-tech tourist office, facing the Douro 1km west of the station, supplies information about the town and the region, including local accommodations and vineyards.

ℹ GETTING THERE & AWAY

Rodonorte (www.rodonorte.pt) buses go twice daily to Lamego (€5.90, 20 minutes).

There are around 13 trains daily from Porto (€10, two hours); some continue up the valley to Pinhão (€2.80, 25 minutes) and Pocinho (€6.50, 1½ hours).

Lamego

Most people come to this prim, prosperous town 10km south of the Rio Douro to see (and possibly climb) the astonishing

baroque stairway that zigzags its way up to the Igreja de Nossa Senhora dos Remédios. The old town centre itself has a mix of winding narrow lanes and tree-lined boulevards, with spotlit medieval landmarks looming from almost every angle.

Lamego is a natural base for exploring the half-ruined monasteries and chapels in the surrounding environs, one of which dates back to the time of the Visigoths.

◎ SIGHTS

Museu de Lamego   Museum

(www.museudelamego.gov.pt; Largo de Camões; adult/reduced €3/1.50; ⊙10am-6pm) Occupying a grand, 18th-century episcopal palace, the Museu de Lamego is one of Portugal's finest regional museums. The collection features five entrancing works by renowned 16th-century Portuguese painter Vasco Fernandes (Grão Vasco), richly worked Brussels tapestries from the same period, and an extraordinarily diverse collection of heavily gilded 17th-century chapels rescued in their entirety from the long-gone Convento das Chagas.

VENEMAMA/GETTY IMAGES ©

Mosteiro de São Gonçalo

Igreja de Nossa
Senhora dos Remédios   Church

(⏱7.30am-8pm May-Sep, to 6pm Oct-Apr) One
of the country's most important pilgrimage sites, this twin-towered, 18th-century
church has a trim blue-and-white stucco
interior with a sky-blue rococo ceiling
and a gilded altar. The church, however,
is quite overshadowed by the zigzagging
monumental **stairway** that leads up to it.
The 600-plus steps are resplendent with
azulejos (hand-painted tiles), urns, fountains and statues, adding up to one of the
greatest works in Portuguese rococo style.

🍽 EATING

Mercado Municipal   Market €

(Avenida 5 de Outubre; ⏱7.30am-6pm Mon-Sat)
The *mercado municipal* (local market) sells
Lamego's famous hams and wines – ideal
picnic food. Thursdays are especially busy.

Manjar do Douro   Portuguese €€

(☎254 611 285; www.manjardodouro.pt;
Avenida Dr Alfredo de Sousa 43; mains €9-16;
⏱11.30am-midnight) Well-known traditional

restaurant frequented by business folk at
lunchtime and dishing out well-prepared
Portuguese mainstays.

🛈 GETTING THERE & AWAY

The most appealing route to Lamego from any-
where in the Douro valley is by train to Peso da
Régua and by bus or taxi from there. A taxi from
Régua costs from about €15 to €20.

From Lamego's bus station, Rede Expressos
(www.rede-expressos.pt) has a daily bus service
to Peso da Régua (€6, 15 minutes) and Lisbon
(€19.50, five hours).

Amarante

Handsomely set on a bend in the Rio
Tâmega, the sleepy village of Amarante
is dominated by a striking church and
monastery, which sit theatrically beside a
rebuilt medieval bridge that still bears city
traffic. The willow-lined riverbanks lend a
pastoral charm, as do the balconied houses and switchback lanes that rise quickly
from the narrow valley floor.

◎ SIGHTS & ACTIVITIES

Museu Amadeo de Souza-Cardoso   Museum

(www.amadeosouza-cardoso.pt; Alameda Teixeira de Pascoaes; adult/child €1/free; ☺10am-12.30pm & 2-6pm Tue-Sun Jun-Sep, 9.30am-12.30pm & 2-5.30pm Oct-May) Hidden in one of the Mosteiro de São Gonça-lo's cloisters is this delightfully eclectic collection of modernist and contemporary art, a pleasant surprise in a town of this size. The museum is named after Amarante's favourite son, artist Amadeo de Souza-Cardoso (1889–1918) – one of the best-known Portuguese artists of the 20th century, who abandoned naturalism for home-grown versions of impressionism and cubism. The museum is full of his sketches, cartoons, portraits and abstracts.

Mosteiro de São Gonçalo   Monastery

(Praça da República; ☺9am-7pm Jun-Sep, to 5.30pm Oct-May) Founded in 1543 by João III, the Mosteiro de São Gonçalo and **Igreja de São Gonçalo** weren't completed until 1620. Above the church's photogenic, Italian Renaissance side portal is an arcaded gallery, 30m high, with 17th-century statues of Dom João and the other kings who ruled while the monastery was under construction: Sebastião, Henrique and Felipe I.

Rio Tâmega   Boating, Walking

(boat hire per 30min/1hr €5/10; ☺boat hire 9am-sunset) For an idyllic river stroll, take the cobbled path along the north bank. A good picnic or daydreaming spot is the rocky outcropping overlooking the rapids 400m east of the bridge. You can also potter about the peaceful Rio Tâmega in a paddle or row boat; boat hire is available along the riverbank.

✗ EATING & DRINKING

Adega Regional Quelha   Portuguese €€

(☏255 425 786; Rua de Olivença; mains €7.50-19.50; ☺11.30am-2pm & 7-10pm Mon-Thu, 11.30am-10pm Fri-Sun) One of several low-key *adegas* (wine taverns) along the river's south bank, Quelha is a good place to sample regional delicacies such as Amarante's fine smoked meats and cheeses.

Bar do Hostel   Bar

(☏255 095 951; Rua Candido dos Reis 53; ☺10am-midnight) Attached to the **Hostel des Arts** (www.hosteldesarts.com; dm €17-24, s €52-59, d €62-69; 🛜), this vibrantly decorated bar serves a full lineup of coffee, local wines and mixed drinks to a young and artsy crowd. Grab a spot on the sofa in the high-ceilinged main room, or catch some rays on the welcoming riverview terrace. Tapas and well-priced daily lunch specials (€7.50) may tempt you to linger.

❶ GETTING THERE & AWAY

At the small but busy **Estacão Quelmado** (Rua Antonio Carneiro), Rodonorte (www.rodonorte. pt) buses from Porto (€7.60, one hour) stop at least five times daily. There are also daily buses to Braga (€9, one to 1½ hours) and Lisbon (€20.40, 4¼ to 5¾ hours).

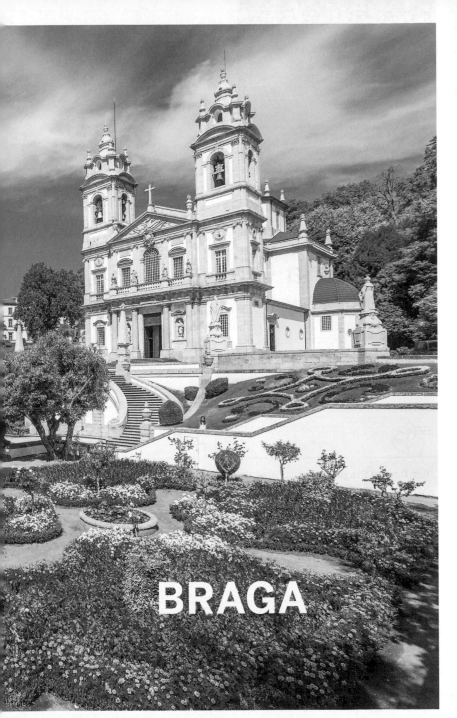

BRAGA

Braga at a Glance...

Portugal's third-largest city is an elegant town laced with ancient narrow lanes closed to vehicles, strewn with plazas and a splendid array of baroque churches. The constant chiming of bells is a reminder of Braga's age-old devotion to the spiritual world. Its religious festivals – particularly the elaborately staged Semana Santa (Holy Week) – are famous throughout Portugal. But don't come expecting piety alone: Braga's upscale old centre is packed with lively cafes and trim boutiques, some excellent restaurants and low-key bars catering to students from the Universidade do Minho.

Two Days in Braga

On day one head straight for Braga's remarkable **cathedral** (p212), the city's must-see. After lunch take in some of the city's other, smaller churches before finishing off the day with dinner at **Casa de Pasto das Carvalheiras** (p219) or **Anjo Verde** (p218). Spend day two exploring the **Museu dos Biscainhos** (p214) and shopping and cafe-hopping in the lively city centre.

Four Days in Braga

Make sure one of the days you are here is a Thursday so you can make it to the sprawling **Feira de Barcelos market** (p220), 22km west of Braga. On day four make a pilgrimage to **Bom Jesus do Monte** (p216), a church 5km east of the city. In the evening join Braga's students for a few cold drinks in one of the city's great bars.

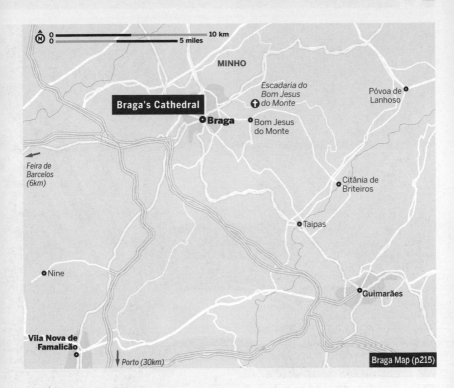

Braga's Cathedral

Braga Map (p215)

Arriving in Braga

Braga has frequent train connections to Porto (€3.25, about one hour); there's also train service to Coimbra (€21, 1¾ to 2¾ hours, four to seven daily) and Lisbon (€34, four hours, two to four daily).

If driving, it's best to park outside the centre. Try the side streets east of Avenida da Liberdade.

Where to Stay

Braga has a wide range of accommodation, from backpacker hostels to luxury guest houses, though most hotels fall into the lower to midrange category. The majority of Braga's accommodation options are located in the city centre, a short walk from most of the sights, restaurants and shopping.

For the quietest night's snooze, choose hotels and guest houses around the Sé.

Organs of the cathedral

Braga's Cathedral

Top billing in Braga goes to its cathedral, the Sé, whose asymmetrical towers loom high over the picturesque city-centre streets. A working church, it is the seat of the Archdiocese of Braga.

Great For...

☑ Don't Miss

The Chapel of Piety (Capela da Piedade), a beautiful 16th-century Renaissance tomb.

The History

Braga's extraordinary cathedral, the oldest in Portugal, was begun when the archdiocese was restored in 1070 and completed in the following century. It's a wonderfully rambling complex made up of differing styles, and architecture buffs could spend half a day happily distinguishing the Romanesque bones from Manueline musculature and baroque frippery. Allow at least three hours to see everything.

The Design

The Sé's original Romanesque style is the most interesting and survives in the cathedral's overall shape, the southern entrance and the marvellous west portal, which is carved with scenes from the medieval legend of Reynard the Fox (now sheltered

Cathedral exterior

IMAGEBROKER/ALAMY STOCK PHOTO ©

Braga

R Dom Diogo de Sousa

Braga 🏛
Cathedral
R Dom Afonso
Henriques

🟥 Braga

ℹ Need to Know

Map p215; www.se-braga.pt; Rua Dom Paio
Mendes; ⊙9.30am-12.30pm & 2.30-6.30pm
Apr-Oct, to 5.30pm Nov-Mar 🔲

✕ Take a Break

A short stroll from the cathedral, Peca-
do da Sé (p219) serves excellent lunch
specials.

★ Top Tip

Come for Sunday mass (11.30am) to
hear the Sé's organ in action.

inside a Gothic porch). The most appealing
external features are the filigree Manueline
towers and roof – an early work by João
de Castilho, who went on to build Lisbon's
illustrious Mosteiro dos Jerónimos. You
can enter the cathedral through the west
portal or via a courtyard and cloister that's
lined with Gothic chapels on the north side.
The church itself features a fine Manueline
carved altarpiece, a tall chapel with *azulejos* (hand-painted tiles) telling the story of
Braga's first bishop (São Pedro de Rates),
and fantastic twin baroque organs (held up
by formidable satyrs and mermen).

Treasury

Connected to the church is the treasury,
housing a goldmine of ecclesiastical booty,
including the lovely Nossa Senhora do Leite
of the Virgin suckling Christ, attributed

to 16th-century French sculptor Nicolas
Chanterène. Another remarkable highlight
is the iron cross that was used in 1500 to
celebrate the very first Mass in Brazil.

Choir

To visit the choir, visitors must purchase
a separate ticket and join a guided tour
(some guides speak English), which gives
an up-close look at the mesmerising
organs and gilded choir stalls. Visitors will
then be led downstairs and into the cathedral's showpiece, Capela dos Reis (Kings'
Chapel), home to the tombs of Henri of
Burgundy and Dona Teresa, parents of the
first king of Portugal, Afonso Henriques.
You'll also visit the *azulejo*-covered Capela
de São Geraldo (dating from the 12th
century but reworked over the years) and
the 14th-century Capela da Glória, whose
interior was painted in unrepentantly
Moorish geometric motifs in the 16th
century.

◎ SIGHTS

GNRation
Cultural Centre

(Map p215; ☏253 142 200; www.gnration.
pt; Praça Conde de Agrolongo 123; ⊙9.30am-
6.30pm Mon-Fri) FREE This spiffy modern
cultural centre lives inside an 18th-century
building that once housed police headquarters. Enter through the sliding glass
doors and you're inside an incubator of
the city's creative industry, with galleries,
concerts, film screenings, workshops and
theatre performances. Free guided tours
are available with advance notice (call or
contact info@gnration.pt).

Museu dos Biscainhos
Museum

(Map p215; www.culturanorte.pt/pt/patrimonio/
museu-dos-biscainhos; Rua dos Biscainhos;
adult/student €2/1, first Sun of the month
free; ⊙10am-12.30pm & 2-5.30pm Tue-Sun)
An 18th-century aristocrat's palace is
home to Braga's enthusiastic municipal
museum, with a nice collection of Roman
relics and 17th- to 19th-century pottery
and furnishings. The palace itself – with its
polychrome, chestnut-panelled ceilings and

18th-century *azulejos* depicting hunting
scenes – and the gorgeously landscaped
gardens out back are reason enough to
visit. The ground floor is paved with deeply
ribbed flagstones on which carriages would
have once rattled through to the stables.

Centro Interpretativo das Memórias da Misericórdia de Braga
Museum

(Map p215; www.scmbraga.pt/cimmb-palácio-
do-raio; Rua do Raio 400; ⊙10am-1pm &
2.30-6.30pm Tue-Sat) FREE Braga's newest
museum is housed inside Palácio do Raio,
whose exuberantly tiled rococo facade (by
André Soares) is must-see material for any
aficionado of the colour blue. The gorgeous
interiors, also clad in *azulejos*, showcase
works of sacred art, textiles, paintings,
sculptures, jewellery, pottery and old medical instruments, all bearing witness to 500
years of the building's history.

Praça da República
Square

(Map p215) The cafes and restaurants on
this broad plaza are a pleasant place to
start or finish your day. An especially

Centro Interpretativo das Memórias da Misericórdia de Braga

ANTON_IVANOV/SHUTTERSTOCK ©

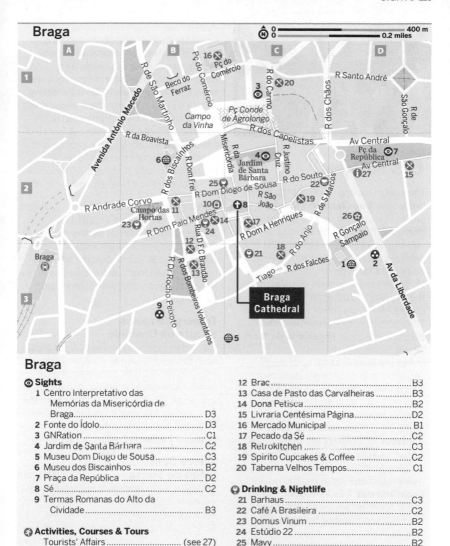

Braga

mellow atmosphere descends in the evening, when coloured lights spring up and people of all ages congregate to enjoy the night air.

The square-shaped, crenellated tower behind the cafes is the walled-up **Torre de Menagem**, which is all that survives of a fortified medieval palace.

Stairway to Heaven

The goal of legions of penitent pilgrims every year, **Bom Jesus do Monte** is one of Portugal's most recognisable icons. A rather windswept and glamorous pilgrimage site, lying 5km east of central Braga, the sober neoclassical church stands atop a forested hill that offers grand sunset views across the city. But most people don't come simply for the church or even the view. They come to see the extraordinary baroque staircase, **Escadaria do Bom Jesus** (Monte do Bom Jesus).

The photogenic climb up to Bom Jesus is made up of tiered staircases, dating from different decades of the 18th century. The lowest is lined with chapels representing the Stations of the Cross. **Escadaria dos Cinco Sentidos** (Stairway of the Five Senses) features allegorical fountains with water gurgling from the ears, eyes, nose and mouth of different statues. Highest is **Escadaria das Três Virtudes** (Stairway of the Three Virtues), with chapels and fountains representing faith, hope and charity.

City bus 2 runs from Braga's Avenida da Liberdade to the bottom of the Bom Jesus steps (€1.65, 20 minutes) – the end of the line – every half-hour all day (hourly on Sunday).

Escadaria do Bom Jesus
LEV LEVIN/SHUTTERSTOCK ©

Fonte do Ídolo   Ruins

(Idol Spring; Map p215; Rua do Raio; adult/student €1.85/0.95; ☺9.30am-1pm & 2-5.30pm Mon-Fri, 11am-5.30pm Sat) Tucked away below street level and concealed by a modern lobby is this evocative ancient spring, one of Braga's unexpected treasures. An essential community water source in the city's early days, the spring and its surrounding rock face were carved into a fountain during pre-Roman times by Celicus Fronto, an immigrant from the city-state of Arcobriga. One carving is of a toga-clad pilgrim thought to be holding the horn of plenty. An introductory video provides historical background.

Jardim de Santa Bárbara   Gardens

(Map p215; Rua Justino Cruz) FREE This 17th-century square has narrow paths picking their way through a sea of flowers and topiary. On sunny days the adjacent pedestrianised Rua Justino Cruz and Rua Francisco Sanches fill with buskers and cafe tables.

Termas Romanas do Alto da Cividade   Ruins

(Map p215; ☎253 278 455; Rua Dr Rocha Peixoto; adult/student €1.85/0.95; ☺9.30am-1pm & 2-5.30pm Mon-Fri, 11am-5.30pm Sat) These ruins of an extensive bathing complex – with an attached theatre – dating from the 2nd century AD, were probably abandoned in the 5th century. See the seven-minute introductory video in English or Portuguese.

Museu Dom Diogo de Sousa   Museum

(Map p215; www.culturanorte.pt/pt/patrimonio/museu-de-arqueologia-d-diogo-de-sousa; Rua dos Bombeiros Voluntários; adult/student €3/1.50, Sun free; ☺9.30am-6pm Tue-Sun Jun–mid-Sep, to 5.30pm mid-Sep–May) The archaeological museum houses a nicely displayed collection of fragments from Braga's earliest days. The four rooms feature pieces from Palaeolithic times (arrowheads, funerary objects and ceramics) through Roman rule and on up to the period dominated by the Suevi-Visigoth kingdom (5th through 7th centuries). Especially fascinating are the huge *miliários* (milestones),

Jardim de Santa Bárbara

carved with Latin inscriptions, that marked the Roman roads.

TOURS

Tourists' Affairs   Tours

(Map p215; ☑ 927 504 470; www.thetourists affairs.com) Excellent tour agency run by a pair of young, enthusiastic locals, an architect and an archaeologist, it specialises in all things Minho. Their focus is on tailor-made à la carte tours of Minho and beyond, but they also do walking tours of Braga – call ahead to reserve a spot and confirm a meeting point (often at Braga's tourist office).

SHOPPING

Som da Sé   Musical Instruments

(Map p215; ☑ 917 270 735; www.somdase.pt; Rua Dom Paio Mendes 77; ⏰ 10am-7pm Mon-Sat) A vision of bliss for any music buff who's ever dreamed of owning a *guitarra portuguêsa* – the pear-shaped guitar used in Portuguese fado music – this shop stocks a huge array

of instruments made in Braga, which you can play on-site before choosing which to bring home. *Violas braguesas, cavaquinhos* (ukeleles) and other traditional Portuguese stringed instruments are also available.

EATING

Braga's historic centre is packed with restaurants, cafes and snack spots. The boisterous **mercado municipal** (Map p215; Praça do Comércio; ⏰ 8am-3pm Mon-Fri, 6am-1pm Sat) buzzes on weekdays and Saturday mornings, and is ideal for self-caterers. You can also hit one of several fruit-and-vegetable shops along Rua de São Marcos.

Livraria Centésima Página   Cafe €

(Map p215; Avenida Central 118-120; snacks €3-5; ⏰ 9am-7.30pm Mon-Sat) Tucked inside Centésima Página, an absolutely splendid bookshop with foreign-language titles, this charming cafe serves a rotating selection of tasty quiches along with salads and desserts, and has outdoor tables in the pleasantly rustic garden. Its lunch specials are a steal.

Praça da República (p214)

Anjo Verde   Vegetarian €

(Map p215; ☏253 264 010; Largo da Praça Velha 21; mains €8.50-9.50; ◷noon-3pm & 7.30-10.30pm Mon-Sat; ✍) Braga's vegetarian offering serves generous, elegantly presented plates in a lovely, airy dining room. Vegetarian lasagne, soy stroganoff, risotto and vegetable tarts are among the specialities here. Mains can be bland, but the spiced chocolate tart is a superstar.

Dona Petisca   Tapas €

(Map p215; ☏253 052 480; www.facebook. com/donapetisca; Rua Dom Paio Mendes 32; sandwiches & snacks €3.50-5.50; ◷noon-midnight Tue-Thu, noon-1am Fri & Sat, 5pm-midnight Sun) This gourmet food shop with a narrow upstairs seating area sells all manner of sandwiches and snacks built around DOP and DOC Portuguese products – from ham and smoked sausage to cheeses, olives and wild mushrooms, all accompanied by quality wines. It's a great place to grab a bite any time of day or night.

Retrokitchen   Portuguese €

(Map p215; ☏253 267 023; www.facebook.com/ retrokitchenbraga; Rua do Anjo 96; mains €9-12; ◷10am-midnight Mon & Wed-Sat) A vintage theme runs through this funky, laid-back restaurant featuring tasty daily specials and a display of eclectic retro items curated by the friendly owner couple. The lunch menu is a steal (main course, bread and coffee for €5, or €6 with soup).

Spirito Cupcakes
& Coffee   Ice Cream €

(Map p215; www.spiritocupcakes.com; Largo São João do Souto 19; cups & cones from €2; ◷1.30-7pm Mon-Thu, 1.30-7pm & 9pm-midnight Fri & Sat) Don't miss the artisanal gelato at this always buzzing shop, where lines form out the door for a cup or cone of oatmeal-, cookie- or bubblegum-flavoured ice cream, and great cupcakes and coffees, too.

Casa de Pasto
das Carvalheiras   Fusion €€

(Map p215; ☏253 046 244; www.facebook.com/ casadepastodascarvalheiras; Rua Dom Afonso

Henriques 8; small plates €5-15; ⊘noon-3pm & 7pm-midnight Mon-Fri, noon-midnight Sat & Sun) This colourful eatery with a long bar serves up delectable, weekly changing *pratinhos* (small plates), from codfish confit with bok choy and noodles, to mushrooms with creamy polenta, to tasty cakes of *alheira* (a light garlicky sausage of poultry or game) and turnip greens. Weekday lunch menus go for €9 or €12, depending on the number of dishes you order.

Pecado da Sé Portuguese €€

(Map p215; ☑919 990 990; Rua do Forno 22; mains €10-17; ⊘noon-3pm Mon, noon-3pm & 8pm-midnight Tue-Thu, noon-3pm & 8pm-2am Fri & Sat) Down a side street from Braga's cathedral, this mod little hideaway mixes traditional Portuguese home cooking with international culinary influences, from classic *bacalhau com broa* (codfish with cornbread) and grilled Bisaro pork to fried chicken, prawn curry and Brazilian *picanha* (steak) with black beans. At lunchtime, it serves excellent all-inclusive menus (€10).

Brac Portuguese €€

(Map p215; ☑253 610 225; Campo das Carvalheiras; mains €14-17; ⊘11am-midnight Mon-Sat) This gourmet hotspot offers tasty *entradas* (appetisers) at the backlit bar, along with more elaborate dishes – Brazilian-style *moqueca* (seafood stew), rice with black pork and pleurotus mushrooms – in the swank stone-columned dining room. Come at lunchtime for the all-you-can eat buffet (€9 to €12.50 Monday through Saturday, €19.50 Sunday), best enjoyed on the front terrace overlooking a leafy park.

Taberna Velhos Tempos Portuguese €

(Map p215; ☑253 214 368; Rua do Carmo 7; mains €7.50-11; ⊘noon-2.30pm & 8-10.30pm Mon-Sat) Under the motto 'rural cuisine for urban people', this wood-beamed tavern

🏛 Semana Santa

Braga hosts the most elaborate Easter celebrations in Portugal. It kicks off with Semana Santa, when Gregorian chants are piped throughout the city centre and makeshift candlelit altars light the streets. The action heats up during Holy Thursday's Procissão do Senhor Ecce Homo, when barefoot, hooded penitents – members of private Catholic brotherhoods – march through the streets spinning their eerie rattles.

The Good Friday celebration in the cathedral is a remarkable, elaborately staged drama with silk canopies, dirge-like hymns, dozens of priests and a weeping congregation. On Saturday evening, the Easter Vigil Mass begins dourly, the entire cathedral in shadow, only to explode in lights and jubilation. Finally, on Sunday, the people of Braga blanket their thresholds with flowers, inviting passing priests to enter and give their home a blessing.

decorated with rustic bric-a-brac serves a tasty menu of traditional mainstays. Try the *bacalhau com natas* (baked codfish with potatoes and cream) or *arroz de pato com pinhão* (rice with duck and pine nuts). Full servings are huge; consider the half portions unless you've got a voracious appetite.

 Feira de Barcelos

The largest, oldest and most celebrated of the Minho's markets is the **Feira de Barcelos** (Barcelos Market; Campo da República; ☺sunrise-sunset Thu), held every Thursday in Barcelos on the banks of the Rio Cávado. Despite attracting travellers, the market retains its rural soul. Villagers hawk everything from scrawny chickens to hand-embroidered linen, and Roma women bellow for business in the clothes section. Snack on sausages and homemade bread as you wander among the brass cowbells, hand-woven baskets and carved ox yokes. Pottery is what most outsiders come to see.

Traditional pottery at Feira de Barcelos
MAURICIO ABREU/ALAMY STOCK PHOTO ©

🍷 DRINKING & NIGHTLIFE

While it's no counterpart to Lisbon or Porto, Braga has a pretty buzzy nightlife, though it's mostly limited to the clutch of cafes and bars in the city centre. As it's a student town the crowd is generally young.

Domus Vinum Wine Bar
(Map p215; Largo da Nossa Senhora da Boa Luz 12; tapas €4-7; ☺6pm-2am Wed-Mon) With Brazilian beats, a lantern-lit front patio and excellent wines by the glass, Domus Vinum draws a stylish crowd. The Portuguese and Spanish tapas are excellent. It's just west of the old-town entrance portal, Arco da Porta Nova.

Mavy Bar
(Map p215; www.facebook.com/espacomavy; Rua D. Diogo de Sousa 133; ☺noon-2am Sun-Thu noon-4am Fri & Sat) From early evening into the wee hours, a youthful crowd congregates at this bar in Braga's pedestrian zone for drinks, late-night comfort food and alternative music. There's a great selection of beers on tap, along with bargain-priced burgers, quiches and toasted sandwiches (€2 to €4).

Café A Brasileira Cafe
(Map p215; ☎253 262 104; www.facebook.com/CafeABrasileiraBraga; Largo Barão São Martinho 17; ☺8am-midnight Sun-Thu, to 2am Fri & Sat) A Braga classic, this 19th-century cafe is a converging point for old and new generations. Try the *café de saco* (a small shot of filtered coffee).

Barhaus Bar
(Map p215; ☎914 426 833; www.facebook.com/barhaus.net; Rua Dom Gonçalo Pereira 58; ☺3pm-2am Mon-Thu, 3pm-4am Fri & Sat, 7pm-1am Sun) This popular spot with two indoor bars and a huge open-air patio draws a crowd with posh pretensions for DJs and live shows.

Estúdio 22 Bar
(Map p215; ☎253 053 751; www.facebook.com/Estudio22cafebargaleria; Rua Dom Paio Mendes 22; ☺2pm-2am Sun-Thu, to 4am Fri & Sat) Loungey cafe-bar on a bustling strip by the cathedral, great for sampling the speciality gin and tonics at night to the sound of live bands or DJs.

🎭 ENTERTAINMENT

Teatro Circo de Braga Theatre
(Map p215; ☎253 203 800; www.theatrocirco.com; Avenida da Liberdade 697) One of the most dazzling theatres in the country, inside a grand fin de siècle building, where you can catch concerts, theatre and dance, with offerings ranging from the staid to the truly avant-garde.

GLEN BERLIN/SHUTTERSTOCK ©

Café A Brasileira

INFORMATION

Turismo (Map p215; 253 262 550; www.
visitbraga.travel; Avenida da Liberdade 1; ⊙9am-
6.30pm Mon-Fri, 9.30am-1pm & 2-5.30pm Sat
& Sun) Braga's helpful tourist office is in an
art deco–style building facing busy Praça da
República.

GETTING THERE & AWAY

BUS

Braga has a centralised bus station that serves
as a major regional hub.

Airport Bus (📞253 262 371; www.getbus.eu)
About 10 buses daily do the 50-minute run
between the Porto airport and Braga, in each direction. The one-way fare is €8 (€4 for children),
return is €14 (€8 for children).

Rede Expressos (📞707 223 344; www.rede-
expressos.pt) Has up to 15 daily buses to Lisbon
(€21, 4½ hours).

Transdev (📞225 100 100; www.transdev.pt) Has
at least eight buses per day to Barcelos (€2.70,
one hour) and Porto (€4.85, one hour). Service
drops by half at weekends.

TRAIN

Braga is at the end of a branch line from Nine
and also within Porto's *suburbano* network,
which means commuter trains travel every hour
or so from Porto (€3.25, about one hour).

COIMBRA

Coimbra at a Glance...

Rising scenically from the Rio Mondego, Coimbra is an animated city steeped in history. It was Portugal's medieval capital for more than a century and it's home to the country's oldest and most prestigious university. The historic centre dates to Moorish times and is wonderfully atmospheric with dark cobbled lanes and a monumental cathedral. On summer evenings, the city's old stone walls reverberate with the haunting metallic notes of the guitarra (Portuguese guitar) and the full, deep voices of fado singers.

During the university term, students bring a youthful energy to the streets, thronging bars and partying late into the weekend.

Two Days in Coimbra

Head straight up through the Old Town to the famed **Universidade de Coimbra** (p226) – the unrivalled highlight of any visit. Spend the rest of the day exploring the historical centre. Day two could be spent dipping in and out of Coimbra's old churches and monasteries and taking in a performance of the city's own version of fado.

Four Days in Coimbra

On day three it's time to get out of the city to explore the wonderful Roman ruins at **Conímbriga** (p231), a short bus ride south. Spend your fourth day in Coimbra shopping for the city's distinctive pottery, kayaking on the **Rio Mondego** (p232) or hanging out with students in some of the learned bars and clubs.

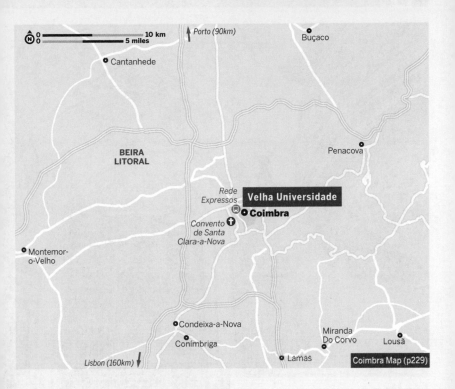

Arriving in Coimbra

Train Coimbra has two train stations: Coimbra-B and the more central Coimbra A (called just 'Coimbra' on timetables). There are regular services to Lisbon (from €20, two hours) and Porto (€13.50, 1¼ hours).

Bus There are direct services to Lisbon (€14.50, 2½ hours), Porto (€12.50, 1½ hours), Braga (€14, 2¾ hours, six daily), and Faro (€28, six to 8½ hours, two daily).

Where to Stay

Accommodation in Coimbra is generally good value for money with several excellent budget and midrange options. Recent years have seen the opening of a number of smart, modern hostels, offering stylish hotel-standard rooms alongside cheaper dorms.

If you stay in the upper town, note that parking is difficult there and you'll almost certainly have to lug your luggage at least some of the way.

Capela de São Miguel

ALVARO GERMAN VILELA/SHUTTERSTOCK ©

Velha Universidade

Coimbra's Unesco-listed university, one of the world's oldest, was originally founded in Lisbon in 1290. Its showpiece centre is the Pátio das Escolas, a vast courtyard surrounded by majestic 16th- to 18th-century buildings.

Overview

There's a lot to see at the Velha Universidade, so you should allow at least two hours. The sights include the Paço das Escolas (Royal Palace), clock tower, Prisão Académica (prison), Capela de São Miguel (chapel) and the highlight of any visit to Coimbra, the Biblioteca Joanina (library).

Biblioteca Joanina

This extraordinary library, a gift from João V in the early 18th century, seems too extravagant and distracting for study, with its rosewood, ebony and jacaranda tables, elaborately frescoed ceilings and gilt chinoiserie bookshelves. Its 60,000 ancient books deal with law, philosophy and theology. A lower floor has more tomes and the Prisão Académica, an erstwhile lock-up for misbehaving students.

Great For...

☑ **Don't Miss**

The superb view across Coimbra from the Pátio das Escolas.

Biblioteca Joanina

ALEX RAGEN/SHUTTERSTOCK ©

🛈 Need to Know

Map p229; ☎239 242 744; www.uc.pt/turismo; Pátio das Escolas; adult/child incl Paço das Escolas, Biblioteca Joanina, Capela de São Miguel & Museu da Ciência €12.50/free, without Biblioteca €7/free; ⏱9am-7.30pm Mar-Oct, 9am-1pm & 2-5pm Nov-Feb

✗ Take a Break

Enjoy the view and the first-rate cooking at the Loggia (p234).

★ Top Tip

Visitors are only allowed into the library in small groups every 20 minutes.

Capela de São Miguel

Part of the main university complex, this ornate 16th-century chapel has a brightly painted ceiling, lavish tilework, Manueline features and a gilded 18th-century organ with about 2000 pipes. Concerts are still held here on occasion.

Other Attractions

Housed in a former royal palace, the Paço das Escolas is where traditional academic ceremonies are still held. The main ceremonial hall is the Sala dos Capelos (named after the academic cape awarded to graduating doctorate students), a former examination room hung with dark portraits of Portugal's kings and crimson quilt-like decoration. Nearby, the Sala do Exame Privado (Private Examination Room) is where graduates would be secretly examined at night.

Another of the university's signature landmarks, the 18th-century tower – and its clock and bells – regulates academic life. Built between 1728 and 1733, on the premise that there could be no order without a clock, it was cursed as 'a cabra' ('goat'; or 'bitch' in contemporary lingo) as it rang out to end the day's classes, signifying the curfew (in the days when students had to be home by 7pm or face prison). It's well worth making the ascent for the fabulous views.

Tickets & Tours

Admission tickets come in two forms: one giving access to all university buildings (except the Torre) and the Museu da Ciência, and a second one that does not include the Biblioteca Joanina. Buy them at the office outside Porta Férrea. Note also that library visits are in groups at set times.

◉ SIGHTS

Many of Coimbra's headline sights are in the hilltop university area and the upper old town. This atmospheric district cascades down the hill in a tangle of steep cobbled lanes, medieval towers and graffiti-daubed student houses. The new town, known as the 'Baixa', sits at the foot of the hill by the Rio Mondego.

Museu Nacional de Machado de Castro
Museum

(Map p229; 📞239 853 070; www.museumacha docastro.pt; Largo Dr José Rodrigues; adult/child €6/3, cryptoportico only €3; ⏰2-6pm Tue, 10am-6pm Wed-Sun) This great museum is a highlight of central Portugal. Housed in a 12th-century bishop's palace, it stands over the city's ancient Roman forum, remains of which can be seen in the maze of spooky tunnels under the building – the *cryptoporticus*. Once you emerge from this, you can start on the fascinating art collection, which runs the gamut from Gothic religious sculpture to 16th-century Flemish painting and ornately crafted furniture.

Particularly spectacular is the vast recreation of a chapel from the Convento de São Domingos but highlights abound. These include a section of the delicate cloister of São João de Almedina and some exquisite alabaster pieces from England. Sculptural works trace the development of Portuguese sculpture from the 11th century, showing how the arrival of Renaissance masters from across Europe paved the way for a distinctive Coimbra tradition.

You can admire terracotta figures from a 16th-century *Last Supper* by the mysterious French artist Hodart and some stunning panels by the Flemish painter Quentin Metsys. A collection of gold monstrances, furniture and Moorish-influenced pieces are almost too much by the time you reach them.

Museu da Ciência
Museum

(Map p229; 📞239 242 744; www.museudaciencia. org; Largo Marquês de Pombal; adult/child incl Paço das Escolas, Biblioteca Joanina & Capela de São Miguel €12.50/free, without Biblioteca €7/free; ⏰10am-7pm Tue-Sun Mar-Oct, to 6pm Nov-Feb) Coimbra's science museum is quite wonderful, with everything from kid-friendly

Museu da Ciência

ROSA IRENE BETTANCOURT 13/ALAMY STOCK PHOTO ©

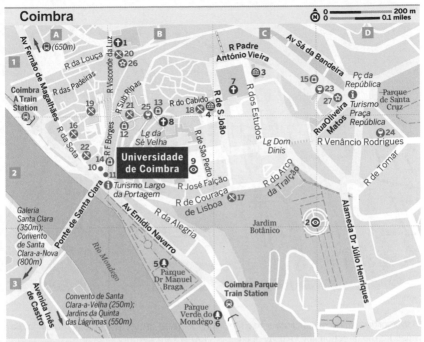

Coimbra

interactive machines to early scientific instruments, fossils and skeletons. The eclectic collection is spread over three sections in two buildings: the chemistry labs where the ticket office is, and, over the road, the physics and natural history galleries. Highlights include a section on light and matter and a riveting display of exquisitely crafted physics' apparatus, many dating from the 17th to 19th centuries.

Sé Velha

We particularly love the centaur used to measure the direction and velocity of an arrow.

After the physics displays, the natural history section takes you back to the Victorian era with cabinets crammed with stuffed animals, jars of preserved specimens and huge skeletons, including one of a *baleia comum* (common whale).

Sé Velha   Cathedral

(Old Cathedral; Map p229; ☏239 825 273; www.sevelha-coimbra.org; Largo da Sé Velha, Rua do Norte 4; €2.50; ◷10am-6pm Mon-Sat, 1-6pm Sun) Coimbra's 12th-century cathedral is one of Portugal's finest examples of Romanesque architecture. The main portal and facade are particularly striking, especially on warm summer evenings when the golden stone seems to glow in the soft light. Its construction was financed by Portugal's first king, Afonso Henriques, and completed in 1184 at a time when the nation was still threatened by the Moors, hence its crenellated exterior and narrow, slit-like lower windows. Interior highlights include an ornate late-Gothic retable and a lovely 13th-century cloister.

Inside, the high, barrel-vaulted nave preserves its main Romanesque features; side altars and well-preserved Gothic tombs of bishops are backed by bright Andalusian tiles. Over the main altar, the flamboyant gilt retable depicts the Assumption of Mary. Contrast this with the grey tones of the Renaissance Capela do Santíssimo Sacramento alongside.

Convento de
Santa Clara-a-Nova   Convent

(☏239 441 674; www.rainhasantaisabel.org; Calçada de Santa Isabel; €2; ◷9am-6.45pm Mon-Sat, to 6pm Sun Nov-Feb, 9am-7pm Mon-Sat, to 6.30pm Sun Mar-Oct) On the west side of the river, this imposing convent was built in the 17th century to replace the original Convento de Santa Clara-a-Velha (p231), which often suffered flooding. It's devoted almost entirely to Queen Isabel (Coimbra's patron saint) whose remains are encased in a silver casket above the altar. Paintings along the aisles illustrate her life story.

Also of note is the convent's attractive 18th-century cloister.

Convento de
Santa Clara-a-Velha
Convent

(☑239 801 160; Rua das Parreiras; adult/student €4/2; ⊗10am-7pm Tue-Sun Apr-Sep, to 6pm Oct-Mar) This Gothic convent was founded in 1330 by the saintly Queen Isabel, Dom Dinis' wife; it served as her final resting place until flooding forced her to be moved uphill. The adjacent **museum** displays archaeological finds and shows two films, one about the nuns who lived here, the other documenting the 20-year renovation that cleared the river ooze that had buried it since the 17th century.

Jardim Botânico
Gardens

(Map p229; ☑239 855 215; www.uc.pt/jardim botanico; ⊗9am-8pm Apr-Sep, 9am-5.30pm Oct-Mar) **FREE** A serene place to catch your breath, the lovely university-run botanic garden sits in the shadow of the 16th-century **Aqueduto de São Sebastião**. Founded by the Marquês de Pombal, the garden combines formal flower beds, meandering paths and elegant fountains.

Sé Nova
Cathedral

(New Cathedral; Map p229; ☑239 823 138; Largo da Sé Nova; €1; ⊗8.30am-6.30pm) The landmark 'new' cathedral, started by the Jesuits in 1598 and completed a century later, dominates the square of the same name high in the old town. Its two-tier white facade gives onto a cavernous interior adorned with gilt side panels and an ornate baroque altarpiece. It also features a gallery of reliquaries featuring bones and worse from minor saints and bishops, including St Francis Xavier and St Luke (so it's claimed!). Climb to the platform for uplifting city views.

Jardins da
Quinta das Lágrimas
Gardens

(Rua Vilarinho Raposo; adult/under 15yr/family €2.50/1/5; ⊗10am-5pm Tue-Sun mid-Oct–mid-Mar, 10am-7pm mid-Mar–mid-Oct) According to legend, this lovely pocket of parkland is where Dona Inês de Castro (aka Portugal's

 ## Conímbriga
Roman Ruins

Set in the lush countryside southwest of Coimbra, this is Portugal's largest and most impressive **Roman site** (☑239 949 110; www.conimbriga.pt; Condeixa-a-Velha; ruins & museum adult/child €4.50/free; ⊗10am-7pm Mar–Oct, to 6pm Nov–Feb). Ancient Conímbriga was an important city in the Roman province of Lusitania and its ruins are extensive and wonderfully well preserved. Highlights include villas paved with elaborate floor mosaics – in particular the Casa dos Repuxos (House of Fountains) – and a 3rd-century defensive wall built in an attempt to keep out invading barbarians.

Transdev runs buses from near Coimbra A station to the ruins (€2.55, 45 minutes, three times daily). You'll need to check the precise hours, though, as they change seasonally. Coimbra's *turismo* can provide timetables.

FRANCESCO DE MARCO/SHUTTERSTOCK ©

Juliet to the Infante Pedro's Romeo) was murdered on the orders of King Afonso IV, Pedro's father. Nowadays it's home to a five-star hotel but anyone can take a turn about the romantic grounds and track down the **Fonte dos Amores** (Lovers' Fountain), which reputedly marks the spot where Inês was struck down. Look also for a sequoia tree planted by the Duke of Wellington.

Parque Verde do Mondego
Park

(Map p229; 🏛) **FREE** At the base of the old town, this park extends from **Parque Dr Manuel Braga** (Map p229) along the riverfront. It has wooden walkways as well as a giant green bear and kids' playgrounds. A pedestrian bridge, the 275m-long Peter and Inês Bridge, spans the Rio Mondego.

TOURS

Go Walks   Walking

(Map p229; ☑910 163 118; www.gowalks
portugal.com; Rua Visconde da Luz 75; tours
per person €25-40) Offers various themed
walking tours – from fado to Jewish Coimbra – led by enthusiastic, knowledgeable
students who speak good English (French
and Spanish also bookable). It also runs
tours further afield in central Portugal.

O Pioneiro do Mondego   Kayaking

(☑239 478 385; www.opioneirodomondego.com;
per person €22.50-24.50) Take to the waters
of the Mondego river on a kayak tour.
Routes include the 18km stretch between
Penacova and Torres de Mondego (three
to four hours) and the 25km descent between Penacova and Coimbra (four to five
hours). Pickups in Coimbra are available on
request.

Tuk a Day   Tours

(Map p229; ☑964 486 445, 962 826 855; per
person €15; ◷9am-7pm) Travellers love
these 1¼-hour tuk-tuk tours of Coimbra.
The multilingual drivers know their stuff
and are highly entertaining guides. Tours
(minimum three people) begin at Largo
da Portagem.

SHOPPING

Carlos Tomás   Ceramics

(Map p229; ☑239 812 945; carlostomas_
ceramicaartesanal@hotmail.com; Largo da Sé
Velha 4; ◷9am-8pm) Lovely hand-painted
ceramics by Senhor Tomás. If you can't
find anything from the stacks of mugs,
jars, plates tiles, objets d'art on sale,
he can do custom-made orders to your
designs.

Anthrop   Design

(Map p229; ☑963 705 464; www.facebook.com/
Anthrop.portugal; Rua Fernandes Tomás 2-6;
◷11am-7.30pm Mon-Fri, 2-7.30pm Sat) Ceramicist Célia Guerreiro set up this welcoming
shop to promote Portuguese designers.

Sé Nova (p231)

Jardim Botânico (p231)

The result is a browser's delight, with a small but curated selection of clothes, homewares, artisanal jewellery, handcrafted bags and original soaps, some made from olive oil and goat's milk.

Concept Store
Concept Store

(Map p229; ☑239 092 989; www.facebook.com/coimbraconceptstore; Av Sá da Bandeira 116; ⊙10am-8pm Mon-Sat) This laid-back store, attractively housed in a tall townhouse, provides a showcase for a range of Portuguese designers. Each room is given over to a different brand, with wares covering everything from stylish crockery to vintage sunglasses, footwear and retro fashions.

Comur
Food

(Map p229; www.comur.com; Largo da Portagem 25; ⊙10am-10pm) Canned fish becomes baroque art at this bright, hard-to-miss shop. The interior, a blast of kitsch gold, camp frescoes and red carpet, is crammed with elaborately designed cans of sardines and all manner of preserved fish. But while the packaging is gleefully over-the-top, the produce is high quality, produced at the historic Comur cannery near Aveiro.

EATING

Coimbra is packed with restaurants, bars, cafes and takeaways catering to all budgets. Hotspots include the area between Praça do Comércio and Coimbra A train station, which is full of characterful, old-school Portuguese eateries, and the upper town, which boasts a number of contemporary tapas-style places.

Justiça e Paz
Cafeteria €

(Map p229; ☑239 822 483; www.justicaepaz. com/restaurante-e-bar.php; Rua de Couraça de Lisboa 30; fixed-price menus €5.50-7; ⊙8.30am-11.30pm Mon-Fri, 9am-7pm Sat) Part of the university's Law Faculty, this busy cafeteria is one of Coimbra's best-kept secrets. An excellent option for the budget traveller, it's open to everyone and serves a selection of daily dishes, cheap snacks and drinks. Best of all, it has a lovely sun terrace with views over the city's botanic garden.

MARCIN JAMKOWSKI/ADVENTURE PICTURES/ALAMY STOCK PHOTO ©

Café Santa Cruz

Loggia
Modern Portuguese €€

(Map p229; ☑239 853 076; www.loggia.pt; Largo Dr José Rodrigues, Museu Nacional de Machado de Castro; mains €13-18; ☉10am-6pm Tue & Sun, to 10.30pm Wed-Sat) As much as its confident modern cuisine, the Loggia's big draw is its setting, on a panoramic terrace overlooking the old town. There's open-air seating for romantic sunset dinners or you can sit inside and admire the views from its glass-walled dining room. Its lunch buffet (€9.50) is great value.

Sete
Restaurante
Modern Portuguese €€

(Map p229; ☑239 060 065; www.facebook.com/seterestaurante; Rua Dr. Martins de Carvalho 10; mains €11-19; ☉1-4pm & 7pm-midnight Wed-Mon) Squeezed into a corner behind the **Igreja de Santa Cruz** (Map p229; Praça 8 de Maio; adult/child €3/free; ☉9.30am-4.30pm Mon-Sat, 1-5pm Sun), this intimate restaurant is one of the most popular in town. Its casual wine-bar vibe, personable service and modern take on Portuguese cuisine ensure it's almost always buzzing. Book ahead to avoid disappointment.

Tapas Nas Costas
Tapas €€

(Map p229; ☑239 157 425; Rua Quebra Costas 19; tapas €4-7.50; ☉11am-midnight Tue-Sat, to 4pm Sun) All the rage right now, this sophisticated tapas restaurant boasts a prime location on the steep steps up the historic centre. Refined decor and friendly service set the tone for fine Portuguese wines and gourmet tapas such as *costeletinhas de borrego* (lamb chops with honey and almonds). Reservations a must.

Zé Manel dos Ossos
Portuguese €€

(Map p229; ☑239 823 790; Beco do Forno 12; mains €8-16; ☉12.30-3pm & 7.30-10pm Mon-Sat) Tucked down a nondescript alley, this hole-in-the-wall gem, papered with scholarly doodles and scribbled poems, is much loved for its hearty meat specialities. Typical of its culinary approach is *feijoada de jovali*, a thick casserole of wild boar, beans and black pudding. Come early or be prepared to wait in line.

Restaurante Zé Neto
Portuguese €€

(Map p229; ☑239 826 786; Rua das Azeiteiras 8; mains €7-14; ☉noon-3pm & 7-11pm Mon-Sat)

This marvellous family-run place specialises in homemade Portuguese standards such as *chanfana* (goat) cooked in red wine and *dobrada* (tripe) served with beans and rice. It's well known locally and fills quickly, particularly at weekends when you'd do well to make a booking.

A Cozinha da Maria Tasca **€€**

(Map p229; ☎968 650 253; www.facebook.com/cozinhadamaria/; Rua das Azeiteiras 65; mains €10-15; ⏲noon-3pm & 7-11pm) With its low wood-beamed ceiling, tiled walls and rustic decor, this is the very picture of a traditional backstreet *tasca* (tavern). In keeping with the look, the cuisine is orthodox, featuring much-loved classics such as fortifying *chanfana* (goat stew) and *bacalhau à brás* (fried flaked cod).

DRINKING & NIGHTLIFE

Coimbra has some action-packed bars. In the old town, around Praça da Sé Velha, students spill on to the cobblestones outside classic pubs, while the area around Praça da República is chock-full of bars, cafes and clubs.

Café Santa Cruz Cafe

(Map p229; ☎239 833 617; www.cafesantacruz.com; Praça 8 de Maio; ⏲7am-2am) Coimbra's historic showpiece cafe is set in a beautiful high-vaulted former chapel, with stained-glass windows and graceful stone arches. Outside, a terrace grants lovely views over Praça 8 de Maio. Don't miss the *crúzios*, egg- and almond-based conventual cakes for which the cafe is famous.

Popular with tourists and locals alike, the cafe also has regular free fado.

Galeria Santa Clara Bar

(☎239 441 657; www.galeriasantaclara.com; Rua António Augusto Gonçalves 67; ⏲2pm-2am Sun-Thu, to 3am Fri & Sat) Arty tea room by day and chilled-out bar by night, this is a terrific place to hang out. Inside, it's all mismatched vintage furniture, books and chandeliers while out back the garden terrace boasts lovely views back over the river to the historic centre. The atmosphere is laid-back and can feel like a house party when things get going.

Fado singing in Coimbra
SERGIO AZENHA/ALAMY STOCK PHOTO ©

Lyrical Coimbra Fado

If Lisbon represents the heart of Portuguese fado music, Coimbra is the head. The 19th-century university was male-only so the town's womenfolk, immortalised in song as *tricanas*, were of great interest to the student body. Coimbra fado developed partly as a way of communicating with these heavily chaperoned females, usually in the form of serenades sung under bedroom windows. For this reason, fado is traditionally sung only by men, who must be students or ex-students.

The Coimbra style is considered more lyrical and pure than the Lisbon variety, even if it has absorbed musical influences from across Portugal and the Portuguese-speaking world. It ranges from hauntingly beautiful serenades and lullabies to more boisterous drinking-type songs. The singer is normally accompanied by a 12-string *guitarra* (Portegese guitar) and perhaps also a Spanish (classical) guitar. Due to the clandestine nature of these bedroom-window concerts, audience appreciation is traditionally indicated by softly coughing rather than clapping.

Aqui Base Tango Bar

(Map p229; ☎916 882 731; www.facebook.com/aquibasetango; Rua Venâncio Rodrigues 8;

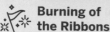

Burning of the Ribbons

In the first week of May, Coimbra celebrates the end of the academic year with the **Queima das Fitas** (www.facebook.com/queimadasfitascoimbra; ☺May). This bacchanalian week-long party takes its name – literally the 'Burning of the Ribbons' – from the student custom of ritually torching the colour-coded ribbons they wear to represent their faculties.

Festivities kick off at midnight on the first Friday with the Serenata Monumental, a hauntingly beautiful fado performance on the steps of the Sé Velha (p230). The program continues with sports events, black-tie balls, concerts at the so-called Queimodromo across the Ponte de Santa Clara, and a beer-soaked parade called the Cortejo dos Grelados from the university down to Largo da Portagem.

Student at Queima das Fitas
SERGIO AZENHA/ALAMY STOCK PHOTO ©

☺4pm-6am Mon-Sat) This offbeat house is one of Coimbra's most enticing hangouts, a quirky space with original decor and a relaxed, inclusive vibe. Music ranges from jazz to alternative rock and there's always something going on. It's gay-friendly, too. Check its Facebook page for upcoming events.

AAC Bar
Bar

(Bar Associação Académica de Coimbra; Map p229; www.facebook.com/baraac; Rua Padre António Vieira 1; ☺10am-4am Mon-Fri, from 3pm Sat & Sun) Join the black-caped students at their union bar, where beers are cheap and everyone is welcome. The esplanade out back, with wood decking and a grassy lawn, makes an agreeable refuge.

Bar Quebra Costas
Bar

(Map p229; ☎239 841 174; Rua Quebra Costas 45; ☺noon-3am Mon-Sat, to 9pm Sun) This Coimbra classic has a sunny, cobbled terrace, an artsy interior, friendly service, and a chilled-out jazzy soundtrack. It's perfectly placed for people-watching over an ice-cold beer after a day pounding the streets.

✪ ENTERTAINMENT

Á Capella
Fado

(Map p229; ☎239 833 985; www.acapella.com.pt; Rua do Corpo de Deus; entry with/without drink €10/5; ☺7pm-2am, shows 9.30pm) A 14th-century chapel turned intimate cocktail lounge, this place hosts nightly performances by the city's most renowned fado musicians. Shows cater directly to a tourist crowd, but the music is excellent and the intimate setting creates a wonderful atmosphere, abetted by heart-rendingly good acoustics.

Fado ao Centro
Fado

(Map p229; ☎239 837 060; www.fadoaocentro.com; Rua Quebra Costas 7; show incl drink €10; ☺show 6pm) At the bottom of the old town, this friendly cultural centre is a good place to acquaint yourself with fado. The evening 6pm show includes plenty of explanation, in Portuguese and English, about the history of the music and the meaning of each song. It's tourist-oriented, but the performers enjoy it and do it well.

You can chat with the musicians afterwards over a glass of port (included with your ticket).

Teatro Académico de Gil Vicente
Theatre, Concert Venue

(TAGV; Map p229; ☎239 855 630; www.tagv.pt; Praça da República; ☺box office 5-10pm Mon-Sat) This university-run auditorium is an important venue, staging a varied program of theatre, cinema, dance and music.

Mondego River, Coimbra

🛈 INFORMATION

Turismo Largo da Portagem (Map p229; ☏239 488 120; www.turismodecoimbra.pt; Largo da Portagem; ⊙9am-6pm Mon-Fri, 9.30am-1pm & 2-5.30pm Sat & Sun), Coimbra's main tourist office, can provide information on the city and surrounding areas. **Turismo Praça República** (Map p229; ☏939 010 084; www.turismode coimbra.pt; Praça da República; ⊙9.30am-6pm Mon-Fri) is another handy spot for info.

🛈 GETTING THERE & AWAY

The **bus station** (Av Fernão de Magalhães; ⊙ticket office 8am-10pm) is a 15-minute walk northwest of the centre. **Rede Expressos** (☏239 855 270; www.rede-expressos.pt) runs buses to Lisbon, Porto, Braga and other destinations.

Long-distance trains stop only at Coimbra B station, north of the city. Cross the platform for quick, free connections to more-central Coimbra A.

🛈 GETTING AROUND

Half-lift, half-funicular, the two-part **Elevador do Mercado** (Largo do Mercado; ticket €1.60; ⊙7.30am-9pm Mon-Sat, 10am-9pm Sun) whisks you up from the lower new town to the university district.

Useful routes include bus 27, 28 and 28 from Coimbra B train station to Praça República via the main bus station.

Tickets can be bought on board (€1.60), at the **SMTUC office** (www.smtuc.pt; Largo do Mercado; ⊙7am-7pm Mon-Fri, 8am-1pm Sat) by the Elevador, at official kiosks, and at some *tabacarias* (tobacconists-newsagents).

Bike and electronic bikes are available to rent from **By Bike** (☏919 080 216; www.facebook. com/bybikecoimbra; bike per hr/half-day/day €5/10/15, E-bikes €10/20/30).

AVEIRO

Aveiro at a Glance...

Situated on the edge of an extensive coastal lagoon system, Aveiro (uh-vey-roo) is a prosperous town with a good-looking centre and a youthful, energetic buzz. It's occasionally dubbed the Venice of Portugal thanks to its small network of picturesque canals. But where the Italian city has gondolas, Aveiro has moliceiros – colourful boats traditionally used for seaweed-harvesting but now used for canal cruises.

There are several beaches within easy striking distance and the nearby São Jacinto nature reserve provides walking and birdwatching – Aveiro's name is possibly derived from the Latin aviarium (place of birds).

Two Days in Aveiro

The first thing you'll probably want to do is hop on board a *moliceiro* for a laid-back tour (p242). Spend the rest of the day exploring the old centre or sampling the town's traditional sweets – *ovos moles*. Spend day two in the town's museums, shopping and enjoying Aveiro's mouthwatering seafood.

Four Days in Aveiro

Spend day three taking a trip to the **Museu Marítimo de Ílhavo** (p244), 8km south of Aveiro, which delves into Portugal's maritime history. On day four, go for a walk amid dunes and forest, followed by some downtime on a pretty beach at the **Reserva Natural das Dunas de São Jacinto** (p246).

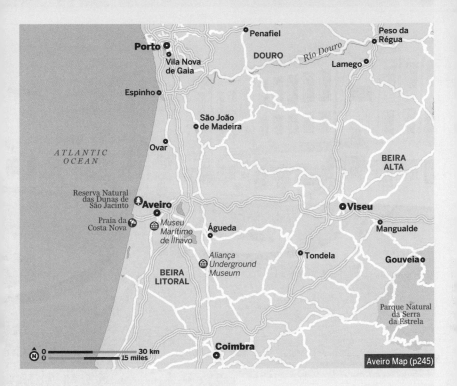

Aveiro Map (p245)

Arriving in Aveiro

Train Aveiro is within Porto's *urbano* network, which means there are commuter trains at least every half hour (€3.50, one hour). There are also at least hourly trains to Coimbra (from €5.20, 30 to 60 minutes) and Lisbon (€26.70, two hours).

Bus Rede Expresso has services to/ from Lisbon (€16, three to four hours, six to 12 daily) and Coimbra (€6, 45 minutes, four daily).

Where to Stay

Hotels are dotted around the outer edge of the town centre, though there are few beds in the historical centre. A couple of more upmarket places offer river views. Many tackle Aveiro as a day trip from elsewhere, including Porto and Coimbra. While you'll rarely have problems securing a room, it pays to book ahead for the busy summer holidays.

Moliceiros on the canal

ACNAKELSY/GETTY IMAGES ©

Boat Trips

At the top of every Aveiro itinerary is a tour on the town's traditional, brightly decorated seaweed-harvesting boats. These relaxing trips head along the river and each boat has a guide on board.

Great For...

☑ **Don't Miss**

The brightly painted prows of the *moliceiros* – some of which tend toward rather racy themes.

Story of the Moliceiro

Aveiro's *moliceiros* date from the 19th century and were originally used to gather seaweed from the bottom of the canals. This gooey mess was spread out on threshing floors to dry, and used as fertiliser on the poor soil that farmers worked around the town. With the development and introduction of chemical fertilisers over the course of the 20th century, the demand for this natural product declined and the boat owners slowly transformed their craft into a tourist attraction. The boats themselves are still made and repaired in the traditional way. As in the olden days, the bow and stern are brightly painted, most often today with some naughty seaside scene, oddly resembling Britain's 'dirty' postcards – some of the images are rather risqué. Each boat seats

PAUL BIRIS/GETTY IMAGES ©

❶ Need to Know

Tickets cost €10. Boats leave every 30 minutes and tours take 45 minutes.

✕ Take a Break

There are numerous cafes lining the riverfront. A seafood lunch at Maré Cheia (p247) continues the nautical theme.

★ Top Tip

All the boat companies (around 10 of them) charge the same amount.

around 20 to 30 people on benches along both sides, and the ride, powered these days by diesel motor, is smooth.

Boat Trips

There are around 10 companies offering *moliceiro* rides, all of them gathered around the bridge over the Canal Central, between the main bus stop and the big Fórum Aveiro shopping mall. Touts try to lure you into their boats, but as all charge the same fare (€10 for adults, €5 for children), condition of the craft, the friendliness of the boatsmen and extras such as welcome drinks come before cost when choosing which outfit to go with.

Tours run around every 30 minutes and the 45-minute cruises explore the town's system of canals. The boatsmen usually double up as guides and are surprisingly

clued up when it comes to Aveiro's history. If you are really fortunate, they may even burst into song. Contact the Regional Turismo (p248) for a rundown of the companies offering *moliceiro* trips. A few reliable favourites include **Viva a Ria** (Map p245; ☑969 008 687; www.vivaaria.com; adult/child €10/5) and **Aveitour** (Map p245; ☑916 658 100; www.aveitour.com; ⊘boat tour adult/child €10/5).

The Canals

Describing Aveiro as the 'Portuguese Venice' might be a slight exaggeration, but the canals and gondola-like *moliceiros* passing beneath the small footbridges that span them certainly create a vaguely similar scene. Canal Central is Aveiro's Grand Canal, with others such as the Canal do Coio, the Canal de São Roque and Canal do Paraiso extending from it. These canals are man-made and were built when the town was cut off from the lagoon by shifting sandbanks.

◉ SIGHTS

Aliança Underground Museum
Museum, Winery

(📞234 732 045, 916 482 226; www.bacalhoa.
pt; Rua do Comércio 444, Sangalhos; guided tour
€3; ◷tours 10am, 11.30am, 2.30pm, 4pm) Between Aveiro and Coimbra, in the village of
Sangalhos in the Bairrada wine-producing
region, this magnificent place is part *adega*
(winery), part art museum. Guided tours
take you beneath the winery to a vast 1.5km
network of tunnels housing an extraordinary collection of African and Portuguese
art. Also down here are cellars crammed
with huge oak barrels of maturing wines
and brandies.

Exhibit highlights include a haunting
collection of funerary objects from the Niger
and a marvellous selection of contemporary
Zimbabwean shona sculpture. Other key
'stops' – maps of the museum are set out
like the London Underground – are the fossil
and mineral collections, and the display of
Portuguese ceramics. These include a range
of azulejos (hand-painted tiles) and quirky
animals by former ceramics company Bordallo Pinheiro (still an icon in Portugal).

The scale of the wine production is
also impressive – the largest oak barrels,
all specially made on-site, are capable of
holding up to 17,000 litres of brandy.

Tours, which must be booked in advance,
are available in English, Spanish, French and
German, and include a glass of sparkling
wine.

Museu de Aveiro/ Santa Joana
Museum

(Map p245; 📞234 423 297; www.facebook.
com/museuaveiro; Avenida Santa Joana; adult/
child €5/free; ◷10am-12.30pm & 1.30-6pm
Tue-Sun) This fine museum, housed in the
15th-century Mosteiro de Jesus, owes its
finest treasures to Princesa Joana (later
canonised), daughter of Afonso V. In 1472,
11 years after the convent was founded,
Joana 'retired' here and, though forbidden to take full vows, she stayed until her
death in 1490. Her tomb, a 17th-century
masterpiece of inlaid marble mosaic,
takes centre stage in a lavishly decorated
room (the remodelled lower choir stalls),

African art at Aliança Underground Museum

SERGIO AZENHA/ALAMY STOCK PHOTO ©

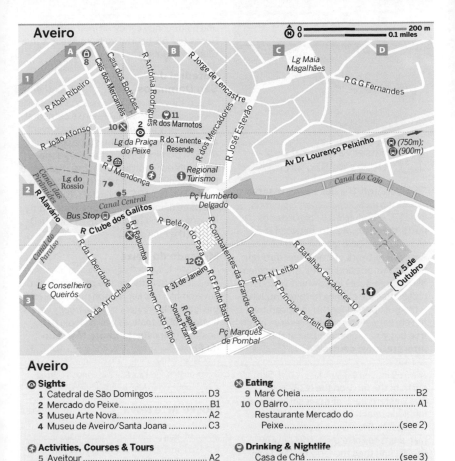

Aveiro

Sights
1 Catedral de São Domingos	D3
2 Mercado do Peixe	B1
3 Museu Arte Nova	A2
4 Museu de Aveiro/Santa Joana	C3

Activities, Courses & Tours
5 Aveitour	A2
6 Oficina do Doce	B2
7 Viva a Ria	A2

Shopping
8 Cais à Porta	A1

Eating
9 Maré Cheia	B2
10 O Bairro	A1
Restaurante Mercado do Peixe	(see 2)

Drinking & Nightlife
Casa de Chá	(see 3)
11 Má Ideia	B1

Entertainment
12 Teatro Aveirense	B3

while an adjacent gold-leafed chapel displays *azulejos* (hand-painted tiles) depicting her life.

Museu Marítimo de Ílhavo Museum
(☑234 329 990; www.museumaritimo.cm-ilhavo. pt; Avenida Dr Rocha Madahil, Ílhavo; adult/child €6/3; ☺10am-6pm Tue-Sat, 2-6pm Sun) The wonderful Museu Marítimo de Ílhavo is in a modern, award-winning building in the town of Ílhavo, 8km south of Aveiro. It covers the history of Portugal's maritime identity, from cod fishing (with superb fishing vessels from the 19th and 20th centuries) to oil paintings on the bows of the *moliceiros*. A highlight is the codfish *(bacalhau)* aquarium, showcasing the Atlantic cod, which the Portuguese have been fishing (and munching on) for centuries.

 Reserva Natural das Dunas de São Jacinto

This gloriously tranquil nature **reserve** (www.natural.pt/portal/en/Infraestrutura/Item/176; ☉9am-1pm & 2-5pm) extends north from São Jacinto, between the sea and the placid lagoon west of Aveiro. A network of trails runs through the pine woods and dunes, including an 8km (three-hour) loop, whilst various hides offer the chance for birdwatching – the best period for this is November to February. Access to the reserve is free but you should register at the **interpretative centre** (📞960 335 438, 234 331 282; www.icnf.pt; Estrada Nacional 327; ☉9am-1pm & 2-5pm Mon-Sat) 1.5km north of the ferry on the N327 road. The western flank of the reserve has a fabulous beach.

To get to the reserve from Aveiro, take a bus to Forte da Barra (return €5.05) and then the ferry to São Jacinto (return passenger/car €3.30/9.30). Check schedules at www.aveirobus.pt. By car, you can avoid the ferry by circumnavigating the lagoon and approaching from the north, but it's a much longer journey.

WESTEND61/GETTY IMAGES ©

Praia da Costa Nova   Beach
The closest beaches to Aveira are the surfing hangouts of **Praia da Barra** and **Costa Nova**, 13km west of Aveiro. Both are developed and busy in summer but Costa Nova is the prettier of the two with its beachside strip of cafes, kitsch gift shops and picturesque candy-striped cottages. Buses (€2.55, hourly) go from Aveiro's Rua Clube dos Galitos.

Catedral de São Domingos   Cathedral
(Map p245; www.paroquiagloria.org; Rua Batalhão Caçadores 10; ☉9am-7pm) Aveiro's cathedral was formerly part of a Dominican convent and contains a Manueline stone cross of Saint Domingo. The cathedral's sober white interior contrasts with the impressive facade centred on a portal flanked by two pairs of unusual Doric pilasters. Note also the three figures – Faith, Hope and Charity – along with the coat of arms of Infante D Pedro (the King's son).

Mercado do Peixe   Market
(Map p245; Largo da Praça do Peixe; ☉7am-1pm Tue-Sat) Right in the centre of town, Aveiro's covered fish market is a fun place to watch the local fishmongers sell their daily wares. If you want to taste as well as look, head upstairs to the **Restaurante Mercado do Peixe** (Map p245; 📞234 351 303; www.restaurantemercadodopeixeaveiro.pt; Largo da Praça do Peixe; mains €12-22; ☉noon-3pm & 7.30-11pm, closed Mon & Sun dinner).

Museu Arte Nova   Museum
(Map p245; 📞234 406 485; http://mca.cm-aveiro.pt; Rua Dr Barbosa de Magalhães 9; adult/child €2/free; ☉10am-12.30pm & 1.30-6pm Tue-Sun) Set in Aveiro's most eye-catching art nouveau building, this small museum above a cafe has a modest one-room exhibition on art nouveau design and architecture. Larger temporary displays rotate every three months. Ask for the multilingual brochures detailing all the town's art nouveau highlights, or better still, the audio guides in Portuguese, English and Spanish outlining the same (€10 deposit).

🏃 ACTIVITIES
Several companies run canal trips in *moliceiros*. You'll find them pitching for business down by the central canal.

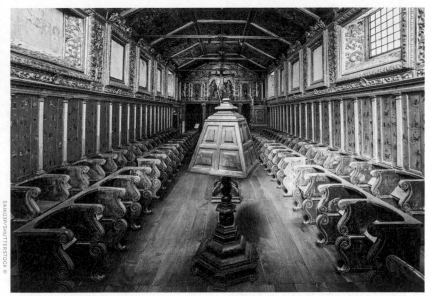

SAIKO3P/SHUTTERSTOCK ©

Museu de Aveiro/Santa Joana (p244)

Oficina do Doce   Food

(Map p245; ☑234 098 840; www.oficinado
doce.com; Rua João Mendonça 23; tours adult/
child €2.75/1.75; ⊗9am 7pm) Part living
museum, part workshop, Oficina do Doce
introduces visitors to Aveiro's proudest
culinary tradition – *ovos moles*, eggy,
sugary sweets originally developed by
local nuns. You can watch as modern-day
confectioners work their magic, or learn
about the process first-hand by filling
your own. Reserve your visit (tours are 45
minutes) by visiting the premises, or book
through the website.

O Cicerone   Walking

(☑234 094 074; www.o-cicerone-tour.com; from
per person €22.50) Year-round, O Cicerone
leads various (half- and full-day) walking
tours in Aveiro and surrounds.

🔒 SHOPPING

Cais à Porta   Concept Store

(Map p245; ☑234 063 085; www.facebook.com/
caisaporta; Cais das Falcoeiras 6; ⊗10am-8pm)

This warehouse concept store down by the
canalside is a browsers delight. Carrying
a selection of Portuguese brands and
artisanal wares, it stocks everything from
men's shirts and sun specs to frocks, bags,
costume jewellery, shoes, original prints
and locally-distilled liqueurs. It's well worth
searching out.

✖ EATING

There are plenty of appealing restaurants
and eateries dotted around town, many
specialising in fresh seafood. Another
local speciality are *ovos moles*, crisp wafer
parcels filled with a sticky-sweet egg-yolk-
and-sugar mix.

A Peixaria   Seafood €€

(☑234 331 165; www.restauranteapeixaria.
pt; Rua Mestre Jorge Pestana, São Jacinto;
mains €14-18; ⊗noon-3pm & 7-10pm Tue-Sun)
It might not be the easiest to get to, but
there's never a shortage of diners at this
no-frills fish restaurant, reckoned by many
to be the best in the area. Situated a block

back from the waterfront in São Jacinto, it specialises in locally-caught Atlantic fish, served fresh and simply cooked.

Maré Cheia
Seafood €€

(Map p245; Rua José Rabumba 8-12; mains €14-35; ⊙noon-3pm & 7-10.30pm Thu-Tue) *Maré cheia* means 'high tide' in Portuguese, but *cheia* (full) applies equally to this popular seafood eatery. You'll often have to elbow your way through a crowd of locals just to get your name on the waiting list. Its giant seafood platters are magnificent, or try the local *enguias* (eels), served fried, grilled or *caldeirada* (stewed).

O Bairro
Portuguese €€

(Map p245; ☑234 338 567; www.obairro.pt; Largo da Praça do Peixe 24; mains €15-22; ⊙12.30-3pm & 7.30-11pm Thu-Sun) Classic Portuguese cuisine gets a fusion makeover at this smart tiled eatery near the fish market. Bag a table in the spacious, light-filled interior and go for innovative dishes such as tiger prawns *(camarão)* served with lime and risotto, or lamb *(cordeiro)* with a pistachio crust.

🍷 DRINKING & NIGHTLIFE

A big student population and summer-holiday crowds make for a raucous nightlife. Action radiates out from Largo da Praça do Peixe, with several bars clustered on Rua do Tenente Resende.

Casa de Chá
Bar

(Map p245; Rua Dr Barbosa de Magalhães 9; ⊙10am-2am Tue-Fri, 12.30pm-3am Sat, 12.30-9pm Sun; 🛜) With its elegant walled courtyard and classy location in Aveiro's landmark art nouveau building, this cafe absolutely looks the part. Stop by for tea and a snack during the day or come late for cocktails and *caipirinhas* (national cocktail of Brazil, made with cachaça, limes, sugar). It's at its liveliest on warm summer nights.

Má Ideia
Craft Beer

(Map p245; www.facebook.com/maideia.aveiro; Rua dos Marnotos 56; ⊙3pm-2am) With books to browse, art on the walls and a laid-back cafe vibe, this is the place for craft beer in Aveiro. Choose from the selection of

Museu Arte Nova (p246)

Praia da Costa Nova (p245)

international guest beers, lovingly curated by the knowledgeable English-speaking owner, and settle down for an evening's tasting. Also serves tapas-style food.

⭐ ENTERTAINMENT

Teatro Aveirense Theatre

(Map p245; ☎234 400 920; www.teatro aveirense.pt; Rua Belém do Para; ⊙box office 9.30am-12.30pm & 2-6pm Mon-Fri, 2-6pm Sat) Celebrating more than 125 years at the heart of Aveiro's cultural scene, this historic theatre stages regular concerts, dance performances and theatre shows.

ℹ INFORMATION

Regional Turismo (Map p245; ☎234 420 760; www.turismodocentro.pt; Rua João Mendonça 8;

⊙9am-7pm Mon-Fri, to 6pm Sat & Sun Jun-Sep, 9am-6pm Mon-Fri, 9.30am-1pm & 2-5.30pm Sat & Sun Oct-May) In an art nouveau building on the main canal. Has town maps and information on Portugal's central region.

ℹ GETTING THERE & AWAY

Catch buses at the **stop** (Map p245) on Rua Clube dos Galitos or the **bus station** east of the centre. **Rede Expresso** (☎234 383 479; www.rede-expressos.pt) has services to/from Lisbon (€16, three to four hours, six to 12 daily) and Coimbra (€6, 45 minutes, four daily).

Trains run frequently to Porto (€3.50, one hour), plus hourly to Coimbra.

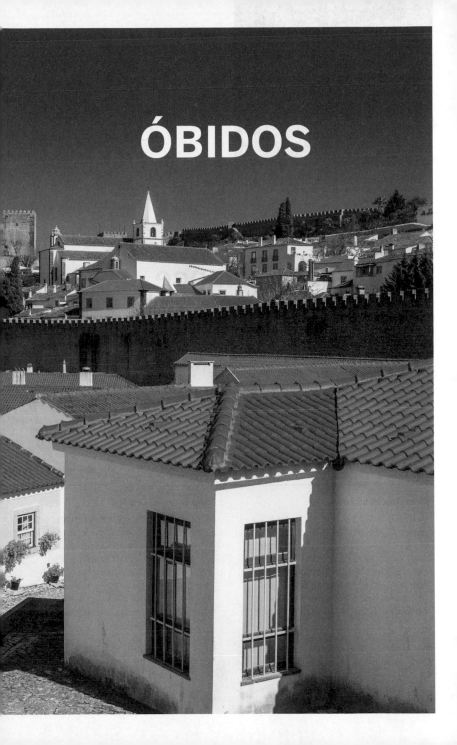

ÓBIDOS

Óbidos at a Glance...

Surrounded by a classic crenellated wall, Óbidos' gorgeous historic centre is a labyrinth of cobblestoned streets and flower-bedecked, whitewashed houses livened up with dashes of vivid yellow and blue paint. It's a delightful place to pass an afternoon, but there are plenty of reasons to stay overnight, as there's excellent accommodation, including a hilltop castle now converted into one of Portugal's most luxurious pousadas (upmarket inns).

Hill-town aficionados looking to savour Óbidos' 'lost in time' qualities may find the main street ridiculously touristy, especially on weekends and during festivals. There are pretty bits outside the walls too.

One Day in Óbidos

With just a day to spare in Óbidos, exploring the old centre should be your top priority. The town's top sights are without doubt the Castelo, the walls and the aqueduct but the **Igreja de Santa Maria** (p255), the **Museu Municipal** (p255) and the **Santuário do Senhor da Pedra** (p255) are also worth a visit.

Two Days in Óbidos

With a second day in the region, consider heading to the coast to catch some rays (and perhaps go surfing) at the gorgeous beaches of **Peniche** (p258) and **Baleal** (p258). Alternatively soak up the atmosphere of this wonderful spot, dipping in and out of the boutiques, bookshops and cafes as you go.

Previous page: Aerial view of Óbidos
SLAVKO SEREDA/SHUTTERSTOCK ©

Óbidos Historic Centre

Arriving in Óbidos

Bus stop On the main road just outside Porta da Vila. There are frequent buses to Lisbon and coastal destinations like Peniche.

Train station Handles trains to Lisbon, with at least six departures daily. The station is located outside the north-eastern section of the castle walls. It's a pretty but uphill walk to town.

Where to Stay

Although touristy, Óbidos has an excellent array of accommodation, from an atmospheric *pousada* to cosy guest houses and some cutting-edge boutique hotels. It's also possible to base yourself elsewhere and visit on a day trip (Lisbon is about a one-hour drive to the south).

Óbidos Castelo

TAROMON/SHUTTERSTOCK ©

Óbidos Historic Centre

Aimless wandering is a delight in walled Óbidos, but the town does have some very worthwhile attractions. You'll need to be fit as there's a lot of climbing involved.

Great For...

☑ Don't Miss

A scenic walk along the town walls with views over the bucolic countryside beyond the village roofs.

Castelo, Walls & Aqueduct

If you've got the legs for it, you can take a stroll around the unprotected *muro* (wall) for uplifting views over the town and surrounding countryside. The walls date from Moorish times though they have been restored since; the *castelo* (castle) itself is one of Dom Dinis' 13th-century creations. It's a stern edifice, with lots of towers, battlements and big gates. It was converted into a palace in the 16th century (some Manueline touches add levity) but today it serves as a deluxe hotel, the **Pousada do Castelo** (📞210 407 630; www.pousadas.pt; Paço Real; d/ste from €200/320; ❄️📶).

The impressive 3km-long aqueduct, southeast of the main gate, dates from the 16th century. Unlike other aqueducts in Portugal, Óbidos' is fully intact and in remarkably serviceable condition. It once

Igreja de Santa Maria

BPPERRY/GETTY IMAGES ©

Museu Municipal

Located in an 18th-century manor house next to Igreja de Santa Maria, the town's **museum** (Rua Direita 97; ☉10am-1pm & 2-6pm Tue-Sun) **FREE** houses a small collection of paintings spanning several centuries. The highlight is Josefa de Obides' haunting portrait, *Beneficiado Faustino das Neves* (1670), remarkable for its dramatic use of light and shade.

Santuário do Senhor da Pedra

Below town this imposing, if a little ramshackle, **church** (Largo do Santuário; ☉9am-12.30pm & 2.30-7pm Tue-Sun May-Sep, to 5pm Oct-Apr) **FREE** is an 18th-century baroque gem in need of some tender loving care. It's worth the stroll down here for the unusual hexagonal interior; in the altar is the stone sculpture of Christ crucified that gives the place its name.

provided water to the town's fountains as well as drinking water to its residents.

Igreja de Santa Maria

The town's elegant main **church** (Praça de Santa Maria; ☉9.30am-12.30pm & 2.30-7pm summer, to 5pm winter), near the northern end of Rua Direita, stands out for its interior, with a wonderful painted ceiling and walls done up in beautiful blue-and-white 17th-century *azulejos* (hand-painted tiles). Paintings by the renowned 17th-century painter Josefa de Óbidos are to the right of the altar. There's a fine 16th-century Renaissance tomb on the left, probably carved by French sculptor Nicolas Chanterène. The church is closed on Mondays.

History

When Dom Dinis first showed Óbidos to his wife Dona Isabel in 1228, it must have already been a pretty sight because she fell instantly in love with the place. The king decided to make the town a wedding gift to his queen, initiating a royal tradition that lasted until the 19th century.

Any grace it had in 1228 must be credited to the Moors, who had laid out the streets and had only recently abandoned the strategic heights. The Moors had chased out the Visigoths, who in turn had evicted the Romans, who also had a fortress here.

◉ SIGHTS

Bacalhôa
Buddha Eden   Sculpture, Gardens
(www.buddhaeden.com; Quinta dos Loridos, Carvalhal; €5; ⊙9am-6pm) What have the Taliban got to do with a rural winery 12km south of Óbidos? Well, when they blew up the Buddhas of Bamiyan in Afghanistan in 2001, the millionaire art collector José Berardo was so incensed at the wanton destruction of culture that he decided to do something to balance it out and created a large sculpture park on the grounds of his winery. The result, Bacalhôa Buddha Eden, is an astonishing sight.

The wildly out-of-place, thoroughly fascinating park features monumental Buddhist statues standing proudly above the cork trees, a phalanx of electric blue terracotta warriors looking down on a duck-filled lake, modern contemporary sculpture among the vines, and a little tourist train (adult/child €4/free) doing the rounds for the sore-of-foot. It's a great place to relax, and there's a cafe here, as well as a wine shop. To make a day of it, there's an appealing restaurant in the nearby village – **Mãe d'Água** (www.restaurantemaedagua. com; Rua 13 Maio 26, Sobral do Parelhão; mains €10.50-16.50; ⊙noon-4pm & 7pm-late Tue-Sun) does confident modern Portuguese fare in a contemporary setting within a noble old building.

To get here, take the A8 motorway south from Óbidos and exit at junction 12, then follow signs for Carvalhal.

ⓐ SHOPPING

Olaria São Pedro   Ceramics
(www.olariaspedro.com; Travessia São Pedro 2; ⊙9am-8pm Jul & Aug, to 6.30pm Sep-Jun) The original of two shops showcasing Caldas da Rainha–based ceramicist Sónia Borga's contemporary, distinctly unkitschy ceramic, pottery, porcelain and jewellery designs that stand out amid a sea of typical tourist wares – the other is in **Sintra** (Map p93; www.olariaspedro.com; Rua Consiglieri Pedroso 9; ⊙9.30am-7pm). Buy something here you won't regret a year down the road.

Bacalhôa Buddha Eden

Livraria de Santiago   Books

(Largo de São Tiago do Castelo; ⊙10am-1pm & 2-7pm) This bookstore managed by the Ler Devagar chain uniquely occupies the 18th-century São Tiago church, originally built in 1186 but rebuilt in 1772 after it was destroyed by the devastating Lisbon earthquake. Upstairs, Peniche bobbin lacemaker and poet Natália Santos demonstrates her talents for visitors. English books (and Lonely Planet guides) available.

EATING

After years of catering to tourist crowds, Óbidos is trying to come into its own, though eating here remains an exercise in tourist trap evasion.

Senhor da Pedra   Portuguese €

(📞914 604 362; Largo do Santuário; mains €6-9.50; ⊙11.30am-10pm Mon-Sat, 11am-4pm Sun) Behind the striking church of Senhor da Pedra below town, this simple white-tiled eatery (the one on the right as you look at the row of restaurants) is a recommended place to try low-priced authentic Portuguese cuisine. It's a classic affair with mum in the kitchen and dad on the tables. Don't expect fast service.

Ja!mon Ja!mon   Portuguese €€

(📞916 208 162; Rua da Biquinha S/N; mains €10-14; ⊙noon-3pm & 7-10pm Tue-Sat, noon-3pm Sun) With the cheery Andre, his family and a young, enthusiastic staff at the helm, the hospitality is oh-so Portuguese (read: happy and generous) at this excellent *tasca* (tavern) featuring a wonderful terrace with lush hillside views.

Poço dos Sabores   Portuguese €€

(📞262 950 086; www.facebook.com/poco dossabores; Rua Principal 83B, Usseira; mains €13-22; ⊙12.30-2.30 & 7.30-10.15pm Tue-Sun Sep-Jun, 12.30-2.30pm Jul & Aug; 🔊) Ditch the tourist onslaught in Óbidos for this village charmer 5km away in Usseira, where Joaquim and sister Angela combine restaurant skills honed in France and Switzerland to create a modern Portuguese destination

Óbidos Festivals

Chocolate lovers, medieval fans and literary fiends shouldn't miss these annual events happening in tiny Óbidos.

The two-week **Mercado Medieval** (📞262 955 561; www.mercadomedieval obidos.pt; adult/child €7/free) includes live entertainment, jousting matches (yes, on horses!), plenty of grog and pigs roasting on spits, and the chance to try your hand at scaling the town walls with the help of a harness and rope. Get into the spirit of things by dressing in medieval attire!

Launched in 2015, **Folio** (Festival Literário Internacional de Óbidos; www. obidosvilaliteraria.com/folio-festival-literario-internacional-de-obidos; Sep-Oct) is a month-long literary festival that celebrates distinguished writers and poets, as well as artists and musicians, with readings and performances around town.

The **Festival Internacional do Chocolate** (📞262 955 561; www.festivalchocolate. cm-obidos.pt; adult/child €6.50/free; ⊙Mar/Apr; 👫) is a scrumptiously decadent celebration that draws over 200,000 people with events for every age and taste, including a kids' playhouse made entirely from chocolate.

Mercado Medieval
SHAUN EGAN/GETTY IMAGES ©

worth shuffling your itinerary around for. The decor is full of village character (walls stacked with memorabilia, bric-a-brac, arts and crafts). The food? At once classic but creative.

Peniche & Baleal

Popular for its long, fabulous town beach, nearby surf strands and also as a jumping-off point for the beautiful Ilhas Berlengas nature reserve, **Peniche** is spectacularly set on a headland surrounded by sea. It remains a working port, giving it a slightly grittier, more 'lived in' feel than its resort neighbours. The seaside **Fortaleza de Peniche** (☎262 780 116; Campo da República; ⏰9am-12.30pm & 2-5.30pm Tue-Fri, from 10am Sat & Sun) **FREE**, where Salazar's regime detained political prisoners, is a must-see for anyone interested in Portuguese history

Outdoors enthusiasts will love the beaches and the spectacular, heavily eroded limestone cliffs that jut out from the tip of the headland at **Cabo Carvoeiro**.

About 5km to the northeast of Peniche, **Baleal** is a scenic island-village, connected to the mainland village of Casais do Baleal by a narrow causeway (note: it's accessed through a car park). The fantastic sweep of sandy beach here offers some fine surfing. Surf schools dot the sands, as do several bar-restaurants.

Peniche is an easy 25km drive west of Óbidos or a 40-minute bus ride (€3.30, six to eight daily).

Baleal beach
JOYFULL/SHUTTERSTOCK ©

Tasca Torta   Portuguese €€
(☎262 958 000; Rua Direita 81; mains €9-19; ⏰12.30-2.25pm & 7-10.25pm) A pleasant hum, appealing aromas and colourful plates sum

up this stylish, contemporary spot. There's a cosy line of tables down one side, a kitchen on the other, and black-and-white photos of Portuguese fishermen. Everything from delicious salmon and spinach lasagna to a trilogy of seafood (salted cod, octopus and fish) pleases palates. Delicious starters are arranged on a slate plate.

Pousada do Castelo   International €€€
(☎210 407 630; www.pousadas.pt; Paço Real; mains €19-31; ⏰1-3pm & 7.30-10.30pm; 🛜) In an austere castle dining room with wide-eyed countryside views through medieval ramparts, the restaurant at Pousada do Castelo (p254) is one of Óbidos' few sure-fire foodie haunts.

🍷 DRINKING & NIGHTLIFE

You can't possibly miss Óbidos' most famous alcoholic concoction: *Ginjinha de Óbidos* (sour cherry liqueur), which is sold along the main street from countless stalls. You can even sip it from a chocolate cup! Otherwise, the town is a bit sleepy, more a wine and cheese sort of place than rounds of *medronho* shots.

Belgituda   Pub
(www.belgituda.com; Estrada Nacional 8; ⏰6pm-late Thu-Sun, closed late Dec–mid-Feb; 🛜) With more than 70 types of Belgian beer by the bottle, this bar just outside the walls is the place in Óbidos for those who set the beer bar higher than Sagres and Super Bock. But the quirky Belgian owner is threatening to close – let's not let him!

Esplanada Santa Maria   Cafe
(Praça de Santa Maria; ⏰10am-8pm) In the shadow of Santa Maria church and a couple of 500-year-old Japanese maple trees, this cash only, open-air esplanade offers some of Óbidos' most atmospheric tipple tables. No fancy mixology here – just cold Estrella Damm on draught and a few select standard cocktails (*porto tonicos*, caipirinhas, gin and tonics; €7.50) – served out of a made-over shipping container.

Santuário do Senhor da Pedra (p255)

Troca-Tintos   Bar

(www.facebook.com/trocatintosobidos; Rua
Dom João de Ornelas; ⊙6pm-2am Mon-Thu, to
3am Fri & Sat; 🔊) A fado shawl and guitar
on the wall sets the precedent for what's
to come in this intimate space, a former
chapel: a warm, friendly wine bar serving
up a good selection of Portuguese wines,
petiscos (tapas; €4.50 to €12) and *tábuas*
(cheese and charcuterie plates; €13 to
€20) and live music, including fado on
Monday and ballads/blues on Tuesday
evenings.

ℹ INFORMATION

Posto de Turismo (📞262 959 231; www.
obidos.pt; Rua da Porta da Vila S/N; ⊙9.30am-
7.30pm May-Sep, to 6pm Oct-Apr) Just outside
Porta da Vila, near the bus stop, with helpful
multilingual staff offering town brochures and
maps in five languages, plus information on
concerts and more.

ℹ GETTING THERE & AWAY

BUS

There are frequent departures for Peniche
(€3.30, 40 minutes) and Lisbon (€7.85, 65 minutes) from the **bus stop** (📞262 767 676; www.
rodoviariadooeste.pt; Rua da Praça S/N) on the
west side of Rua da Praça.

CAR

There are five car parks in Óbidos outside the
gates, two of which are fee-charging (from €5
per day). The best and biggest free **car park**
(N114) is behind Caixa Geral de Depósitos, 220m
southeast of Porta da Vila.

TRAIN

There are at least six daily trains to Lisbon
(€8.90 to €9.05, 2½ hours), mostly via connections at Mira Sintra-Meleças station on the
suburban Lisbon line. The **train station** (www.
cp.pt; Estrada da Estação S/N) is located outside
the northeastern section of the castle walls,
1.1km north of Porta da Vila. It's a pretty, but
uphill, walk to town.

BATALHA

Batalha at a Glance...

Among the achievements of Manueline architecture, Batalha's monastery transports visitors to another world, where solid rock has been carved into myriad forms. This extraordinary abbey was built to commemorate the 1385 Battle of Aljubarrota. Most of the monument was completed by 1434 in Flamboyant Gothic, but Manueline exuberance steals the show, thanks to additions made in the 15th and 16th centuries.

At the Battle of Aljubarrota, around 6500 Portuguese repulsed a 30,000-strong force of Juan I of Castile, who had come claiming the throne of João d'Avis. João called on the Virgin Mary for help and vowed to build a superb abbey in return for victory.

One Day in Batalha

Take at least half a day to explore Batalha's exquisite **abbey** (p264), making sure you don't miss the Unfinished Chapels. Also don't forget that a special ticket also covers Alcobaça and the Convento de Cristo in Tomar, all of which you can reach if you have a hire car at your disposal.

Two Days in Batalha

With two days to fill in Batalha, you can explore the rest of the town at your leisure, checking out the **Batalha de Aljubarrota Centro de Interpretação** (p266) and the **MCCB** (p266). End your day with a hearty dinner of Estremadura dishes at **Burro Velho** (p266).

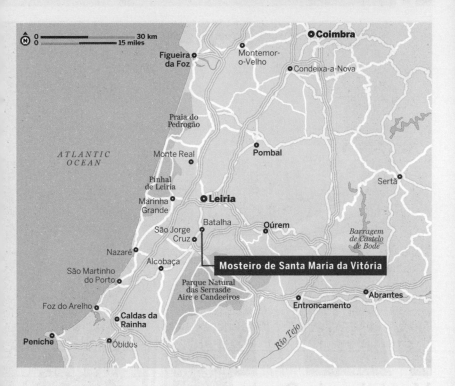

Arriving in Batalha

Buses with Rodoviária do Lis (www.rodoviariadolis.pt) and Rede Expressos (www.rede-expressos.pt) arrive at the bus stop on Rua do Moinho da Via, near the Intermarché supermarket, behind the police station. Express services go to major cities, including Lisbon (€11.40, two hours) four to five times daily – buy tickets online or at Cafe Frazão behind the church nearby.

Where to Stay

Batalha has several places to stay – all excellent value for money – and there are other good options in surrounding villages. The tourist office is the best place to start if you choose to turn up unannounced, though this is not recommended at the height of summer.

Unfinished Chapels

TAKASHI IMAGES/SHUTTERSTOCK ©

Mosteiro de Santa Maria da Vitória

Visiting this architecturally rich abbey and Unesco World Heritage Site is one of the highlights of the Estramadura. Allow at least half a day to do the place justice.

Great For...

☑ Don't Miss

The tomb of Prince Henry the Navigator, Portugal's most important monarch.

Exterior

The glorious limestone exterior bristles with pinnacles and parapets, flying buttresses and balustrades, and late-Gothic carved windows, as well as octagonal chapels and massive columns. The spectacular western doorway's layered arches pack in apostles, angels, saints and prophets, all topped by Christ and the Evangelists.

Interior

The vast, vaulted Gothic interior is plain, long and high (the highest in Portugal), warmed by light from the deep-hued stained-glass windows. Some of the interior was originally painted. To the right as you enter is the intricate Capela do Fundador (Founder's Chapel), an achingly beautiful, lofty, star-vaulted square room

Architectural details of the Unfinished Chapels

M.KO383/GETTY IMAGES ©

the architect Mateus Fernandes overshadow everything else. Although Fernandes' plan was never finished, the staggering ornamentation is all the more dramatic for being open to the sky.

Cloisters

Afonso Domingues, master of works during the late 1380s, built the fabulous Claustro Real (Royal Cloister) in a Gothic style, but it's the later Manueline embellishments by the great Mateus Fernandes that really take your breath away. Every arch is a tangle of detailed stone carvings of Manueline symbols, such as armillary spheres and crosses of the Order of Christ, entwined with writhing vegetation, exotic flowers and marine motifs. Three graceful cypresses echo the shape of the Gothic spires atop the adjacent chapter house. (And we challenge you to spot the ancient graffiti on the walls!)

Anything would seem austere after the Claustro Real, but the simple Gothic Claustro de Dom Afonso V is like being plunged into cold water – sobering you up after all that frenzied decadence. Between the two cloisters there is an interpretation centre.

lit by an octagonal lantern. In the centre is the joint tomb (the first pantheon to be built in Portugal) of João I and his English wife, Philippa of Lancaster, whose marriage in 1387 cemented the alliance that still exists between Portugal and England. The tombs of their four youngest sons line the south wall of the chapel, including that of Henry the Navigator (second from the right).

The Unfinished Chapels

The roofless Capelas Imperfeitas are perhaps the most astonishing aspect of Batalha. Only accessible from outside the abbey, the octagonal mausoleum with its seven chapels was commissioned in 1437. However, the later Manueline additions by

 Mosteiro de Santa Maria de Alcobaça

One of Iberia's great monasteries utterly dominates the town of **Alcobaça** (262 505 120; www.mosteiroalcobaca. pt; Praça 25 de Abril; €6, with Tomar & Batalha €15, free 1st Sun of the month to 2pm for residents, church free; 9am-7pm Apr-Sep, to 6pm Oct-Mar). Hiding behind the imposing baroque facade lies a high, austere, monkish church with a forest of unadorned 12th-century arches. But make sure you visit the rest too: the atmospheric refectory, vast dormitory and other spaces bring back the Cistercian life, which, according to sources, wasn't quite as austere here as it should have been.

After visiting the monastery, have a memorable meal at the **Restaurante António Padeiro** (262 582 295; www. facebook.com/restauranteantoniopadeiro. alcobaca; Rua Dom Maur Cocheril 27; mains €10-17; noon-3pm & 7-10pm), a Portuguese classic going strong for over 70 years.

Nearby, the enticing **Estremadura Café** (www.facebook.com/EstremaduraCafe; Praça 25 de Abril 80; noon-4pm & 7-midnight Sun, Mon & Thu, noon-4pm & 7pm-2am Fri & Sat;) serves excellent cocktails and craft beers.

Alcobaça is about 25km southwest of Batalha; Rodoviária do Oeste (www. rodoviariadooeste.pt) buses travel 11 times daily (weekdays) between the two towns, with infrequent service on weekends (€3.30, 40 minutes).

◉ SIGHTS

Batalha de Aljubarrota Centro de Interpretação   Historic Site

(www.fundacao-aljubarrota.pt; Avenida Nuno Álvares Pereira 120; adult/student/child/family €7/5/3.50/20; 10am-5.30pm Tue-Sun) For Portuguese people Aljubarrota conjures up a fierce sense of national pride, a 1385 battle where they defied the odds to defeat the Castilian force and established the foundations for the Portuguese golden age. The entry fee to the modern interpretation centre here, 3km south of Batalha, might seem steep until you see the multimedia show, a no-expenses-spared blood-and-thunder half-hour medieval epic (showing at 11.30am, 3pm and 4.30pm, audio guide €3) that brings the whole thing to vivid life.

The display on bones is also fascinating – one skull still has the tip of an arrowhead in it. The battlefield itself is freely accessible and has some English explanations, but to really understand what went on here, you'll want the audio guide from the interpretation centre. It's available in eight languages.

MCCB   Museum

(Museu da Comunidade Concelhia da Batalha; www.museubatalha.com; Largo Goa, Damão e Diu 4; adult/child €2.50/1.80; 10am-1pm & 2-6pm Wed-Sun) This modern, award-winning municipal museum in the centre of town is well worth the visit, taking you through the prehistory and history of the region, including some well-presented Roman remains and sections on the Battle of Aljubarrota and Mosteiro de Santa Maria da Vitória's construction.

⊗ EATING

Burro Velho   Portuguese €€

(244 764 174; www.burrovelho.com; Rua Nossa Sra do Caminho 6A; mains €8.50-16.50; noon-3pm & 7-10pm Mon-Sat, noon-3pm Sun;) Batalha's best, a bustling place serving up great modern Portuguese fare – seafood rices for two (€28 to €65), fresh catches of

the day and a *bulhão pato*–style (with olive oil, coriander and garlic) salted cod 'cheeks' starter that will redefine your enthusiasm for *bacalhau*. Carry on later (until 2am; same menu) at the newer and trendier wine bar next door.

It's run by a savvy young guy who not only works the floor but has established the recipe for success: service flair and quality products.

Churrasqueira Vitória   Grill €
(Largo da Misericórdia 4; mains €7-10; ☉noon-3pm & 7-10pm Tue-Sun) Neither outstanding nor terrible, this simple, friendly place serves tasty grilled meat and other Portuguese standards. Grab half a chicken for €7 and go home happy. Good-value lunch menus are only €7.50.

Tromba Rija   Buffet €€€
(☎244 852 277; www.trombarija.com; Estrada Nacional 1, Quinta do Fidalgo; all-you-can-eat €25; ☉1-3.30pm & 8-10.30pm Tue-Sat, 1-3.30pm Sun; ☏) This recent Leiria transplant occupies an old horse stable on a farm near Centro, where it serves an extensive – if pricey – 'Flavours of Portugal' buffet (fairly uncommon in Portugal). Start with eight or so cheeses and a vast salad and starter spread before moving onto a few select hot dishes per day (pork ribs, duck confit, salted cod etc).

Sometimes the presentations are off-putting (codfish dunked in a vat of olive oil, for example) but it all tastes better than it looks and it's nice to watch them transform the main course spread into a well-presented plate (they plate the main courses, not you). Desserts, digestifs, dried fruits and nuts and port are included, but wine and other standard drinks are not. Do not follow Google Maps here – you'll end up lost (and walking here isn't recommended – it involves some dangerous motorway manoeuvring).

🍷 DRINKING & NIGHTLIFE

Tasca da Tinouca   Bar
(Rua Doña Filipa de Lencastre 2440; ☉4pm-2am Tue-Sun; ☏) Somewhat hidden above a Vodafone shop steps from the monastery, you'll find one of Batalha's few bars, a modern – but smoky – *tasca* that draws a lively late afternoon happy-hour crowd for good wine, several conventional beers on draught and a solid tapas menu.

ℹ️ INFORMATION

Posto de Turismo (☎244 765 180; www.descobrirbatalha.pt; Praça Mouzinho de Albuquerque; ☉10am-1pm & 2-6pm) The very helpful, enthusiastic Nelia has worked here for years and knows the lot. It faces the back of the monastery.

ℹ️ GETTING THERE & AWAY

For Alcobaça, Fátima, Leiria, Nazaré and Tomar, connections are few and schedules change frequently, though with forward planning it can be done. Tickets are purchased on board. See helpful Nelia at the Posto de Turismo for the rundown.

ℹ️ GETTING AROUND

The **Gira Batalha** (www.girabatalha.pt; €1) does a 30-minute circular route hourly from the town bus stop to the monastery to Batalha de Aljubarrota Centro de Interpretação six times per day from 10.30am to 4.30pm. A hop-on, hop-off ticket costs €2.95 for 24 hours.

In Focus

Portugal Today

Bounding out of a dire recession with a rejuvenated mojo, Portugal is having a moment; indeed, cities like Lisbon and Porto are hotter than ever. A boom in tourism, improvements in quality of life thanks to quantifiable changes implemented by left-wing Prime Minister António Costa, and investment in green energy have been catalysts for this newfound swagger.

Left Foot Forward

When António Costa seized the reins as prime minister with his left-wing coalition in late 2015, the country seemed to give an audible sigh of relief – this was a new era in Portuguese politics. His objective was clear: achieve economic growth and reduce the deficit while reversing painful austerity measures – a daunting challenge, particularly given the fragile left-wing alliance holding his administration together. And yet he has largely been successful: the government has upped the minimum wage (to €676 per month in 2018), increased state pensions, cut taxes and improved welfare benefits. Unemployment has dropped substantially, at 6.7% in the third quarter of 2018 (markedly down from an all-time high of 17.5% in early 2013).

occupation of workforce
(% of population)

60 Services
28 Industry
12 Agriculture

if Portugal were 100 people

85 would be Roman Catholic
9 would be other
4 would be no religion
2 would be Christian

population per sq km

≈ 30 people

Portugal   USA   UK

As the fiscal future of the country is more optimistic and the economy more robust, word has it that Portugal might soon break free of its 25-year budget deficit – a turning point for the indebted economy.

Going Green

Portugal has invested heavily in renewable energy in recent years, and it now meets more than 50% of its needs with sustainable power, making it one of the leaders in Europe (behind only Austria, Sweden, Iceland and Norway). The Alentejo is home to one of the world's largest solar farms, with 376,000 panels spread across a 130-hectare site with a peak capacity of 46 megawatts.

This promising foundation in renewable energy took a leap forward in March 2018 when Portugal did something astonishing: for the first time in at least four decades, renewables exceeded the mainland power demand, generating 104% of the country's electricity supply – the majority of which came from wind turbines and hydropower.

Recent reports estimate that the production of renewable electricity should account for the total annual electricity consumption of mainland Portugal by 2040. But it will come at a cost, with estimates hovering around the €20 billion mark of what the nation will need to invest to make this dream a reality. Nonetheless, current trends signal bright things for the country's future in sustainable energy production.

Tourism: A Double-Edged Sword

When it comes to tourism, Portugal's star keeps rising, and the boom is visible: boutique hotels, restaurants and bars are popping up quicker than people can keep tabs on them. While the country continues to scoop up global tourism awards left, right and centre, tourism is spurring economic growth and setting national records, contributing €13.2 billion, or 6.8% of Portugal's GDP in 2017. So far, so positive, but the prime minister, António Costa, is aiming higher, seeking to increase tourism's total contribution to Portugal's GDP to the EU average of 10%, quipping 'you can never have too many tourists'.

There is a flip side to the story, however. Some locals are lamenting the fact that short-term rentals are skyrocketing in cities such as Lisbon and Porto because of mass tourism, pushing residents and small businesses further and further out of the centre, as many apartments are now let through home-sharing services. In Lisbon, the local authorities are currently figuring out new legislation that will better control and protect apartments for local residential use. Whether this will actually work remains to be seen.

Praça do Comércio, Lisbon (p50)

TTSTUDIO/SHUTTERSTOCK ©

History

Celts, Romans, Visigoths, Moors and Christian crusaders all made contributions to Portugal's early identity. In the 15th century, sea captains and intrepid explorers helped transform Portugal into the seat of a vast global empire. The centuries that followed saw devastation (the Lisbon earthquake of 1755) and great changes (industrialisation, dictatorship, decolonisation) before Portugal became a stable democracy in the 1980s.

5000 BC
Little-understood neolithic peoples build protected hilltop settlements in the lower Tejo valley.

700 BC
Celtic peoples, migrating across the Pyrenees with their families and flocks, sweep through the Iberian Peninsula.

197 BC
After defeating Carthage in the Second Punic War, the Romans invade Iberia, expanding their empire west.

Padrão dos Descobrimentos, Lisbon

OLIVEROUGE 3/SHUTTERSTOCK ©

Early Peoples

One of Europe's earliest places of settlement, the Iberian Peninsula was first inhabited many millennia ago, when hominids wandered across the landscape some time before 200,000 BC. During the Palaeolithic period, early Portuguese ancestors left traces of their time on earth in stone carvings near Vila Nova de Foz Côa in the Alto Douro. These date back some 30,000 years and were only discovered by accident, during a proposed dam-building project in 1992. Other signs of early human artistry lie hidden in the Alentejo, in the Gruta do Escoural, where cave drawings of animals and humans date back to around 15,000 BC.

Homo sapiens weren't the only bipeds on the scene. Neanderthals coexisted alongside modern humans in a few rare places like Portugal for as long as 10,000 years. In fact, some of the last traces of their existence were found in Iberia.

Neanderthals were only the first of a long line of inhabitants to appear (and later disappear) from the Iberian stage. In the 1st millennium BC Celtic people started trickling into the peninsula, settling northern and western Portugal around 700 BC. Dozens of *citânias*

AD 100	**800**	**1147**
Romans collect taxes to build roads, bridges and other public works. They cultivate vineyards and teach the natives to preserve fish.	The Umayyad dynasty rules the Iberian Peninsula. The region flourishes under the tolerant caliphate.	Christians attain decisive victories over the Moors during the Reconquista. Portugal's first king, Afonso Henriques lays siege to Lisbon.

The Mystery of the Neanderthals

Scientists have never come to an agreement about the fate of the Neanderthals – stout and robust beings who used stone tools and fire, buried their dead and had brains larger than those of modern humans. The most common theory is that *Homo sapiens* drove Neanderthals to extinction. A less-accepted theory is that Neanderthals and humans bred together and produced a hybrid species. This idea gained credence when Portuguese archaeologists found the first complete Palaeolithic skeleton ever unearthed in Iberia just north of Lisbon in 1999. The team, led by João Zilhão, director of the Portuguese Institute of Archaeology, discovered the 25,000-year-old remains of a young boy with traits of both early humans (a pronounced chin and teeth) and of Neanderthals (broad limbs). The boy had been interred in what was clearly a ritual burial.

(fortified villages) popped up, such as the formidable Citânia de Briteiros. Further south, Phoenician traders, followed by Greeks and Carthaginians, founded coastal stations and mined metals inland.

Roman Settlements

When the Romans swept into southern Portugal in 197 BC, they expected an easy victory. But they hadn't reckoned on the Lusitani, a Celtic warrior tribe that settled between the Rio Tejo and Rio Douro and resisted ferociously for half a century. Unable to subjugate the Lusitani, the Romans offered peace instead and began negotiations with Viriato, the Lusitanian leader. Unfortunately for Viriato and his underlings, the peace offer was a ruse, and Roman agents, posing as intermediaries, poisoned him. Resistance collapsed following Viriato's death in 139 BC.

For a vivid glimpse into Roman Portugal, you won't see a better site than Conímbriga, near Coimbra, or the monumental remains of the so-called Temple of Diana, in Évora.

By the 5th century, when the Roman Empire had all but collapsed, Portugal's inhabitants had been under Roman rule for 600 years. They had built roads and bridges. They also brought wheat, barley, olives and vines; large farming estates called *latifúndios* (still found in the Alentejo); a legal system; and, above all, a Latin-derived language. No other invader proved so useful.

Moors & Christians

The gap left by the Romans was filled by barbarian invaders from beyond the Pyrenees: Vandals, Alans, Visigoths and Suevi, with Arian Christian Visigoths gaining the upper hand in 469.

Internal Visigothic disputes paved the way for Portugal's next great wave of invaders, the Moors. In 711 North African Muslims were invited to help a Visigoth faction. The Moors quickly occupied large chunks of Portugal's southern coast.

Southerners enjoyed peace and productivity under the Moors, who established a capital at Shelb (Silves). The new rulers were tolerant of Jews and Christians. Christian smallholding

1297	**1348**	**1411**
The boundaries of the Portuguese kingdom are formalised with neighbouring Castile. The kingdom of Portugal has arrived.	The Plague reaches Portugal (most likely carried on ships that dock in Porto and Lisbon). The disease devastates, killing one in three.	Newly crowned Dom João builds an elaborate monastery to commemorate his victory at Aljubarrota.

farmers, called Mozarabs, could keep their land and were encouraged to try new methods and crops, especially citrus and rice. Arabic words, such as *alface* (lettuce), *arroz* (rice) and dozens of place names (including Fátima, Silves and Algarve), filtered into the Portuguese language, and locals became addicted to Moorish sweets.

Meanwhile, in the north, Christian forces were gaining strength and reached as far as Porto in 868. But it was in the 11th century that the Reconquista (the Christian reconquest) heated up. In 1064 Coimbra was taken and, in 1085, Alfonso VI thrashed the Moors in their Spanish heartland of Toledo; he is said to have secured Seville by winning a game of chess with its emir. But in the following year, Alfonso's troops were driven out by ruthless Moroccan Almoravids who answered the emir's distress call.

Alfonso called for help and European crusaders came running – rallying against the 'infidels'. With the help of Henri of Burgundy, among others, Alfonso made decisive moves towards victory. The struggle continued in successive generations, and by 1139 Afonso Henriques (grandson of Alfonso VI) won such a dramatic victory against the Moors at Ourique (Alentejo) that he named himself Dom – King of Portugal – a title confirmed in 1179 by the Pope (after extra tribute was paid, naturally). Afonso also retook Santarém and Lisbon from the Moors.

By the time he died in 1185, the Portuguese frontier was secure to the Rio Tejo, though it would take another century before the south was torn from the Moors.

The Burgundian Era

During the Reconquista people faced more than just war and turmoil: in the wake of Christian victories came new rulers and settlers. The church and its wealthy clergy were the greediest landowners, followed by aristocratic fat cats. Though theoretically free, most common people remained subjects of the landowning class, with few rights. The first hint of democratic rule came with the establishment of the *cortes* (parliament). This assembly of nobles and clergy first met in 1211 at Coimbra, the then capital. Six years later, the capital moved to Lisbon.

Afonso III (r 1248–79) deserves credit for standing up to the church, but it was his son, the 'Poet King' Dinis (r 1279–1325), who really shook Portugal into shape. A far-sighted, cultured man, he took control of the judicial system, started progressive afforestation programs and encouraged internal trade. He suppressed the dangerously powerful military order of the Knights Templar, refounding them as the Order of Christ. He cultivated music, the arts and education, and he founded a university in Lisbon in 1290, later transferred to Coimbra.

Dom Dinis built or rebuilt some 50 fortresses along the eastern frontier with Castile and signed a pact of friendship with England in 1308, the basis for a future long-lasting alliance.

It was none too soon. Within 60 years of Dinis' death, Portugal was at war with Castile. Fernando I helped provoke the clash by playing a game of alliances with both Castile and the English. He dangled promises of marriage to his daughter Beatriz in front of both nations, eventually marrying her off to Juan I of Castile, thus throwing Portugal's future into Castilian hands.

1415	1418	1443
Dom João's third son, Prince Henry the Navigator, joins his father in the conquest of Ceuta in North Africa.	Shipbuilding advances lead to the development of the caravel, a fast, agile ship that changes the face of sailing.	Explorers bring the first African slaves to Portugal, marking the beginning of a long, shameful era of slavery.

Mosaic at Conímbriga Roman Ruins (p231)

DERICK D MILLER/SHUTTERSTOCK ©

★ Best Roman Sites

Conímbriga (p231; Beiras)

Milreu (p141; Algarve)

Templo Romano (p181; Évora)

Núcleo Arqueológico (p50; Lisbon)

Termas Romanas do Alto da Cividade (p216; Braga)

On Fernando's death in 1383, his wife, Leonor Teles, ruled as regent. But she too was entangled with the Spanish, having long had a Galician lover. The merchant classes preferred unsullied Portuguese candidate João, son (albeit illegitimate) of Fernando's father. João assassinated Leonor's lover, Leonor fled to Castile and the Castilians duly invaded.

The showdown came in 1385 when João faced a mighty force of Castilians at Aljubarrota. Even with Nuno Álvares Pereira (the Holy Constable) as his military right-hand man and English archers at the ready, the odds were stacked against him. João vowed to build a monastery if he won – and he did. Nuno Álvares, the brilliant commander-in-chief of the Portuguese troops, deserves much of the credit for the victory. Within a few hours the Spanish were retreating in disarray and the battle was won.

The victory clinched independence and João made good his vow by commissioning Batalha's stunning Mosteiro de Santa Maria da Vitória (aka the Mosteiro da Batalha or Battle Abbey). It also sealed Portugal's alliance with England, and João wed John of Gaunt's daughter. Peace was finally concluded in 1411.

Age of Discoveries

João's success had whetted his appetite and, spurred on by his sons, he soon turned his military energies abroad. Morocco was the obvious target, and in 1415 Ceuta fell easily to his forces. It was a turning point in Portuguese history, a first step into its golden age.

It was João's third son, Henry, who focused the spirit of the age – a combination of crusading zeal, love of martial glory and lust for gold – into extraordinary explorations across the seas. These explorations were to transform the small kingdom into a great imperial power.

The biggest breakthrough came in 1497 during the reign of Manuel I, when Vasco da Gama reached southern India. With gold and slaves from Africa and spices from the East, Portugal was soon rolling in riches. Manuel I was so thrilled by the discoveries (and resultant cash injection) that he ordered a frenzied building spree in celebration. Top of his list was the extravagant Mosteiro dos Jerónimos in Belém, later to become his pantheon.

1494	**1497**	**1519**
The race for colonial expansion is on: Spain and Portugal carve up the world, with the Treaty of Tordesillas.	Following Bartolomeu Dias' historic journey around the Cape of Good Hope in 1488, Vasco da Gama sails to India and becomes a legend.	Fernão Magalhães (Ferdinand Magellan) embarks on his journey to circumnavigate the globe. He is killed in the Philippines.

Another brief boost to the Portuguese economy at this time came courtesy of an influx of around 150,000 Jewish people, who had been expelled from Spain in 1492.

Spain had also jumped on the exploration bandwagon and was soon disputing Portuguese claims. Christopher Columbus' 1492 'discovery' of America for Spain led to a fresh outburst of jealous conflict. It was resolved by the Pope in the bizarre 1494 Treaty of Tordesillas, which divided the world between the two powers along a line 370 leagues west of the Cape Verde islands. Portugal won the lands east of the line, including Brazil, officially claimed in 1500.

The rivalry spurred the first circumnavigation of the world. In 1519 Portuguese navigator Fernão Magalhães (Ferdinand Magellan), his allegiance transferred to Spain after a tiff with Manuel I, set off in an effort to prove that the Spice Islands (today's Moluccas) lay in Spanish 'territory'. He reached the Philippines in 1521 but was killed in a skirmish there. One of his five ships, under the Basque navigator Juan Sebastián Elcano, reached the Spice Islands and then sailed home via the Cape of Good Hope, proving the earth was round.

As its explorers reached Timor, China and eventually Japan, Portugal cemented its power with garrison ports and trading posts. The monarchy, taking its 'royal fifth' of profits, became stinking rich – indeed the wealthiest monarchy in Europe, and the lavish Manueline architectural style symbolised the exuberance of the age.

It couldn't last. By the 1570s the cost of expeditions and maintaining an empire was taking its toll. The final straw came in 1578. Young, idealistic Sebastião was on the throne and, determined to bring Christianity to Morocco, he rallied a force of 18,000 and set sail from Lagos. He was disastrously defeated at the Battle of Alcácer-Quibir (or the Battle of Three Kings): Sebastião and 8000 others were killed, including much of the Portuguese nobility. Sebastião's aged successor, Cardinal Henrique, drained the royal coffers ransoming those captured.

On Henrique's death in 1580, Sebastião's uncle, Felipe II of Spain (Felipe I of Portugal), fought for and won the throne. This marked the end of centuries of independence, Portugal's golden age and its glorious moment at the centre of the world stage.

Spanish Rule & Portuguese Revival

Spanish rule began promisingly, with Felipe vowing to preserve Portugal's autonomy and attend the long-ignored parliament. But commoners resented Spanish rule and held on to the dream that Sebastião was still alive (as he was killed abroad in battle, some citizens were in denial); pretenders continued to pop up until 1600. Though Felipe was honourable, his successors proved to be considerably less so, using Portugal to raise money and soldiers for Spain's wars overseas and appointing Spaniards to govern Portugal.

An uprising in Catalonia gave fuel to Portugal's independence drive and in 1640 a group of conspirators launched a coup. Nationalists drove the female governor of Portugal and her Spanish garrison from Lisbon. It was then that the duke of Bragança reluctantly stepped forward and was crowned João IV.

With a hostile Spain breathing down its neck, Portugal searched for allies. Two swift treaties with England led to Charles II's marriage to João's daughter, Catherine of Bragança,

1572	1578	1622
Luís Vaz de Camões writes *Os Lusíadas*, an epic poem that celebrates da Gama's historic voyage.	Dom Sebastião raises an army and invades Morocco. The expedition ends at the Battle of Alcácer-Quibir.	Portugal's empire is slipping out of Spain's grasp. The English seize Hormoz.

★ Islamic Sites

Núcleo Islâmico (p145; Tavira)

Castelo de São Jorge (p55; Lisbon)

Museu Municipal de Arqueologia
(p141; Silves)

Castelo de São Jorge (p55), Lisbon

STOCKPHOTOSART/GETTY IMAGES ©

and the ceding of Tangier and Bombay to England. In return the English promised arms and soldiers; however, a preoccupied Spain made only half-hearted attempts to recapture Portugal and recognised Portuguese independence in 1668.

João IV's successors pursued largely absolutist policies (particularly under João V, an admirer of French King Louis XIV). The crown hardly bothered with parliament, and another era of profligate expenditure followed, giving birth to projects such as the wildly extravagant monastery-palace in Mafra.

Cementing power for the crown was one of Portugal's most revered (and feared) statesmen – the Marquês de Pombal, chief minister to the epicurean Dom José I (the latter more interested in opera than political affairs). Described as an enlightened despot, Pombal dragged Portugal into the modern era, crushing opposition with brutal efficiency.

Pombal set up state monopolies, curbed the power of British merchants and boosted agriculture and industry. He abolished slavery and distinctions between traditional and New Christians (converted from Judaism), and overhauled education. When Lisbon suffered an earthquake in 1755, Pombal swiftly rebuilt the city. He was by then at the height of his power, and he dispensed with his main enemies by implicating them in an attempt on the king's life.

He might have continued had it not been for the accession of the devout Dona Maria I in 1777. The anticlerical Pombal was promptly sacked, tried and charged with various offences, though he was never imprisoned. While his religious legislation was repealed, his economic, agricultural and educational policies were largely maintained.

But turmoil was once again on the horizon, as Napoleon was sweeping through Europe.

A Devastating Earthquake

Lisbon in the 1700s was a thriving city, with gold flowing in from Brazil, a thriving merchant class and grand Manueline architecture. Then, on the morning of 1 November 1755, a devastating earthquake levelled much of the city, which fell like a pack of dominoes, never to regain its former status; palaces, libraries, art galleries, churches and hospitals were razed to the ground. Tens of thousands died, crushed beneath falling masonry,

1703	**1717**	**1755**
France and Britain are at war. Facing (disastrous!) wine shortages, the English sign a new treaty with Portugal.	Brazilian gold extraction nears its peak, with over 600,000oz imported annually. Dom João V becomes Europe's richest monarch.	Lisbon suffers Europe's biggest natural disaster. On All Saints' Day, three massive earthquakes destroy the city.

drowned in the tsunami that swept in from the Tejo or killed in the fires that followed.

Enter the formidable, unflappable, geometrically minded Marquês de Pombal. As Dom José I's chief minister, Pombal swiftly set about reconstructing the city, true to his word to 'bury the dead and heal the living'. In the wake of the disaster, the autocratic statesman not only kept the country's head above water as it was plunged into economic chaos but also managed to propel Lisbon into the modern era.

Together with military engineers and architects Eugenio dos Santos and Manuel da Maia, Pombal played a pivotal role in reconstructing the city in a simple, cheap, earthquake-proof way that created today's formal grid, and the Pombaline style was born. The antithesis of rococo, Pombaline architecture was functional and restrained: *azulejos* (hand-painted tiles) and decorative elements were used sparingly, building materials were prefabricated, and wide streets and broad plazas were preferred.

India Ahoy!

Fed up with the Venetian monopoly on overland trade with Asia, Portuguese explorer Vasco da Gama set sail from Lisbon in 1497 with a motley crew aboard his caravel. He skirted the coast of Mozambique and the port of Mombasa before washing up on the shore of Calicut, India, in May 1498. The bedraggled crew received a frosty welcome from the Zamorin (Hindu ruler) and, when tensions flared, they returned whence they came. The voyage was hardly plain sailing – more than half of Vasco da Gama's party perished. For his success in discovering a sea route to India, Manuel I made him a lord when he returned in 1499 and he was hailed 'Admiral of the Indian Ocean'.

Dom José I, for his part, escaped the earthquake unscathed. Instead of being in residence at the royal palace, he had ridden out of town to Belém with his extensive retinue. After seeing the devastation, the eccentric José I refused to live in a masonry building ever again, and he set up a wooden residence outside town, in the hills of Ajuda, north of Belém. What was known as the Real Barraca (Royal Tent) became the site of the Palácio Nacional de Ajuda after the king's death.

The Dawn of a Republic

A French Invasion Unleashes Royal Chaos

In 1793 Portugal found itself at war again when it joined Britain in sending naval forces against revolutionary France. Before long, Napoleon gave Portugal an ultimatum: close your ports to British shipping or be invaded.

There was no way Portugal could turn its back on Britain, upon which it depended for half of its trade and the protection of its sea routes. In 1807 Portugal's royal family fled to Brazil (where it stayed for 14 years), and Napoleon's forces marched into Lisbon, sweeping Portugal into the Peninsular War (France's invasion of Spain and Portugal, which lasted until 1814).

1807	**1815**	**1822**
Napoleon invades Portugal. The Portuguese royal family and several thousand in their retinue pack up and set sail for Brazil.	Having fallen for Brazil, Dom João VI declares Rio the capital of the United Kingdom of Portugal and Brazil and the Algarves.	In Brazil, Prince Regent Pedro leads a coup d'état and declares Brazilian independence, with himself the new 'emperor'.

To the rescue came Sir Arthur Wellesley (later Duke of Wellington), Viscount Beresford and their seasoned British troops, who eventually drove the French back across the Spanish border in 1811.

Free but weakened, Portugal was administered by Beresford while the royals dallied in Brazil. In 1810 Portugal lost a profitable intermediary role by giving Britain the right to trade directly with Brazil. The next humiliation was João's 1815 proclamation of Brazil as a kingdom united with Portugal – he did this to bring more wealth and prestige to Brazil (which he was growing to love) and, in turn, to him and the rest of the royal family residing there. With soaring debts and dismal trade, Portugal was at one of the lowest points in its history, reduced to a de facto colony of Brazil and a protectorate of Britain.

Meanwhile, resentment simmered in the army. Rebel officers quietly convened parliament and drew up a new liberal constitution. Based on Enlightenment ideals, it abolished many rights of the nobility and clergy, and instituted a single-chamber parliament.

Faced with this fait accompli, João returned and accepted its terms – though his wife and his son Miguel were bitterly opposed to it. João's elder son, Pedro, had other ideas: left behind to govern Brazil, he snubbed the constitutionalists by declaring Brazil independent in 1822 and himself its emperor. When João died in 1826, the stage was set for civil war.

Offered the crown, Pedro dashed out a new, less liberal charter and then abdicated in favour of his seven-year-old daughter, Maria, on the provisos that she marry uncle Miguel and that uncle Miguel accept the new constitution. Miguel took the oath but promptly abolished Pedro's charter and proclaimed himself king. A livid Pedro rallied the equally furious liberals and forced Miguel to surrender at Évoramonte in 1834.

After Pedro's death, his daughter Maria, now queen of Portugal at just 15, kept his flame alive with fanatical support of his 1826 charter. The radical supporters of the liberal 1822 constitution grew vociferous over the next two decades, bringing the country to the brink of civil war. The Duke of Saldanha, however, saved the day, negotiating a peace that toned down Pedro's charter while still radically modernising Portugal's infrastructure.

A Hopeful New Era

The latter half of the 19th century was a remarkable period for Portugal, and it became known as one of the most advanced societies in southern Europe. Casual visitors to Lisbon, such as Hans Christian Andersen, were surprised to find tree-lined boulevards with gas street lamps, efficient trams and well-dressed residents. The educational reformer João Arroio dramatically increased the number of schools, doubling the number of boys' schools and quadrupling the number of girls' schools. Women gained the right to own property; slavery was abolished throughout the Portuguese empire, as was the death penalty; and even the prison system received an overhaul – prisoners were taught useful trades while in jail so they could integrate into society upon their release.

Professional organisations, such as the Literary Guild, emerged and became a major force for the advancement of ideas in public discourse, inspiring debate in politics, religious life and the art world.

1865	1890	1908
Portugal enjoys a period of peace and prosperity. Advancements are made in industry, agriculture, health and education.	Portugal takes a renewed interest in its African colonies. Britain wants control of sub-Saharan Africa and threatens Portugal with war.	Dom Carlos and his eldest son, Luís Filipe, are assassinated. Two years later Portugal is declared a republic.

As elsewhere in Europe, this was also a time of great industrial growth, with a dramatic increase in textile production, much of it to be exported. Other significant undertakings included the building of bridges and a nationwide network of roads, as well as the completion of major architectural works such as the Palácio Nacional da Pena above Sintra.

Dark Days & a King's Death

By 1900, discontent among workers began to grow. With increased mechanisation, workers began losing their jobs (some factory owners began hiring children to operate the machines), and their demands for fair working conditions went unanswered. Those who went on strike were simply fired and replaced. At the same time, Portugal experienced a dramatic demographic shift: rural areas were increasingly depopulated in favour of cities, and emigration (especially to Brazil) snowballed.

Much was changing, and more and more people began to look towards socialism as a cure for the country's inequalities. Nationalist republicanism swept through the lower-middle classes, spurring an attempted coup in 1908. It failed, but the following month Dom Carlos and Crown Prince Luís Filipe were brutally assassinated in Lisbon.

Carlos' younger son, Manuel II, tried feebly to appease republicans, but it was too little, too late. On 5 October 1910, after an uprising by military officers, a republic was declared. Manuel, dubbed 'the Unfortunate', sailed into exile in Britain, where he died in 1932.

The Rise & Fall of Salazar

After a landslide victory in the 1911 elections, hopes were high among republicans for dramatic changes, but the tide was against them. The economy was in tatters, an issue only exacerbated by a financially disastrous decision to join the Allies in WWI. In the postwar years the chaos deepened: republican factions squabbled, unions led strikes and were repressed, and the military grew more powerful.

The new republic soon had a reputation as Europe's most unstable regime. Between 1910 and 1926 there were an astonishing 45 changes of government, often resulting from military intervention. Another coup in 1926 brought forth new names and faces, most significantly António de Oliveira Salazar, a finance minister who would rise through the ranks to become prime minister in 1932 – a post he would hold for the next 36 years.

Salazar hastily enforced his 'New State' – a corporatist republic that was nationalistic, Catholic, authoritarian and essentially repressive. All political parties were banned except for the loyalist National Union, which ran the show, and the National Assembly. Strikes were forbidden and propaganda, censorship and brute force kept society in order. The sinister new Polícia Internacional e de Defesa do Estado (PIDE) secret police inspired terror and suppressed opposition using imprisonment and torture. Various attempted coups during Salazar's rule came to nothing. For a chilling taste of life as a political prisoner under Salazar, you could visit the 16th-century Fortaleza at Peniche – used as a jail by the dictator.

1916	1932	1935
Despite initial neutrality, Portugal gets drawn into WWI. The war effort devastates the economy, creating a long postwar recession.	António de Oliveira Salazar seizes power. The Portuguese economy grows but at enormous human cost.	The largely unpublished 47-year-old poet Fernando Pessoa dies, leaving a trunk containing a staggering collection of writing.

Museu de Portimão (p154)

The only good news was the dramatic economic turnaround. Through the 1950s and 1960s, Portugal experienced an annual industrial growth rate of 7% to 9%.

Internationally, the wily Salazar played two hands, unofficially supporting Franco's nationalists in the Spanish Civil War and, despite official neutrality, allowing the British to use Azores airfields during WWII and engaging in illegal sales of tungsten to Germany. It was later discovered that Salazar had also authorised the transfer of Nazi-looted gold to Portugal – 44 tonnes, according to Allied records.

But it was something else that finally brought the Salazarist era to a close – decolonisation. Refusing to relinquish the colonies, he was faced with ever more costly and unpopular military expeditions. In 1961 Goa was occupied by India, and nationalists rose up in Angola. Guerrilla movements also appeared in Portuguese Guinea and Mozambique. Salazar, however, didn't have to face the consequences. In 1968 he had a stroke, and he died two years later.

His successor Marcelo Caetano failed to ease unrest. Military officers sympathetic to African freedom fighters grew reluctant to fight colonial wars – the officers had seen the horrible conditions in which the colonies lived beneath the Portuguese authorities. Several hundred officers formed the Movimento das Forças Armadas (MFA), which in 1974 carried out a nearly bloodless coup in Lisbon, later nicknamed the Revolution of the Carnations (after victorious soldiers stuck carnations in their rifle barrels). Carnations are still a national symbol of freedom.

From Revolution to Democracy

Despite the coup's popularity, the following year saw unprecedented chaos. It began where the revolution had begun: in the African colonies. Independence was granted immediately to Guinea-Bissau, followed by the speedy decolonisation of the Cape Verde islands, São Tomé e Príncipe, Mozambique and Angola. The transition wasn't smooth: civil war racked Angola, and East Timor, freshly liberated in 1975, was promptly invaded by Indonesia. Within Portugal, too, times were turbulent, with almost a million refugees from African colonies flooding into the country.

1943
Portugal, neutral during WWII, becomes a crossroads for the intelligence activities of Allied and Axis operatives.

1961
Portugal's empire crumbles as India seizes Goa. Independence movements are under way in Portugal's former African colonies.

1974
Army officers overthrow Salazar's successor in the Revolution of the Carnations. Portugal veers to the left.

The nation was an economic mess, with widespread strikes and a tangle of political ideas and parties. The communists and a radical wing of the MFA launched a revolutionary movement, nationalising firms and services. Peasant farmers seized land to establish communal farms that failed because of infighting and poor management. While revolutionaries held sway in the south, the conservative north was led by Mário Soares and his Partido Socialista (PS; Socialist Party).

In the early post-Salazar days, radical provisional governments established by the military failed one after the other, as did an attempted coup led by General António de Spínola in 1975. A period of relative calm finally arrived in 1976, when Portugal adopted a new constitution and held its first elections for a new parliament. General António Ramalho Eanes was elected president the same year and helped steer the country toward democracy. He chose as his prime minister Soares, who took the reins with enormous challenges facing Portugal, including soaring inflation, high unemployment and downward-spiralling wages.

The Rocky Road to Stability

Portugal was soon committed to a blend of socialism and democracy, with a powerful president, an elected assembly and a Council of the Revolution to control the armed forces.

Mário Soares' minority government soon faltered, prompting a series of attempts at government by coalitions and nonparty candidates, including Portugal's first female prime minister, Maria de Lourdes Pintasilgo. In the 1980 parliamentary elections, a new political force took the reins: the conservative Aliança Democrática (AD; Democratic Alliance), led by Francisco Sá Carneiro. After Carneiro's almost immediate (and suspicious) death in a plane crash, Francisco Pinto Balsemão stepped into his shoes. He implemented plans to join the European Community (EC).

It was partly to keep the EC and the International Monetary Fund (IMF) happy that a new coalition government under Soares and Balsemão implemented a strict program of economic modernisation. The belt-tightening wasn't popular. The loudest critics were Soares' right wing partners in the Partido Social Democrata (PSD; Social Democrat Party), led by the dynamic Aníbal Cavaco Silva. Communist trade unions organised strikes, and the appearance of urban terrorism by the radical left-wing Forças Populares 25 de Abril (FP-25) deepened unrest.

In 1986, after nine years of negotiations, Portugal joined the EC. Flush with new funds, it raced ahead of its neighbours with unprecedented economic growth. The new cash flow also gave Prime Minister Cavaco Silva the power to push ahead with radical economic plans. These included labour-law reforms that left many workers disenchanted. The 1980s were crippled by strikes – including one involving 1.5 million workers – though they were to no avail: the controversial legislation was eventually passed.

The economic growth, however, wouldn't last. In 1992 EC trade barriers fell and Portugal suddenly faced new competition. Fortunes dwindled as a recession set in, and disillusionment grew as Europe's single market revealed the backwardness of Portugal's agricultural sector.

1986	**1998**	**2004**
Mário Soares becomes Portugal's first civilian head of state in 60 years. Portugal joins the EC, along with Spain.	Lisbon hosts Expo '98, showcasing new developments, including Santiago Calatrava's cutting-edge train station.	Hosting the UEFA European Championship, Portugal makes it to the final only to suffer an agonising loss to Greece.

Strikes, crippling corruption charges and student demonstrations over rising fees only undermined the PSD further, leading to Cavaco Silva's resignation in 1995. The general elections that year brought new faces to power, with the socialist António Guterres running the show. Despite hopes for a different and less conservative administration, it was business as usual, with Guterres maintaining the budgetary rigour that qualified Portugal for the European Economic & Monetary Union (EMU) in 1998. Indeed, for a while Portugal was a star EMU performer, with steady economic growth that helped Guterres win a second term. But corruption scandals, rising inflation and a faltering economy soon spelt disaster. The next 10 years were ones of hardship for the Portuguese economy, which saw little or negative GDP growth, and rising unemployment from 2001 to 2010. As elsewhere in Europe, Portugal took a huge hit during the global financial crisis. Ultimatums from the EU governing body to rein in its debt brought unpopular austerity measures that led to protests and strikes.

Hard Times

Portugal's economy wasn't particularly strong in the years before the economic crisis, making the economic fire all the more destructive. Lumped in with other economically failing eurozone nations, the group of them collectively known as PIIGS (Portugal, Italy, Ireland, Greece and Spain), Portugal – in dire financial straits – accepted an EU bailout worth €78 billion in 2011. The younger generation has borne the heaviest burden following the crisis, with unemployment above 40% for workers under the age of 25. In addition, there are the underemployed and those scraping by on meagre wages.

The EU bailout came with the stipulation that Portugal improve its budget deficit by reducing spending and increasing tax revenues. Austerity measures followed and the public took to the streets to protest against higher taxes and slashed pensions and benefits, in the context of record-high unemployment. Mass demonstrations and general strikes grew, with the largest attracting an estimated 1.5 million people nationwide in 2013 – an astounding figure given Portugal's small size. Those in industries most affected by government policy – including education, healthcare and transportation – joined the ranks of the unemployed and pensioners to amass in the largest gatherings since the Revolution of the Carnations in 1974.

Despite the bailout package Portugal remained in its most severe recession since the 1970s. Every day, Portuguese were confronted with headlines announcing freezes on public spending, cuts in healthcare, removal of free school lunches, curtailing of police patrols and rising suicides, among other issues. Pensioners living on 200-odd euros a month struggled to feed themselves, and poverty and hunger affected millions; according to TNS Global, roughly three out of four people in Portugal struggled to make their money last through the month.

What began as a financial crisis soon turned into a political crisis, as successive government ministers failed to ameliorate the growing problems. With anger mounting on the streets, the public clamoured for the resignation of Prime Minister Pedro Passos Coelho. Indeed, his time in power would come to an abrupt end in 2015, with a left-wing Socialist Party government, led by António Costa, taking control and ushering in a new era in Portuguese politics.

2010	**2013**	**2017**
Portugal legalises same-sex marriage, becoming the sixth country in Europe (and the eighth in the world) to do so.	Fed up with rising unemployment, soaring taxes and spending cuts, 1.5 million protesters take to the streets of Portugal.	Fires ravage 45,000 hectares and kill 66 people – the largest loss of life to wildfires in Portugal's history.

A Sagrada Família com São João Batista, Santa Isabel e Anjos, by Josefa de Óbidos (p292)

ART COLLECTION 4/ALAMY STOCK PHOTO ©

Art & Architecture

Portugal has a long and storied art history. Everyone from Neolithic tribes to early Christian crusaders have left their mark. The Age of Discoveries, a rich era of grand cathedrals and lavish palaces, began around 1500. In the 500 years that followed, Portugal became a showcase for a dizzying array of architectural styles. Meanwhile, painters, sculptors, poets and novelists all made contributions to Portugal's artistic heritage.

The Palaeolithic Palette

The Cromeleque dos Almendres, a most mysterious group of 95 huge monoliths, forms a strange circle in an isolated clearing among Alentejan olive groves near Évora. It's one of Europe's most impressive prehistoric sites.

All over Portugal, but especially in the Alentejo, you can visit such ancient funerary and religious structures, built during the neolithic and mesolithic eras. Most impressive are the dolmens: rectangular, polygonal or round funerary chambers, reached by a corridor of stone slabs and covered with earth to create an artificial mound. King of these is Europe's largest dolmen, the Anta Grande do Zambujeiro, near Évora, with six 6m-high stones forming a huge chamber. Single monoliths, also known as menhirs, often carved with phallic

A Serendipitous Discovery

In 1989 researchers were studying the rugged valley of the Rio Côa to understand the environmental impact of a planned hydroelectric dam that was to flood the valley. There they made an extraordinary discovery: a number of petroglyphs (rock engravings) dating back 10,000 to 40,000 years. In 1998 the future of the collection was safeguarded when Unesco designated the valley a World Heritage Site.

Today Rio Côa (p203) holds one of the largest-known collections of open-air Palaeolithic art in the world. Most of the petroglyphs depict animals: stylised horses, aurochs (extinct ancestors of cattle) and long-horned ibex. The most intriguing engravings consist of overlapping layers, with successive artists adding their touches thousands of years after the first strokes were applied.

or religious symbols, also dot the countryside like an army of stone sentinels. Their relationship to promoting fertility seems obvious.

With the arrival of the Celts (800–200 BC) came the first established hilltop settlements, called *castros*. The best-preserved example is the Citânia de Briteiros, in the Minho, where you can literally step into Portugal's past. Stone dwellings were built on a circular or elliptical plan, and the complex was surrounded by a drystone defensive wall. In the *citânias* (fortified villages) further south, dwellings tended to be rectangular.

The Romans

The Romans left Portugal their typical architectural and engineering feats – roads, bridges, towns complete with forums (marketplaces), villas, public baths and aqueducts. These have now largely disappeared from the surface, though the majority of Portugal's cities are built on Roman foundations. Today you can descend into dank subterranean areas under new buildings in Lisbon and Évora, and see Roman fragments around Braga. At Conímbriga, the country's largest Roman site, an entire town is under excavation. Revealed so far are city walls, some spectacular mosaics, along with structural or decorative columns, the original stone heating ducts for the thermal baths, the tunnels of the amphitheatre, carved entablatures and classical ornamentation, giving a sense of the Roman high life.

Portugal's most famous and complete Roman ruin is the Templo Romano, the so-called Temple of Diana in Évora, with its flouncy-topped Corinthian columns nowadays echoed by the complementary towers of Évora's cathedral. This is the finest temple of its kind on the Iberian Peninsula, its preservation the result of having been walled up in the Middle Ages and later used as a slaughterhouse.

Architectural Movements

Great Gothic

Cistercians introduced the Gothic trend, which reached its pinnacle in Alcobaça, in one of Portugal's most ethereally beautiful buildings. The austere abbey church and cloister of the Mosteiro de Santa Maria de Alcobaça, begun in 1178, has a lightness and simplicity strongly influenced by Clairvaux Abbey in France. Its hauntingly simple Cloisters of Silence were a model for later cathedral cloisters at Coimbra, Lisbon, Évora and many other places. This was the birth of Portuguese Gothic, which flowered and transmuted over the coming years as the country gained more and more experience of the outside world after centuries of being culturally dominated and restricted by Spain and the Moors.

By the 14th century, when the Mosteiro de Santa Maria da Vitória (commonly known as Mosteiro da Batalha or Battle Abbey) was constructed, simplicity was a distant, vague memory. Portuguese, Irish and French architects worked on this breathtaking monument for more than two centuries. The combination of their skills and the changing architectural fashions of the times, from Flamboyant (late) Gothic to Renaissance and then Manueline, turned the abbey into a seething mass of carving, organic decorations, lofty spaces and slanting stained-glass light. A showcase of High Gothic art, it exults in the decorative (especially in its Gothic Royal Cloisters and Chapter House) and its flying buttresses tip their hat to English Perpendicular Gothic.

Secular architecture also enjoyed a Gothic boom, thanks to the need for fortifications against the Moors and to the castle-building fervour of 13th-century ruler Dom Dinis. Some of Portugal's most spectacular, huddled, thick-walled castles – for example, Estremoz, Óbidos and Bragança – date from this time, many featuring massive double-perimeter walls and an inner square tower.

Manueline

Manueline is a uniquely Portuguese style: a specific, crazed flavour of late Gothic architecture. Ferociously decorative, it coincided roughly with the reign of Dom Manuel I (r 1495–1521) and is interesting not just because of its extraordinarily imaginative designs, burbling with life, but also because this dizzyingly creative architecture skipped hand in hand with the era's booming confidence.

During Dom Manuel's reign, Vasco da Gama and fellow explorers claimed new overseas lands and new wealth for Portugal. The Age of Discoveries was expressed in sculptural creations of eccentric inventiveness that drew heavily on nautical themes: twisted ropes, coral and anchors in stone, topped by the ubiquitous armillary sphere (a navigational device that became Dom Manuel's personal symbol) and the cross of the Order of Christ (symbol of the religious military order that largely financed and inspired Portugal's explorations).

Manueline first emerged in Setúbal's Igreja de Jesus, designed in the 1490s by French expatriate Diogo de Boitaca, who gave it columns like trees growing into the ceiling and ribbed vaulting like twisted ropes. The style quickly caught on, and soon decorative carving was creeping, twisting and crawling over everything (aptly described by 19th-century English novelist William Beckford as 'scollops and twistifications').

Outstanding Manueline masterpieces are Belém's Mosteiro dos Jerónimos, masterminded largely by Diogo de Boitaca and João de Castilho; and Batalha's Mosteiro de Santa Maria da Vitória's otherworldly Capelas Imperfeitas (Unfinished Chapels).

Other famous creations include Belém's Torre de Belém, a Manueline-Moorish cake crossed with a chess piece by Francisco de Arruda; his brother Diogo de Arruda's fantastical organic, seemingly barnacle-encrusted window in the Chapter House of Tomar's Convento de Cristo; and the convent's fanciful 16-sided Charola – the Templar church, resembling an eerie *Star Wars* set. Many other churches sport a Manueline flourish against a plain facade.

The style was enormously resonant in Portugal, and reappeared in the early 20th century in exercises in mystical romanticism, such as Sintra's Quinta da Regaleira and Palácio Nacional da Pena, and Luso's over-the-top and extraordinary neo-Manueline Palace Hotel do Buçaco.

Baroque

With independence from Spain re-established and the influence of the Inquisition on the wane, Portugal burst out in a fever of baroque – an architectural style that was exuberant and theatrical and fired straight at the senses. Nothing could rival the Manueline flourish, but the baroque style – named after the Portuguese word for a rough pearl, *barroco* –

Palácio Nacional da Pena (p91), Sintra

cornered the market in flamboyance. At its height during the 18th century (almost a century later than in Italy), it was characterised by curvaceous forms, huge monuments, spatially complex schemes and lots and lots and lots of gold.

Financed by the 17th-century gold and diamond discoveries in Brazil, and encouraged by the extravagant Dom João V, local and foreign (particularly Italian) artists created mind-bogglingly opulent masterpieces. Prodigious *talha dourada* (gilded woodwork) adorns church interiors all over the place, but it reached its extreme in Aveiro's Mosteiro de Jesus, Lisbon's Igreja de São Roque and Porto's Igreja de São Francisco.

The baroque of central and southern Portugal was more restrained. Examples include the chancel of Évora's cathedral and the massive Palácio Nacional de Mafra. Designed by the German architect João Frederico Ludovice to rival the palace-monastery of San Lorenzo de El Escorial (near Madrid), the Mafra version is relatively sober, apart from its size – which is such that at one point it had a workforce of 45,000, looked after by a police force of 7000.

Meanwhile, Tuscan painter and architect Nicolau Nasoni (who settled in Porto around 1725) introduced a more ornamental baroque style to the north. Nasoni is responsible for Porto's Torre dos Clérigos and Igreja da Misericórdia, and the whimsical Palácio de Mateus near Vila Real (internationally famous as the image on Mateus rosé wine bottles).

In the mid-18th century a school of architecture evolved in Braga. Local artists such as André Soares built churches and palaces in a very decorative style, heavily influenced by Augsburg engravings from southern Germany. Soares' Casa do Raio, in Braga, and much of the monumental staircase of the nearby Bom Jesus do Monte, are typical examples of this period's ornamentation.

Only when the gold ran out did the baroque fad fade. At the end of the 18th century, architects flirted briefly with rococo (best exemplified by Mateus Vicente's Palácio de Queluz, begun in 1747, or the palace at Estói) before embracing neoclassicism.

The Modern Era

The Salazar years favoured decidedly severe, Soviet-style state commissions (eg Coimbra university's dull faculty buildings, which replaced elegant 18th-century neoclassical ones). Ugly buildings and apartment blocks rose on city outskirts. Notable exceptions dating from the 1960s are Lisbon's Palácio da Justiça in the Campolide district and the gloriously sleek Museu Calouste Gulbenkian. The beautiful wood-panelled Galeto cafe-restaurant is a time capsule from this era.

The tendency towards urban mediocrity continued after the 1974 revolution, although architects such as Fernando Távora and Eduardo Souto de Moura have produced impressive schemes. Lisbon's postmodern Amoreiras shopping complex, by Tomás Taveira, is another striking contribution.

Portugal's most prolific contemporary architect is Álvaro Siza Vieira. A believer in clarity and simplicity, he takes an expressionist approach that is reflected in projects such as the Pavilhão de Portugal for Expo '98, Porto's splendid Museu de Arte Contemporânea and the Igreja de Santa Maria at Marco de Canavezes, south of Amarante. He has also restored central Lisbon's historic Chiado shopping district with notable sensitivity, following a major fire in 1988.

Spanish architect Santiago Calatrava designed the lean, organic monster Gare do Oriente for Expo '98, architecture that is complemented by the work of many renowned contemporary artists. The interior is more state-of-the-art spaceship than station. In the same area lies Lisbon's architectural trailblazer the Parque das Nações, with a bevy of unique designs, including a riverfront park and Europe's largest aquarium. The longest bridge in Europe, the Ponte de Vasco da Gama, built in 1998, stalks out across the river from nearby.

Since the turn of the millennium, Portugal has seen a handful of architecturally ambitious projects come to fruition. One of the grander projects is Rem Koolhaas' Casa da Música in Porto (2005). From a distance, the extremely forward-looking design appears to be a solid white block of carefully cut crystal. Both geometric and defiantly asymmetrical, the building mixes elements of tradition – like *azulejos* (hand-painted tiles) hidden in one room – with high modernism, such as the enormous curtains of corrugated glass flanking the concert stage.

Two Legendary Architects

Porto is home to not one but two celebrated contemporary architects: Álvaro Siza Vieira (born 1933) and Eduardo Souto de Moura (born 1952). Both remain fairly unknown outside their home country, which is surprising given their loyal following among fellow architects and their long and distinguished careers. Both have earned the acclaimed Pritzker Prize, the Nobel of the architecture world (Siza Vieira in 1992, Souto de Moura in 2011). The two men are quite close, and they even have offices in the same building. They have collaborated on a handful of projects and, prior to going out on his own, Souto de Moura also worked for Siza Vieira.

Azulejos

Portugal's favourite decorative art is easy to spot. Polished painted tiles called *azulejos* (after the Arabic *al zulaycha*, meaning polished stone) cover everything from churches to train stations. The Moors introduced the art, having picked it up from the Persians, but the Portuguese wholeheartedly adopted it.

Portugal's earliest tiles are Moorish, from Seville. These were decorated with interlocking geometric or floral patterns (figurative representations aren't an option for Muslim artists for religious reasons). After the Portuguese captured Ceuta in Morocco in 1415, they began exploring the art themselves. The 16th-century Italian invention of majolica, in which colours are painted directly onto wet clay over a layer of white enamel, gave works a fresco-like brightness and kicked off the Portuguese *azulejo* love affair.

The earliest homegrown examples, polychrome and geometric, date from the 1580s and may be seen in churches such as Lisbon's Igreja de São Roque, where they provide an ideal counterbalance to fussy, gold-heavy baroque.

The late 17th century saw a fashion for huge panels depicting everything from saints to seascapes. As demand grew, mass production became necessary and the Netherlands' blue-and-white Delft tiles started appearing.

Portuguese tile makers rose to the challenge of this influx, and the splendid work of virtuosos António de Oliveira Bernardes and his son Policarpo in the 18th century springs

Mosteiro de São Vicente de Fora, Lisbon (p59)

TRABANTOS/SHUTTERSTOCK ©

from this competitive creativity. You can see their work in Évora, in the impressive Igreja de São João.

By the end of the 18th century, industrial-scale manufacture began to affect quality. There was also massive demand for tiles after the 1755 Lisbon earthquake. (Tiling answered the need for decoration and was cheap and practical – a solution for a population that had felt the ground move beneath its feet.)

From the late 19th century, the art nouveau and art deco movements took *azulejos* by storm, providing fantastic facades and interiors for shops, restaurants and residential buildings. Today, *azulejos* still coat contemporary life, and you can explore the latest in *azulejos* in the Lisbon metro. Maria Keil (1914–2012) designed 19 of the stations, from the 1950s onwards – look out for her wild modernist designs at the stations of Rossio, Restauradores, Intendente, Marquês de Pombal, Anjos and Martim Moniz. Oriente also showcases extraordinary contemporary work by artists from five continents.

Literary Giants

In 2010 Portugal lost one of its greatest writers when José Saramago died at the age of 87. Known for his discursive, cynical and darkly humorous novels, Saramago gained worldwide attention after winning the Nobel Prize in 1998. His best works mine the depths of the human experience and are often set in a uniquely Portuguese landscape. Sometimes his quasi-magical tales revolve around historic events – like the Christian Siege of Lisbon or the building of the Palácio Nacional de Mafra – while at other times he takes on grander topics (writing, for instance, of Jesus' life as a fallible human being) or even creates modern-day fables (in *Blindness*, everyone on earth suddenly goes blind). As a self-described libertarian communist, Saramago had political views that sometimes landed him in trouble. After his name was removed from a list of nominees for a European literary prize, he went into self-imposed exile, spending the last years of his life in the Canary Islands.

In the shadow of Saramago, António Lobo Antunes is Portugal's other literary great – and many of his admirers say the Nobel committee gave the prize to the wrong Portuguese writer. Antunes produces magical, fast-paced prose, often with dark undertones and vast historical sweeps; some critics compare his work to that of William Faulkner. Antunes' writing reflects his harrowing experience as a field doctor in Angola during Portugal's bloody colonial wars, and he often turns a critical gaze on Portuguese history – setting his novels around colonial wars, the dark days of the Salazar dictatorship and the 1974 revolution. He gained an international following slowly, but Antunes is still active today, and many of his earlier novels have finally been translated into English.

Fernando Pessoa

'There's no such man known as Fernando Pessoa', swore Alberto Caeiro, who, truth be told, didn't really exist himself. He was one of more than a dozen heteronyms (identities) adopted by Fernando Pessoa (1888–1935), Portugal's greatest 20th-century poet.

Heralded by literary critics as one of the icons of modernism, Pessoa was also among the stranger characters to wander the streets of Lisbon. He worked as a translator by day (having learned English while living in South Africa as a young boy) and wrote poetry by night – but not just Pessoa's poetry. He took on numerous personas, writing in entirely different styles, representing different philosophies, backgrounds and levels of mastery. Of Pessoa's four primary heteronyms, Alberto Caeiro was regarded as the great master by other heteronyms Alvaro de Campos and Ricardo Reis. (Fernando Pessoa was the fourth heteronym, but his existence, as alluded to earlier, was denied by the other three.) Any one style would have earned Pessoa renown as a major poet of his time, but considered together, the variety places him among the greats of modern literature.

Paula Rego

The conservative Salazar years of the mid-20th century didn't create the ideal environment to nurture contemporary creativity, and many artists left the country. These include Portugal's best-known living artist, Paula Rego, who was born in Lisbon in 1935 but has been a resident of the UK since 1951. Rego's signature style developed around fairy-tale paintings with a nightmarish twist. Her works deal in ambiguity and psychological and sexual tension, such as *The Family* (1988), where a seated businessman is either being tortured or smothered with affection by his wife and daughter. Domination, fear, sexuality and grief are all recurring themes in Rego's paintings, and the mysterious and sinister atmosphere, heavy use of chiaroscuro (stark contrasting of light and shade) and strange distortion of scale are reminiscent of the work of surrealists Max Ernst and Giorgio de Chirico.

For many, Pessoa is inextricably linked to Lisbon. He spent his nights in cafes, writing, drinking and talking until late into the evening, and many of his works are set in Lisbon's old neighbourhoods. Among Pessoa's phobias were lightning and having his photograph taken. You can see a few of the existing photos of him at the Café Martinho da Arcada, one of his regular haunts.

Despite his quirks and brilliance, Pessoa published very little in his lifetime, with his great work *Livro do Desassossego* (Book of Disquiet) only appearing in 1982, 50 years after it was written. In fact, the great bulk of Pessoa's writing was discovered after his death: thousands of manuscript pages lay hidden inside a wooden trunk. Scholars are still poring over his elusive works.

Painting

The Early Masters

As Gothic art gave way to more humanistic Renaissance works, Portugal's 15th-century painters developed their own style. Led by the master Nuno Gonçalves, the *escola nacional* (national school) took religious subjects and grounded them against contemporary backgrounds. In Gonçalves' most famous painting, the panels of Santo Antonio (in Lisbon's Museu Nacional de Arte Antiga), he includes a full milieu of Portuguese society – nobles, Jews, fisherfolk, sailors, knights, priests, monks and beggars.

Some of Portugal's finest early paintings emerged from the 16th-century Manueline school. These artists, influenced by Flemish painters, developed a style known for its incredible delicacy, realism and luminous colours. The most celebrated painter of his time was Vasco Fernandes, known as Grão Vasco (1480–1543). His richly hued paintings (still striking five centuries later) hang in a museum in Viseu dedicated to his work – as well as that of his Manueline school colleague Gaspar Vaz. Meanwhile, sculptors, including Diogo de Boitaca, went wild with Portuguese seafaring fantasies and exuberant decoration on some of Portugal's icons.

The Star of Óbidos

The 17th century saw a number of talented Portuguese artists emerge. One of the best was Josefa de Óbidos, who enjoyed success as a female artist – an extreme rarity in those days. Josefa's paintings were unique in their personal, sympathetic interpretations of religious subjects and for their sense of innocence. Although she studied at an Augustine convent as a young girl, she left without taking the vows and settled in Óbidos (where she got her nickname). Still she maintained close ties to the church, which provided many of her commissions, and remained famously chaste until her death in 1684. Josefa left one of the finest legacies of work of any Portuguese painter. She excelled in richly coloured still lifes and detailed religious works, ignoring established iconography.

Naturalism

In the 19th century naturalism was the dominant trend, with a handful of innovators pushing Portuguese art in new directions. Columbano Bordalo Pinheiro, who hailed from a family of artists, was a seminal figure among the Portuguese artists of his time. He played a prominent role in the Leã d'Ouro, a group of distinguished artists, writers and intellectuals who gathered in the capital and were deeply involved in the aesthetic trends of the day. A prolific artist, Pinheiro painted some of the luminaries of his time, including the novelist Eça de Queirós and Teófilo Braga (a celebrated writer who later became president of the early republic). One of his best-known works is a haunting portrait of the poet Antero de Quental, who later died by suicide.

The 20th Century

Building on the works of the naturalists, Amadeo de Souza-Cardoso lived a short but productive life, experimenting with new techniques emerging in Europe. Raised in a sleepy village outside Amarante, he studied architecture at the Academia de Belas Artes in Lisbon but soon dropped out and moved to Paris. There he found his calling as a painter and mingled with the leading artists and writers of the time, including Amedeo Modigliani, Gertrude Stein, Max Jacob and many others. He experimented with impressionism, and later cubism and futurism, and created a captivating body of work, though he is little known outside Portugal.

José Sobral de Almada Negreiros delved even deeper into futurism, inspired by the Italian futurist Filippo Tommaso Marinetti. His work encompassed richly hued portraits with abstract geometrical details – an example is his famous 1954 portrait of Fernando Pessoa – and he was also a sculptor, writer and critic. He managed to walk a fine line during the Salazar regime, creating large-scale murals by public commission as well as socially engaged works critical of Portuguese society.

Celebration at the anniversary of the Fátima apparitions (p295)

FRANCISCO LEONG/AFP/GETTY IMAGES ©

Religion

Christianity has been a powerful force in shaping Portugal's history, and religion still plays an important role in the lives of its people. Churches are sprinkled across the country, and Portugal's biggest celebrations revolve around religious events. Portugal is also home to a number of pilgrimage sites, the most important of which, Fátima, attracts several million pilgrims each year.

Church & State

Portugal has a deep connection to the church. Even during the long rule of the Moors, Christianity flourished in the north – which provided a strategic base for Christian crusaders to retake the kingdom. Cleric and king walked hand in hand, from the earliest papal alliances of the 11th century through to the 17th century, when the church played a role both at home and in Portugal's expanding empire.

Things ran smoothly until the 18th century, when the Marquês de Pombal, a man of the Enlightenment, wanted to curtail the power of the church – specifically that of the Jesuits, whom he expelled in 1759. He also sought to modernise the Portuguese state (overseeing one of the world's first urban 'grid' systems) and brought education under the state's control. State–church relations seesawed over the next 150 years, with power struggles

Life Under Muslim Rule

The Moors ruled southern Portugal for almost 400 years: some scholars describe that time as a golden age. The Arabs introduced irrigation, previously unknown in Europe. The Moors opened schools and created campaigns to achieve mass literacy (in Arabic, of course), as well as the teaching of mathematics, geography and history. Medicine reached new levels of sophistication. There was also a degree of religious tolerance, but this evaporated when Christian crusaders came to power. Much to the chagrin of Christian slave owners, slavery was not permitted in the Islamic kingdom – making it a refuge for runaway slaves. Muslims, Christians and Jews all peacefully coexisted, and at times even collaborated, creating one of the most scientifically and artistically advanced societies the world had ever known.

including the outright ban of religious orders in 1821 and the seizing by the state of many church properties.

The separation of church and state was formally recognised during the First Republic (1910–26). But in practice the church remained intimately linked to many aspects of people's lives. Health and education were largely under religious auspices, with Catholic schools and hospitals the norm. Social outlets for those in rural areas were mostly church related. And the completion of any public-works project always included a blessing by the local bishop.

In 1932 António de Oliveira Salazar swept into power, establishing a Mussolini-like Estado Novo (New State) that lasted until the 1974 Revolution of the Carnations. Salazar had strong ties to the Catholic church – he spent eight years studying for the priesthood before switching to law. His college roommate was a priest who later became the Cardinal Patriarch of Lisbon. Salazar was a ferocious anticommunist, and he used Roman Catholic references to appeal to people's sense of authority, order and discipline. He described the family, the parish and the larger institution of Christianity as the foundations of the state. Church officials who spoke out against him were silenced or forced into exile.

Following the 1974 revolution, the church found itself out of favour with many Portuguese; its support of the Salazar regime spelt its undoing in the topsy-turvy days following the government's collapse. The new constitution, ratified in 1976, again emphasised the formal separation of church and state, although this time the law had teeth, and Portugal quickly transitioned into a more secular society. Today, only about half of all weddings happen inside a church. Divorce is legal, as is abortion (up to 10 weeks; the law went into effect following a 2007 referendum). In 2010 same-sex marriage was legalised, making Portugal the sixth European nation to permit it (with several other nations joining the ranks in recent years).

The Inquisition

'After the earthquake, which had destroyed three-quarters of the city of Lisbon, the wise men of that country could think of no means more effectual to preserve the kingdom from utter ruin than to entertain the people with an auto-da-fe...'
 – Voltaire, *Candide*

One of the darkest episodes in Portugal's history, the Inquisition was a campaign of church-sanctioned terror and execution that began in 1536 and lasted for 200 years, though it was not officially banned until 1821. It was initially aimed at Jews, who were either expelled from Portugal or forced to renounce their faith. Those who didn't embrace Catholicism risked facing the auto-da-fé (act of faith), a church ceremony consisting of a Mass, a procession of the guilty, reading of the sentences and, later, burning at the stake.

'Trials' took place in public squares in Lisbon, Porto, Évora and Coimbra in front of crowds sometimes numbering in the thousands. At the centre, atop a large canopied platform, sat the Grand Inquisitor, surrounded by a staff of aristocrats, priests, bailiffs, torturers and scribes, who meticulously recorded the proceedings.

The victims usually spent years in prison, often undergoing crippling torture, before seeing the light of day. They stood accused of a wide variety of crimes – such as skipping meals on Jewish fast days (signs of 'unreformed' Jews), leaving pork uneaten on the plate, failing to attend Mass or observe the sabbath, as well as blasphemy, witchcraft and homosexuality. No matter how flimsy the 'evidence' – often delivered to the tribunal by a grudge-bearing neighbour – very few were found not guilty and released. After a decade or so in prison, the condemned were finally brought to their auto-da-fé. Before meeting their judgment, they were dressed in a *san benito* (yellow penitential gown painted with flames) and a *coroza* (high conical cap) and brought before the tribunal.

Crypto Jews

When Manuel I banned Judaism, most Jews fled or converted. Some, however, simply hid their faith from public view and wore the facade of being a New Christian (the name given to Jewish converts). Religious ceremonies were held behind closed doors, with the sabbath lamp placed at the bottom of a clay jar so that it could not be seen from outside. Within their Catholic prayer books Jews composed Jewish prayers, and they even overlaid Jewish prayers atop Catholic rituals (like the making of the sign of the cross).

One Crypto-Jewish community in Belmonte managed to maintain its faith in hiding for more than 400 years and was only revealed in 1917. No longer underground (Belmonte now has its own synagogue and Jewish cemetery), members of the community remain quite secretive about the practices they maintained in hiding.

After the sentence was pronounced, judgment was carried out in a different venue. By dawn the next morning, for instance, executioners would lead the condemned to a killing field outside town. Those who repented were strangled before being burnt at the stake. The unrepentant were simply burnt alive.

During the years of the Inquisition, the church executed over 2000 victims and tortured or exiled tens of thousands more. The Portuguese even exported the auto-da-fé to the colonies, burning Hindus at the stake in Goa, for instance.

As Voltaire sardonically suggested, superstition played no small part in the auto-da-fé. Some believers thought that the earthquake of 1755 was the wrath of God upon them, and that they were being punished – not for their bloody auto-da-fés but because the Holy Office hadn't done quite enough to punish the heretics.

The Apparitions at Fátima

For many Portuguese Catholics, Fátima represents one of the most momentous religious events of the 20th century, and it transformed a tiny village into a major pilgrimage site for Catholics across the globe. On 13 May 1917, 10-year-old Lúcia Santos and her two younger cousins, Jacinta and Francisco Marto, were out tending their parents' flocks in the fields outside the village of Fátima. Suddenly a bolt of lightning struck the earth, and a woman 'brighter than the sun' appeared before them. According to Santos, she came to them with a message exhorting people to pray and do penance to save sinners. She asked the children to pray the rosary every day, which she said was key to bringing peace to one's own life and to the world. At the time, peace was certainly on the minds of many Portuguese, who were already deeply

Semana Santa (p22), Braga

ZACARIAS PEREIRA DA MATA/
SHUTTERSTOCK ©

enmeshed in WWI. She then told the children to come again on the 13th of each month, at the same time and place, and that in October she would reveal herself to them.

Word of the alleged apparition spread, although most who heard the tale of the shepherd children reacted with scepticism. Only a handful of observers came to the field for the 13 June appearance, but the following month several thousand showed up. That's when the apparition apparently entrusted the children with three secrets. In the weeks that followed, a media storm raged, with the government accusing the church of fabricating an elaborate hoax to revive its flagging popularity. The church, for its part, didn't know how to react. The children were even arrested and interrogated at one point, but the three refused to change their story.

On 13 October 1917 some 70,000 people gathered for what was to be the final appearance of the apparition. Many witnesses there experienced the so-called Miracle of the Sun, where the sun seemed to grow in size and dance in the sky, becoming a whirling disc of fire, shooting out multicoloured rays. Some spoke of being miraculously healed; others were frightened by the experience; still others claimed they saw nothing at all. The three children claimed they saw Mary, Jesus and Joseph in the sky. Newspapers across the country reported on the event, and soon a growing hysteria surrounded it.

Only Lúcia made it into adulthood. Jacinta and Francisco, both beatified by the church in 2000, were two of the more than 20 million killed during the 1918 influenza epidemic. Lúcia later became a Carmelite nun and died at the age of 97 on 13 February 2005.

Faith on the Decline

The percentage of Portuguese who consider themselves Catholics (around 81%) ranks among the highest in Western Europe. The number of the faithful, however, has been on a steady decline since the 1970s, when over 95% of the nation was Catholic. Today nearly half a million residents describe themselves as agnostic, and less than 20% of the population are practising Catholics.

Regional differences reveal a more complicated portrait: around half of northern Portugal's population still attend Sunday Mass, as do more than a quarter in Lisbon – with noticeably fewer churchgoers on the southern coast.

O Fado, by José Malhoa

Saudade

The Portuguese psyche is complicated, particularly when it comes to elusive concepts like saudade. In its purest form, saudade is the nostalgic, often deeply melancholic longing for something: a person, a place or just about anything that's no longer obtainable. Saudade is profoundly connected to the seafaring nation's history and remains deeply intertwined with Portuguese identity.

Roots of Saudade

Scholars are unable to pinpoint exactly when the term *saudade* first arose. Some trace it back to the grand voyages during the Age of Discoveries, when sailors, captains and explorers spent many months at sea, and the term gave voice to the longing for the lives they left behind. Yet even before the epic voyages across the ocean, Portugal was a nation of seafarers, and *saudade* probably arose from those on terra firma – the women who longed for the men who spent endless days out at sea, some of whom never returned.

Naturally, emigration is also deeply linked to *saudade*. Long one of Europe's poorest peoples, the Portuguese were often driven by hardship to seek better lives abroad. Until recently, this usually meant the men leaving behind their families to travel to northern Europe or America to find work. Families sometimes waited years before being reunited, with

Saudade of the Jews

Until the end of the 15th century, Jews enjoyed a prominent place in Portuguese society. The treasurer of Dom Afonso V (1432–81) was Jewish, as were others who occupied diplomatic posts and worked as trade merchants, physicians and cartographers. Jews from other countries were welcomed in Portugal, including those expelled from Spain in 1492. Eventually, pressure from the church and from Spain forced the king's hand, and in 1497 Manuel I decreed that all Jews convert to Christianity or leave the country. A catalogue of horrors followed, including the massacre of thousands of Jews in 1506 by mobs run riot and two centuries of the bloody Inquisition that kicked off in 1536.

Aside from a secretive Crypto-Jewish group in Belmonte that managed to preserve their faith, the Judaic community slowly withered and perished. Those who converted felt the heart-rending *saudade* of deep loss – essentially the loss of their identity. Once thriving Jewish neighbourhoods died as residents went into exile or perhaps suffered arrest, torture and even execution. The personal losses paralleled the end of a flourishing and tolerant period in Portugal's history and effectively ended the Jewish presence in Portugal.

emigrants experiencing years of painful longing for their homeland – for the familiar faces and foods, and village life. Many did eventually return, but of course things had changed and so *saudade* reappeared, this time in the form of longing for the way things were in the past.

A Nation of Emigrants

The great discoveries of Portuguese seafarers had profound effects on the country's demographics. With the birth and expansion of an empire, Portuguese settled in trading posts in Africa and Asia, but the colony of Brazil drew the biggest numbers of early Portuguese emigrants. They cleared the land (harvesting Brazilwood, which gave the colony its name), set up farms and went about the slow, steady task of nation building – with help, of course, from the millions of slaves brought forcibly from Africa. Numbers vary widely, but an estimated half-a-million Portuguese settled in Brazil during the colonial period, prior to independence in 1822, and more than 400,000 flooded in during the second half of the 19th century.

By the 1900s, Portuguese began emigrating in large numbers to other parts of the world. The US and Canada received over half-a-million immigrants, with huge numbers heading to France, Germany, Venezuela and Argentina. The 1960s saw another surge of emigrants, as young men fled the country in order to avoid the draft that would send them to fight bloody colonial wars in Africa. The 1974 revolution also preceded a big exodus, as those associated with the Salazar regime went abroad rather than face reprisals.

What all these emigrants had in common was the deep sadness of leaving their homeland to struggle in foreign lands. Those left behind were also in a world of heartache – wives left to raise children alone, villages deserted of young men, families torn apart. The numbers are staggering: over three million emigrants between 1890 and 1990. No other European country apart from Ireland has lost as many people to emigration.

Saudade in Literature

One of the first great Portuguese works of literature that explores the theme of *saudade* is *Os Lusíadas* (The Lusiads; The Portuguese). Luís Vaz de Camões mixes mythology with historical events in his verse epic about the Age of Discoveries of the 15th and 16th centuries. The heroic adventurer Vasco da Gama and other explorers strive for glory, but many never return, facing hardships such as sea monsters and treacherous kings along the way. First-hand experience informed Camões' work: he served in the overseas militia, lost an eye in Ceuta in a battle with the Moors, served prison time in Portugal and survived a shipwreck in the Mekong (swimming ashore with his unfinished manuscript held aloft, according to legend).

The great 19th-century Portuguese writer Almeida Garrett wrote an even more compelling take on the Age of Discoveries. In his book *Camões*, a biography of the poet, he describes the longing Camões felt for Portugal while in exile. He also captured the greater sense of *saudade* that so many experienced as Portugal's empire crumbled in the century following the great explorations.

More recent writers also explore the notion of *saudade*, though they take radically different approaches from their predecessors. Contemporary writer António Lobo Antunes deconstructs *saudade* in cynical tales that expose the nostalgic longing for something as a form of neurotic self-delusion. In *As Naus* (The Return of the Caravels; 1988) he turns the discovery myth on its head when, four centuries after da Gama's voyage, the great explorers, through some strange time warp, become entangled with the *retornados* (who returned to Portugal in the 1970s after the loss of the country's African empire) as Renaissance-era achievements collapse in the poor, grubby, lower-class neighbourhoods of Lisbon.

Saudade in Film

Portugal's most prolific film-maker, Manoel de Oliveira (1908–2015), was making films well past his 100th birthday. In a career that spanned 75 years, he became known for carefully crafted, if slow-moving, films that delve deep into the world of *saudade* – of growing old, unrequited loves and longing for things that no longer exist. In *Viagem ao Princípio do Mundo* (Voyage to the Beginning of the World; 1997), several companions make a nostalgic tour of the rugged landscapes and traditional villages of the north – one in search of a past that he knows only in his dreams (having heard of his ancestral land from his Portuguese-born father), another haunted by a world that no longer exists (the places of his childhood having been uprooted). Past and present, nostalgia and reality collide in this quiet, meditative film. It stars a frail, 72-year-old Marcello Mastroianni as Oliveira's alter ego; this was the actor's final film before he died.

One of the finest love letters to the capital is the sweet, meandering *Lisbon Story* (1994), directed by German film-maker Wim Wenders. The story follows a sound engineer who goes in search of a missing director, discovering the city through the footage his friend left behind. Carefully crafted scenes conjure up the mystery and forlorn beauty of Lisbon (and other parts of Portugal, including a wistful sequence on the dramatic cliffs of Cabo Espichel). *Saudade* here explores many different realms, inspired in large part by the ethereal soundtrack by Madredeus – band members also play supporting roles in the film.

Fado

'I don't sing fado. It sings me.' – Amália Rodrigues

Portugal's most famous style of music, fado (Portuguese for 'fate'), couldn't really exist without *saudade*. These melancholic songs are dripping with emotion – and they revel in stories of the painful twists and turns of fate, of unreachable distant lovers, fathomless yearning for one's homeland and wondrous days that have come and gone. The emotional quality of the singing plays just as important a role as technical skill, helping fado to reach across linguistic boundaries. Listening to fado is perhaps the easiest way of understanding *saudade*, in all its evocative variety.

A style born in the capital in the 19th century, fado is Portugal's greatest contribution to world music. In 2011 Unesco recognised fado's significance by adding the genre to its list of the world's Intangible Cultural Heritage. Its origins are unclear – it may have been influenced by the rhythms and chants from around Portugal's empire. However, it's known that it emerged from the working-class neighbourhoods of Mouraria and Alfama in the late 19th century, only to be taken up by the upper classes. Coimbra has its own, quite different style of fado, heard around the university and performed by men only.

Fados are traditionally sung by one performer accompanied by a 12-string Portuguese *guitarra* (pear-shaped guitar). When two *fadistas* perform, they sometimes engage in *desgarrada*, a bit of improvisational one-upmanship where the singers challenge and play off one another. At fado houses there are usually a number of singers, each one traditionally singing three songs.

Amália Rodrigues (1920–99) remains the most famous fado performer, reaching her zenith in the 1940s and '50s.

JACEK_SOPOTNICKI/GETTY IMAGES ©

Survival Guide

Directory A–Z

Accessible Travel

• Although public offices and agencies are required to provide access and facilities for people with disabilities, private businesses are not.

• Lisbon airport is wheelchair accessible, while Porto and Faro airports have accessible toilets.

• Parking spaces are allotted in many places, but are frequently occupied. The EU parking card entitles visitors to the same street-parking concessions given to disabled residents.

• Newer and larger hotels tend to have some adapted rooms, though the facilities may not be up to scratch; ask at the local *turismo*. Most campgrounds have accessible toilets and some hostels have facilities for people with disabilities.

• Lisbon, with its cobbled streets and hills, may be difficult for some travellers with disabilities, but not impossible. The Baixa's flat grid and Belém are fine, and all the sights at Parque das Nações are accessible. Download Lonely Planet's free Accessible Travel guide from http://lptravel.to/AccessibleTravel, or for more information, contact one of the following organisations.

Accessible Portugal (☏211 338 693; www.accessible portugal.com; Rua António Champalimaud, Lote 1) This Lisbon-based association promotes accessible tourism and is the brains behind the excellent TUR4all Portugal app (Android and iOS), which works like a database of accessible tourist resources and services throughout Portugal and Spain.

Secretaria do Nacional de Reabilitação (☏217 929 500; www.inr.pt; Av Conde de Valbom 63) The national governmental organisation representing people with disabilities supplies information, provides links to useful operations and publishes guides (in Portuguese) that advise on barrier-free accommodation, transport, shops, restaurants and sights.

Climate

Lisbon

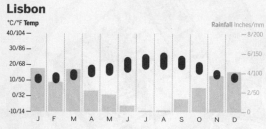

Porto

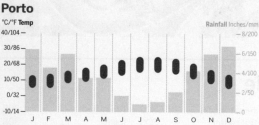

Lagos

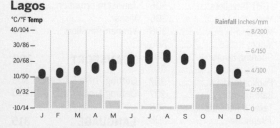

Accommodation

Although you can usually show up in any town and find a room on the spot, it's worthwhile booking ahead, especially for July and August.

Accommodation Types

Guest houses Small, often family-run places, some set in historic buildings; amenities range from simple to luxurious.

Hostels Portugal has a growing network of hostels around the country, with many choices in Lisbon and Porto.

Turihab Properties Options to stay in characterful manor houses, restored farmhouses or self-contained stone cottages.

Pousadas Unique accommodation inside former castles, monasteries and estates; nearly three dozen *pousadas* are spread across the country.

Book Your Stay Online

For more accommodation reviews by Lonely Planet authors, check out http://hotels.lonely planet.com/portugal. You'll find independent reviews, as well as recommendations on the best places to stay. Best of all, you can book online.

Turihab Properties

These charming properties are part of a government scheme, through which you can stay in a farmhouse, manor house, country estate or rustic cottage as the owner's guest.

High-season rates for two people, either in a double room or a cottage, range from €70 to €150. Some properties have swimming pools and most include breakfast (often with fresh local produce).

There are three types of Turihab lodgings:

Aldeias de Portugal (www.aldeiasdeportugal.pt) Lodging in rural villages in the north, often in beautifully converted stone cottages.

Casas no Campo (www.casasnocampo.net) Country houses, cottages and luxury villas.

Solares de Portugal (www.solaresdeportugal.pt) Grand manor houses, some of which date from the 17th or 18th century.

Private rooms and apartments Loads of online listings throughout Portugal.

Seasons

In popular tourist destinations prices rise and fall with the seasons. Mid-June to mid-September are firmly high season (book well ahead); May to mid-June and mid-September to October are midseason; and other times are low season, when you can get some really good deals. Outside the resorts, prices don't vary much between seasons.

In the Algarve, you'll pay the highest premium for rooms from mid-July to the end of August, with slightly lower prices from June to mid-July and in September, and substantially less (as much as 50%) if you travel between November and April. Note that a handful of places in the Algarve close in winter.

Price Ranges

The following price ranges refer to a double room with bathroom in high season. Unless otherwise stated, breakfast is included in the price.

Category	Cost
€	less than €60
€€	€60–€120
€€€	more than €120

Bargaining

Gentle haggling is common in markets (less so in produce markets); in all other instances you're expected to pay the stated price.

Travel Health Websites

It's a good idea to consult your government's travel-health website before departure, if one is available:

Australia (www.smarttraveller.gov.au)

Canada (www.travel.gc.ca)

UK (www.fitfortravel.nhs.uk)

USA (http://wwwnc.cdc.gov/travel)

Discount Cards

○ Portugal's network of *pousadas da juventude* (youth hostels) is part of the HI network. A HI card from your hostelling association at home entitles you to the standard cheap rates.

○ A student card will get you reduced admission to almost all sights. Likewise, those aged over 65 with proof of age will save cash.

○ If you plan to do a lot of sightseeing in Portugal's main cities, the Lisboa Card (www.lisboacard.org) and Porto Card (www.portocard.city) are sensible investments. Sold at tourist offices, these cards allow discounts or free admission to many attractions and free travel on public transport.

Electricity

Portugal uses 230V/50Hz supply. Plugs are the two-pinned European variety.

Emergency & Important Numbers

Country Code	351
International Access Code	00
Ambulance, Fire & Police	112

Etiquette

Greetings When greeting females or mixed company, an air kiss on both cheeks is common courtesy. Men give each other a handshake.

Visiting churches It is considered disrespectful to visit churches as a tourist during Mass. Taking photos at such a time is definitely inappropriate.

'Free' appetisers Whatever you eat, you must pay for, whether or not you ordered it. It's common practice for restaurants to bring bread, olives, cheese and other goodies to the table, but these are never free and will be added to your bill at the end. If you don't want them, a polite

'No, thank you' will see them returned to the kitchen.

Health

Portugal has a high-quality healthcare system, with pharmacies and doctors readily available countrywide. Most pharmacists speak some English. They can also advise when more specialised help is required and point you in the right direction.

Citizens of the EU are eligible for free emergency medical treatment if they have a European Health Insurance Card (EHIC). Citizens from other countries should find out if there is a reciprocal arrangement for free medical care between their country and Portugal. We recommend that you always purchase travel insurance when travelling.

Tap water is generally safe to drink in Portugal.

Health Hazards

Heat Exhaustion & Heat Stroke

Be mindful of heat exhaustion, particularly on hot summer days in the Algarve, and when engaging in vigorous outdoor activities anywhere in the country during the hottest months. Heat exhaustion occurs following excessive fluid loss with inadequate replacement of fluids and salt. Symptoms include headache, dizziness and tiredness. To treat heat exhaustion, replace lost fluids by drinking water and/or fruit juice or an oral rehydration solution, such as Dioralyte, and cool the body with cold water and fans.

Heat stroke is much more serious, resulting in irrational and hyperactive behaviour and eventually loss of consciousness and death. Rapid cooling by spraying the body with water and fanning is ideal. Emergency fluid and electrolyte replacement by intravenous drip is recommended.

Jellyfish & Sea Urchins

In general, jellyfish aren't a major problem in Portuguese waters, though there are rare sightings along the southern beaches. Stings from jellyfish are painful but not dangerous. Douse the wound in vinegar to deactivate any stingers that haven't 'fired'. Applying calamine lotion, antihistamines or analgesics may reduce the reaction and relieve the pain.

Watch for sea urchins around rocky beaches. If you get their needles embedded in your skin, immerse the limb in hot water to relieve the pain. To avoid infection visit a doctor and have the needles removed.

Insurance

Don't leave home without travel insurance that covers

theft, loss and medical problems. You should get insurance for the worst-case scenario, for example, an accident or illness requiring hospitalisation and a flight home.

Check the small print as some policies specifically exclude 'dangerous activities' such as scuba diving, motorcycling or even trekking. If these activities are in your sights, either find another policy or ask for an amendment (usually available for an extra premium) that includes them.

Make sure you keep all documentation for any claims later on. Some policies ask you to call back (reverse charges) to a centre in your home country, where an immediate assessment of your problem is made.

Worldwide travel insurance is available at www.lonelyplanet.com/travel-insurance. You can buy, extend and claim online any time – even if you're already on the road.

Internet Access

Wi-fi access is widespread in Portugal. If you have your own laptop, most hotels, hostels and midrange guest houses offer free wireless access. Many cafes and some restaurants also offer free wi-fi. Cybercafes are now rare.

We use the icon @ to indicate places that have a physical computer where guests can access the internet; the wi-fi icon indicates where wireless access is available.

Another option is using a *biblioteca municipal* (municipal library).

Legal Matters

o Fines for illegal parking are common. If you're parked illegally, your car will be towed away and you will have to pay around €100 to get your car back. Be aware of local road rules, as fines for other transgressions will also be enforced.

o It's illegal in Portugal to drive while talking on a mobile phone.

o Narcotic drugs were decriminalised in 2001 in an attempt to clear up the public-health problems among drug users, and to address the issue as a social rather than a criminal one. You may be brought before a commission and subject to fines or treatment if you are caught with up to 10 doses of a drug.

o Drug dealing is still a serious offence and suspects may be held for up to 18 months before coming to trial. Bail is at the court's discretion.

LGBT Travellers

In 2010 Portugal legalised gay marriage, becoming the sixth European country to do so. Most Portuguese profess a laissez-faire attitude about same-sex couples, although how out you can be depends on where you are in Portugal. In Lisbon, Porto and the Algarve, acceptance has increased, whereas in most other areas same-sex couples would be met with incomprehension. In this conservative Catholic country, homosexuality is still outside the norm. And while homophobic violence is extremely rare, discrimination has been reported in schools and workplaces.

Lisbon has the country's best gay and lesbian network and nightlife. Lisbon and Porto hold Gay Pride marches, but outside these events the gay community keeps a discreet profile.

Maps

National and natural park offices usually have simple park maps, though these are of little use for trekking or cycling. The following offer a good range of maps.

East View Geospatial (www.geospatial.com) US company that sells excellent maps, including 1:25,000 topographic maps.

Stanfords (www.stanfords.co.uk) Good selection of Portugal maps and travel products in the UK.

Media

Newspapers Main newspapers include *Diário de Notícias*, *Público*, *Jornal de Notícias* and the tabloid bestseller *Correio da Manhã*. English-language newspapers include the long-running daily, the *Portugal News* (www.theportugalnews.com).

Radio National radio stations include state-owned Rádiodifusão Portuguesa (RDP), which runs the stations Antena 1, 2 and 3 and plays Portuguese broadcasts and evening music (Lisbon frequencies are 95.7, 94.4 and 100.3). For English-language radio there is the BBC World Service (Lisbon 90.2) and Voice of America (VOA), or a few Algarve-based stations, such as Kiss (95.8 and 101.2).

Television TV channels include Rádio Televisão Portuguesa (RTP-1 and RTP-2), Sociedade Independente (SIC) and TV Independente (TV1), with RTP-2 providing the best selection of foreign films and world-news coverage. Other stations fill the airwaves with a mix of Portuguese and Brazilian soaps, game shows and dubbed or subtitled foreign films.

Video system Portugal uses the PAL video system, incompatible with both the French SECAM system and the North American NTSC system.

Money

Portugal uses the euro, along with most other European nations.

ATMs

ATMs are the easiest way to get cash in Portugal, and they are easy to find in most cities and towns. Tiny rural villages probably won't have ATMs, so it's wise to get cash in advance. Most banks have a Multibanco ATM, with menus in English (and other languages), that accepts Visa, Access, MasterCard, Cirrus and so on. You just need your card and PIN. Keep in mind that the ATM limit is €200 per withdrawal, and many banks charge a foreign transaction fee (typically from 2% to 3%).

Changing Money

Note that banks and *bureaux de change* are free to set their own rates and commissions, so a low commission might mean a skewed exchange rate.

Credit Cards

Most hotels and smarter restaurants accept credit cards; smaller guest houses, budget hotels and smaller restaurants might not, so it's wise to have cash with you.

Tipping

Bars Not expected.

Hotels One euro per bag is standard; gratuity for cleaning staff is at your discretion.

Restaurants In touristy areas, 10% is fine; few Portuguese ever leave more than a round-up to the nearest euro.

Snack bars Not expected.

Taxis Not expected, but it's polite to round up to the nearest euro.

Government Travel Advice

The following government websites offer travel advisories and information on current hotspots.

Australian Department of Foreign Affairs (www.smarttraveller.gov.au)

British Foreign Office (www.gov.uk/foreign-travel-advice)

Canadian Department of Foreign Affairs (www.travel.gc.ca)

US State Department (http://travel.state.gov)

Opening Hours

Opening hours vary throughout the year. We provide high-season opening hours; hours will generally decrease in the shoulder and low seasons.

Banks 8.30am–3pm Monday to Friday

Bars 7pm–2am

Cafes 9am–7pm

Clubs 11pm–4am Thursday to Saturday

Restaurants noon–3pm and 7–10pm

Shopping malls 10am–10pm

Shops 9.30am–noon and 2–7pm Monday to Friday, 10am–1pm Saturday

Post

Post offices are called CTT (www.ctt.pt). *Correio normal* (ordinary mail) goes in the red letterboxes, *correio azul* (airmail) goes in the blue boxes. Automated red postal stands dispense stamps, saving you the hassle of waiting in line at the post office. Post to Europe takes up to five working days, and the rest of the world up to seven. Economy mail (or surface airlift) is about a third cheaper, but takes a week or so longer.

Public Holidays

Banks, offices, department stores and some shops close on the public holidays listed here. On New Year's Day, Easter Sunday, Labour Day and Christmas Day, even *turismos* close.

New Year's Day 1 January

Carnaval Tuesday February/March – the day before Ash Wednesday

Good Friday March/April

Liberty Day 25 April

Labour Day 1 May

Corpus Christi May/June – ninth Thursday after Easter

Portugal Day 10 June – also known as Camões and Communities Day

Feast of the Assumption 15 August

Republic Day 5 October

All Saints' Day 1 November

Independence Day 1 December

Feast of the Immaculate Conception 8 December

Christmas Day 25 December

Safe Travel

o Once behind the wheel of a car, the otherwise mild-mannered Portuguese change personality. Macho driving, such as tailgating at high speeds and overtaking on blind corners, is all too common. Portugal has one of the highest road accident rates in Europe. Police have responded by aggressively patrolling certain dangerous routes, such as the cheerfully named 'highway of death' from Salamanca in Spain.

o Compared with other European countries, Portugal's crime rate remains low, but some types of crime – including car theft – are on the rise. Crime against foreigners is of the usual rush-hour-pickpocketing, bag-snatching and theft-from-rental-cars variety. Take the usual precautions:

don't flash your cash; keep valuables in a safe place; and, if you're challenged, hand it over – it's not worth taking the risk.

○ Take care in the water; the surf can be strong, with dangerous ocean currents.

Taxes & Refunds

Prices in Portugal almost always include 23% VAT (some basic food stuffs and services carry reduced rates of 6% and 13%, respectively). Non-EU passport holders can claim back the VAT on goods from participating retailers – be sure to ask for the tax back forms and get them stamped by customs. Refunds are processed at the airport or via post.

Telephone

To call Portugal from abroad, dial the international access code (🕾00), then Portugal's country code (🕾351), then the number. All domestic numbers have nine digits and there are no area codes.

Mobile phones

Local SIM cards can be used in unlocked European, Australian and quad-band US mobiles. Portugal uses the GSM 900/1800 frequency, the same as that found in Australia,

the UK and the rest of the EU. Mobile-phone usage is widespread in Portugal, with extensive coverage provided in all but the most rural areas. The main domestic operators are Vodafone, Optimus and TMN. All of them sell prepaid SIM cards that you can insert into a GSM mobile phone and use as long as the phone is not locked by the company providing you service. If you need a phone, you can buy one at the airport and shops throughout the country with a package of minutes for under €20. This is generally cheaper than renting a phone.

Time

Portugal, like Britain, is on GMT/UTC in winter and GMT/UTC plus one hour in summer. This puts it an hour earlier than Spain year-round. Clocks are set forward by an hour on the last Sunday in March and back on the last Sunday in October. In 2019, the European Parliament voted to abolish the biannual time change. Starting in 2021, Portugal is likely to maintain GMT/UTC plus one hour all year long.

Toilets

○ Finding public toilets in major cities such as Lisbon and Porto can be difficult. Most towns and villages that draw tourists have free public toilets.

○ The *mercado municipal* (municipal market) often has free toilets. These are generally fairly clean and adequately maintained.

○ In more built-up areas, your best bet is to look for a toilet in a shopping centre or simply duck into a cafe.

Tourist Information

○ Turismo de Portugal, the country's national tourist board, operates a handy website: www.visitportugal.com.

○ Locally managed *postos de turismo* (tourist offices, usually signposted '*turismo*') are everywhere, offering brochures and varying degrees of help with sights and accommodation.

Visas

Nationals of EU countries don't need a visa for any length of stay in Portugal.

Those from Canada, New Zealand, the USA and (by temporary agreement) Australia can stay for up to 90 days in any six-month period without a visa. Others, including nationals of South Africa, need a visa unless they're the spouse or child of an EU citizen.

The general requirements for entry into Portugal also apply to citizens of other signatories of the 1990 Schengen Convention (Austria, Belgium, Denmark, Finland, France, Germany, Greece, Iceland, Italy, Luxembourg, the Netherlands, Norway, Spain and Sweden). A visa issued by one Schengen country is generally valid for travel in all the others, but unless you're a citizen of the UK, Ireland or a Schengen country, you should check visa regulations with the consulate of each Schengen country you plan to visit. You must apply for any Schengen visa while you are still in your country of residence.

Women Travellers

○ Women travelling alone in Portugal report few serious problems. As when travelling anywhere, women should take care – be cautious where you walk after dark and don't hitch.

○ If you're travelling with a male partner, people will expect him to do all the talking and ordering,

and pay the bill. In some conservative pockets of the north, unmarried couples will avoid hassle by saying they're married.

○ If you're a victim of violence or rape while you're in Portugal, you can contact the **Associação Portuguesa de Apoio à Vítima** (APAV, Portuguese Association for Victim Support; ☎213 587 900; www.apav.pt; Rua José Estêvão 135), which offers assistance for rape victims. Visit the website for office locations nationwide.

Transport

An increasingly popular destination, Portugal is well connected to North America and European countries by air. There are also handy overland links by bus and train to and from Spain, from where you can continue on to other destinations on the continent.

Flights, cars and tours can be booked online at lonelyplanet.com/bookings.

Getting There & Away

Air

Most international flights arrive in Lisbon, though Porto and Faro also receive some. For more information,

including live arrival and departure schedules, see www.ana.pt.

TAP (www.flytap.com) is Portugal's international flag carrier as well as its main domestic airline. The three main airports in Portugal are **Faro Airport** (FAO; ☎289 800 800; www.aeroportofaro.pt; ☎), **Lisbon Airport** (Lisbon Airport; ☎218 413 500; www.ana.pt/pt/lis/home; Alameda das Comunidades Portuguesas) and **Porto Airport** (☎229 432 400; www.aeroportoporto.pt; 4470-558 Maia).

Land

Portugal shares a land border only with Spain, but there is both bus and train service linking the two countries, with onward connections to the rest of mainland Europe.

Bus

The major long-distance carriers that serve European destinations are Busabout (www.busabout.com) and Eurolines (www.eurolines.com); although these carriers serve Portugal, they are not currently included in the multicity travel passes of either company.

For some European routes, Eurolines is affiliated with the big Portuguese operators **Internorte** (☎707 200 512; www.internorte.pt) and **Eva Transportes** (☎289 589 055; www.eva-bus.com).

Car & Motorcycle

If you're driving your own car or motorcycle into

Portugal, you need the following:

- vehicle registration (proof of ownership)
- insurance documents
- motor vehicle insurance with at least third-party cover

Train

Trains are a popular way to get around Europe – comfortable, frequent and generally on time. But unless you have a rail pass the cost can be higher than flying.

You will have few problems buying long-distance tickets as little as a day or two ahead, even in summer. For those intending to do a lot of European rail travel, the European Rail Timetable (www.europeanrailtime table.eu) is updated monthly and is available for sale as a digital download on the website. Another excellent resource for train travel around Europe (and beyond) is the Man in Seat Sixty-One website (www.seat61.com).

River

Transporte Fluvial del Guadiana (www.rioguadiana.net) operates car ferries across the Rio Guadiana between Ayamonte in Spain and Vila Real de Santo António in the Algarve every hour (half-hourly in summer) from 9am to 7pm Monday to Saturday, and from 10am to 5pm Sunday. Buy tickets from the waterfront office (€1.90/5.50/1.20 per person/car/bike).

Sea

There are no scheduled seagoing ferries to Portugal, but there are many to Spain. The closest North African ferry connections are from Morocco to Spain; contact FRS (www.frs.es) for details. Car ferries also run from Tangier to Gibraltar.

Getting Around

Transport in Portugal is reasonably priced, quick and efficient. Most journeys are taken by bus as the rail network doesn't reach everywhere.

Air

Flights within mainland Portugal are expensive and, for the short distances involved, not really worth considering. Nonetheless, TAP (www.flytap.com) has multiple daily Lisbon–Porto and Lisbon–Faro flights (taking less than one hour) year-round. For Porto to Faro, change in Lisbon.

Bicycle

Cycling is popular in Portugal, even though there are few dedicated bicycle paths. Possible itineraries are numerous in the mountainous national and natural parks of the north (especially Parque Nacional da Peneda-Gerês), along the coast or across the Alentejo plains. Coastal trips are easiest from north to south, with the prevailing winds. More demanding is the Serra da Estrela (which serves as the Tour de Portugal's 'mountain run'). You could also try the Serra do Marão between Amarante and Vila Real.

Local bike clubs organise regular Passeio BTT trips; check their flyers at rental agencies, bike shops and *turismos*. Guided trips are

Climate Change & Travel

Every form of transport that relies on carbon-based fuel generates CO_2, the main cause of human-induced climate change. Modern travel is dependent on aeroplanes, which might use less fuel per kilometre per person than most cars but travel much greater distances. The altitude at which aircraft emit gases (including CO_2) and particles also contributes to their climate change impact. Many websites offer 'carbon calculators' that allow people to estimate the carbon emissions generated by their journey and, for those who wish to do so, to offset the impact of the greenhouse gases emitted with contributions to portfolios of climate-friendly initiatives throughout the world. Lonely Planet offsets the carbon footprint of all staff and author travel.

often available in popular tourist destinations.

Cobbled roads in some old-town centres may jar your teeth loose if your tyres aren't fat enough; they should be at least 38mm in diameter.

There are numerous places to rent bikes, especially in the Algarve and other touristy areas. Prices range from €10 to €25 per day.

Boat

Other than river cruises along the Rio Douro from Porto, and the Rio Tejo from Lisbon, Portugal's only remaining waterborne transport are cross-river ferries. Commuter ferries include those across the Rio Tejo to/from Lisbon, and across the mouth of the Rio Sado between Setúbal and Tróia.

Bus

A host of small private bus operators, most amalgamated into regional companies, run a dense network of services across the country. Among the largest are: **Rede Expressos** (☏707 223 344; www.rede-expressos.pt), **Rodonorte** (☏259 340 710; www.rodonorte.pt) and the Algarve-line Eva Transportes (www.eva-bus.com).

Bus services are of four general types.

Alta Qualidade A fast deluxe category offered by some companies.

Carreiras Marked 'CR'; slow, stopping at every crossroads.

Expressos Comfortable, fast buses between major cities.

Rápidas Quick regional buses.

Even in summer you'll have little problem booking an *expresso* ticket for the same or next day. A Lisbon–Faro express bus takes about four hours and costs around €20; Lisbon–Porto takes about 3½ hours for around €19. By contrast, local services can thin out to almost nothing on weekends, especially in summer when school is out.

Don't rely on *turismos* for accurate timetable information. Most bus-station ticket desks will give you a little computer printout of fares and services.

Except in Lisbon or Porto, there's little reason to take municipal buses, as most attractions are within walking distance.

Car & Motorcycle

Portugal's modest network of *estradas* (highways) is gradually spreading across the country. Main roads are sealed and generally in good condition. The downside is your fellow drivers: the country's per-capita death rate from road accidents has long been one of Europe's highest, and drinking, driving and dying are hot political potatoes. The good news is that recent years have seen a steady decline in the road toll, thanks to a zero-tolerance police crackdown on accident-prone routes and alcohol limits.

Driving can be tricky in Portugal's small walled towns, where roads may

taper to donkey-cart size before you know it, and fiendish one-way systems can force you out of your way.

A common occurrence in larger towns is down-and-outers, who lurk around squares and car parks, waving you into the parking space you've just found for yourself, and asking for payment for this service. It's wise to do as Portuguese do, and hand over some coins (€0.50) to keep your car out of 'trouble' (scratches, broken windows, etc).

Automobile Associations

Automóvel Club de Portugal (ACP; ☏219 429 113, 24hr emergency assistance 808 222 222; www.acp.pt), Portugal's national auto club, provides medical, legal and breakdown assistance to its members. Road information and maps are available to anyone at ACP offices, including the head office in Lisbon and branches in Aveiro, Braga, Bragança, Coimbra, Évora, Faro, Porto and elsewhere.

If your national auto club belongs to the Fédération Internationale de l'Automobile or the Alliance Internationale de Tourisme, you can also use ACP's emergency services and get discounts on maps and other products. Among clubs that qualify are the AA and RAC in the UK, and the Australian, New Zealand, Canadian and US automobile associations.

Driving Licences

Nationals of EU countries, the USA and Brazil need only

their home driving licence to operate a car or motorcycle in Portugal. Others should get an International Driving Permit (IDP) through an automobile licencing department or automobile club in their home country.

Fuel

Fuel is expensive – about €1.60 for a litre of *sem chumbo* (unleaded petrol) at the time of writing. There are plenty of self-service stations and credit cards are accepted at most. If you're near the border, you can save money by filling up in Spain, where it's around 20% cheaper.

Motorways & Tolls

Top of the range roads are *auto-estradas* (motorways), all of them *portagens* (toll roads); the longest of these are Lisbon–Porto and Lisbon–Algarve. Toll roads charge cars and motorcycles around €0.09 per kilometre (around €22 from Lisbon to Porto and €25 from Lisbon to Lagos). You can calculate prices at www.portugaltolls.com.

Nomenclature can be baffling. Motorway prefixes indicate the following.
A Portugal's toll roads.
E Europe-wide designations.
N Main two-lane *estradas nacionais* (national roads); prefix letter used on some road maps only.
IC *(itinerário complementar)* Subsidiary highways.
IP *(itinerário principal)* Main highways.

Note that Portugal's main toll roads now have automated tollbooths, meaning you won't be able to simply drive through and pay an attendant. Most car-rental agencies hire out the small electronic devices (for around €6 per week, less on subsequent weeks), and it's worth asking if one is available before renting a car.

Via Verde (☏707 500 900; www.viaverde.pt) has information on toll roads and details on where you can hire electronic tag devices throughout the country (useful if your car hire doesn't have them or you're driving your own vehicle).

Hire

● To rent a car in Portugal you should be at least 25 years old and have held your driving licence for more than a year (some companies allow younger drivers at higher rates). The widest choice of car-hire companies is at Lisbon, Porto and Faro airports. Competition has driven Algarve rates lower than elsewhere.

● Some of the best advance-booking rates are offered by internet-based brokers such as Holiday Autos (www.holidayautos.com). Other bargains come as part of 'fly-drive' packages. The worst deals tend to be those done with international firms on arrival, though their prepaid promotional rates are competitive. Book at least a few days ahead in high season. For on-the-spot rental,

domestic firms such as Auto Jardim (www.auto-jardim.com) have some of the best rates.

● The average price for renting the smallest and cheapest available car for a week in high season is around €300 (with tax, insurance and unlimited mileage) if booked from abroad, and a similar amount through a Portuguese firm.

● For an additional fee you can get personal insurance through the rental company, unless you're covered by your home policy. A minimum of third-party coverage is compulsory in the EU.

● Rental cars are especially at risk of break-ins or petty theft in larger towns, so don't leave anything of value visible in the car.

● Motorcycles and scooters can be rented in larger cities, and all over coastal Algarve. Expect to pay from €30/60 per day for a scooter/motorcycle.

Insurance

Your home-country insurance policy may or may not be extendable to Portugal, and the coverage of some comprehensive policies automatically drops to third party outside your home country unless the insurer is notified.

If you hire a car, the rental firm will provide you with registration and insurance papers, plus a rental contract.

If you are involved in a minor 'fender bender' with no injuries, the easiest way for drivers to sort things out with their insurance companies is to fill out a Constat Aimable (the English version is called a European Accident Statement). There's no risk in signing this: it's just a way to exchange the relevant information and there's usually one included in rental-car documents. Make sure it includes any details that may help you prove that the accident was not your fault. To alert the police, dial ☏112.

Parking

Parking is often metered within city centres, but is free on Saturday evening and Sunday. Lisbon has car parks, but these can get expensive (upwards of €20 per day).

Road Rules

o Despite the sometimes chaotic relations between drivers, there are rules. To begin with, cars must drive on the right, overtaking is on the left, and most signs use international symbols. An important rule to remember is that traffic from the right usually has priority. Portugal has lots of ambiguously marked intersections, so this is more important than you might think.

o Except when marked otherwise, speed limits for cars (without a trailer) and motorcycles (without a sidecar) are 50km/h in

towns and villages, 90km/h outside built-up areas and 120km/h on motorways. By law, car safety belts must be worn in the front and back seats, and children under 12 years may not ride in the front. Motorcyclists and their passengers must wear helmets, and motorcycles must have their headlights on day and night.

o The police can impose steep on-the-spot fines for speeding and parking offences, so save yourself a big hassle and remember to toe the line.

o The legal blood-alcohol limit is 0.5g/L, and there are fines of up to €2500 for drink-driving. It's also illegal in Portugal to drive while talking on a mobile phone.

Hitching

Hitching is never entirely safe, and we don't recommend it. Travellers who hitch should understand that they are taking a small but potentially serious risk. In any case, it isn't an easy option in Portugal. Almost nobody stops on major highways, and on smaller roads drivers tend to be going short distances so you might only advance from one field to the next.

Local Transport

Almost all Portugal's larger towns have a city bus service linking the city centre with outlying suburbs and villages. Fares are low, but services fall away on Saturday

afternoons and Sundays. Lisbon has a famous tram system with vintage cars climbing the steep streets of the city centre. Lisbon and Porto also have a metro. Portugal loves cable cars – using them can save you a lot of walking but they are expensive relative to the rest of the public transport system.

Taxi & Rideshare Services

o Taxis offer fair value over short distances, and are plentiful in large towns and cities. Ordinary taxis are usually marked with an 'A' (which stands for *aluguer*, 'for hire') on the door, number plate or elsewhere. They use meters and are available on the street and at taxi ranks, or by telephone for a surcharge of €0.80.

o The fare on weekdays during daylight hours is about €3.25 *bandeirada* (flag fall) plus around €0.80 per kilometre, and a bit more for periods spent idling in traffic. A fare of €6 will usually get you across bigger towns. It's best to insist on the meter, although it's possible to negotiate a flat fare. If you have a sizeable load of luggage you'll pay a further €1.60.

o Rates are about 20% higher at night (9pm to 6am), and on weekends and holidays. Once a taxi leaves the city limits you also pay a surcharge or higher rate.

○ In larger cities, including Lisbon and Porto, meterless taxis marked with a T (for *turismo*) can be hired from private companies for excursions. Rates for these are higher but standardised; drivers are honest and polite, and speak foreign languages.

○ Uber is available in Lisbon and Porto.

Train

Portugal has an extensive railway network, making for scenic travel between destinations; see the **Comboios de Portugal** (☏707 210 220; www.cp.pt) website.

Discounts

○ Children aged under five years travel free; those aged five to 12 years go for half price.

○ A youth card issued by Euro26 member countries gets you a 20% discount on *regional* and *interregional* services on any day. For distances above 100km, you can also get a 20% discount on *intercidade* (express) services and a 10% discount on Alfa Pendular (AP) trains – though the latter applies only from Tuesday to Thursday.

○ Travellers aged 65 years and over can get 50% off

any service by showing some ID.

Information & Reservations

○ You can get hold of timetable and fare information at all stations and from www.cp.pt.

○ You can book *intercidade* and Alfa Pendular tickets up to 30 days ahead, though you'll have little trouble booking for the next or even the same day. Other services can only be booked 24 hours in advance.

○ A seat reservation is mandatory on most *intercidade* and Alfa trains; the booking fee is included in the price.

Train Passes

The One Country Portugal Pass from InterRail (www. interrail.eu) gives you unlimited travel on any three, four, five, six or eight days over a month (2nd class costs €92/114/134/154/190 per three/four/five/six/eight days; 1st class costs about 35% more; and if you're under 28 years, it costs about 15% less). It's available to all travellers who hail from outside Portugal and can be purchased from many travel agents in Portugal or in advance from the website.

Types & Classes of Service

There are four main types of long-distance service. Note that international services are marked IN on timetables.

Regional (R) Slow, stop everywhere.

Interregional (IR) Reasonably fast.

Intercidade (IC) *Rápido* or express trains.

Alfa Pendular Deluxe This service is marginally faster than express and much pricier.

Only the Faro–Porto Comboio Azul and international trains such as Sud-Expresso and Talgo Lusitânia have restaurant cars, though all IC and Alfa trains have aisle service and most have bars.

Lisbon and Porto have their own *urbano* (suburban) train networks. Lisbon's network extends to Sintra, Cascais and Setúbal, and up the lower Tejo valley. Porto's network takes the definition of 'suburban' to new lengths, running all the way to Braga, Guimarães and Aveiro. *Urbano* services also travel between Coimbra and Figueira da Foz. The distinction matters where long-distance services parallel the more convenient, plentiful and considerably cheaper *urbanos*.

Language

Portuguese pronunciation is not difficult because most sounds are also found in English. The exceptions are the nasal vowels (represented in our pronunciation guides by 'ng' after the vowel), which are pronounced as if you're trying to make the sound through your nose; and the strongly rolled 'r' (represented by 'rr' in our pronunciation guides). Also note that the symbol 'zh' sounds like the 's' in 'pleasure'. The stress generally falls on the second-last syllable of a word. In our pronunciation guides stressed syllables are indicated with italics. Portuguese has masculine and feminine forms of nouns and adjectives. Both forms are given where necessary, indicated with 'm' and 'f' respectively.

To enhance your trip with a phrasebook, visit **lonelyplanet.com**.

Basics

Hello.
Olá.   o·*laa*

Goodbye.
Adeus.   a·de·*oosh*

How are you?
Como está?   *ko*·moo shtaa

Fine, and you?
Bem, e você?   beng e vo·*se*

Yes.
Sim.   seeng

No.
Não.   nowng

Please.
Por favor.   poor fa·*vor*

Thank you.
Obrigado.   o·bree·*gaa*·doo (m)
Obrigada.   o·bree·*gaa*·da (f)

You're welcome.
De nada.   de *naa*·da

Excuse me.
Faz favor.   faash fa·*vor*

Sorry.
Desculpe.   desh·*kool*·pe

Do you speak English?
Fala inglês?   *faa*·la eeng·*glesh*

I don't understand.
Não entendo.   nowng eng·*teng*·doo

Accommodation

Do you have a single/double room?
Tem um quarto de   teng oong *kwaar*·too de
solteiro/casal?   sol·*tay*·roo/ka·*zal*

How much is it per night/person?
Quanto custa   *kwang*·too koosh·ta
por noite/pessoa?   poor *noy*·te/pe·*so*·a

Eating

What would you recommend?
O que é que   oo ke e ke
recomenda?   rre·koo·*meng*·da

I don't eat ...
Eu não como ...   e·oo nowng ko·moo ...

  meat   *carne*   *kar*·ne
  chicken   *frango*   *frang*·goo
  fish   *peixe*   *pay*·she

Bring the bill/check, please.
Pode-me trazer   po·de·me tra·*zer*
a conta.   a *kong*·ta

Emergencies

Help!
Socorro!   soo·*ko*·rroo

Go away!
Vá-se embora!   vaa·se eng·*bo*·ra

Call ...!
Chame ...!   *shaa*·me ...

  a doctor   *um médico*   oong *me*·dee·koo
  the police   *a polícia*   a poo·*lee*·sya

I'm lost.
Estou perdido.   shtoh per·*dee*·doo (m)
Estou perdida.   shtoh per·*dee*·da (f)

I'm ill.
Estou doente.   shtoh doo·*eng*·te

Directions

Where's (the station)?
Onde é (a estação)? ong·de e (a shta·*sowng*)

What's the address?
Qual é o endereço? kwaal e oo eng·de·*re*·soo

Can you show me (on the map)?
Pode-me mostrar   po·de·me moosh·*traar*
(no mapa)?   (noo *maa*·pa)

Behind the Scenes

Acknowledgements

Climate map data adapted from Peel MC, Finlayson BL & McMahon TA (2007) 'Updated World Map of the Köppen-Geiger Climate Classification', *Hydrology and Earth System Sciences*, 11, 1633–44.

Cover photograph: Torre de Belém, Lisbon, Carlos Sanchez Pereyra/Getty Images ©

This Book

This 2nd edition of Lonely Planet's *Best of Portugal* guidebook was curated by Regis St Louis, who also researched and wrote it, along with Gregor Clark, Mark Di Duca, Duncan Garwood, Catherine Le Nevez, Kevin Raub and Kerry Walker. The previous edition was curated by Marc Di Duca, and written by Marc, Kate Armstrong, Anja Mutić, Kevin Raub, Regis St Louis and Kerry Walker. This guidebook was produced by the following:

Destination Editor Tom Stainer

Senior Product Editor Genna Patterson, Jessica Ryan

Regional Senior Cartographer Anthony Phelan

Product Editor Amy Lynch

Book Designer Ania Bartoszek

Assisting Editors Katie Connolly, Melanie Dankel, Victoria Harrison, Kellie Langdon, Rosie Nicholson, Lorna Parkes, Sarah Reid

Cartographer Hunor Csutoros

Cover Researcher Naomi Parker

Thanks to Ronan Abayawickrema, Sandra Henriques Gajjar, Anthony Gartland, Kate Kiely, Doug Rimington

Send Us Your Feedback

We love to hear from travellers – your comments keep us on our toes and help make our books better. Our well-travelled team reads every word on what you loved or loathed about this book. Although we cannot reply individually to postal submissions, we always guarantee that your feedback goes straight to the appropriate authors, in time for the next edition. Each person who sends us information is thanked in the next edition, the most useful submissions are rewarded with a selection of digital PDF chapters.

Visit lonelyplanet.com/contact to submit your updates and suggestions or to ask for help. Our award-winning website also features inspirational travel stories, news and discussions.

Note: We may edit, reproduce and incorporate your comments in Lonely Planet products such as guidebooks, websites and digital products, so let us know if you don't want your comments reproduced or your name acknowledged. For a copy of our privacy policy visit lonelyplanet.com/privacy.

Index

A

Symbols & Map Key

Look for these symbols to quickly identify listings:

◎ Sights
⊕ Activities
⊖ Courses
⊙ Tours
⊗ Festivals & Events

⊗ Eating
⊖ Drinking
✪ Entertainment
⊕ Shopping
ⓘ Information & Transport

These symbols and abbreviations give vital information for each listing:

🌿 Sustainable or green recommendation
FREE No payment required

☎ Telephone number
☺ Opening hours
P Parking
⊖ Nonsmoking
✳ Air-conditioning
@ Internet access
🛜 Wi-fi access
🏊 Swimming pool

🚌 Bus
⛴ Ferry
🚃 Tram
🚆 Train
🗒 English-language menu
🥗 Vegetarian selection
👪 Family-friendly

Find your best experiences with these Great For... icons.

 Art & Culture
 Beaches
 Budget
 Cafe/Coffee
 Cycling
 Detour
 Drinking
 Entertainment
 Events
 Family Travel
 Food & Drink

 History
 Local Life
 Nature & Wildlife
📷 Photo Op
🔭 Scenery
🛍 Shopping
🧳 Short Trip
🏀 Sport
🥾 Walking
❄ Winter Travel

Sights

🏖 Beach
🐦 Bird Sanctuary
⛪ Buddhist
🏰 Castle/Palace
✝ Christian
☯ Confucian
🕉 Hindu
☪ Islamic
🛕 Jain
✡ Jewish
🗿 Monument
🏛 Museum/Gallery/ Historic Building
🏚 Ruin
⛩ Shinto
🪯 Sikh
☯ Taoist
🍇 Winery/Vineyard
🐾 Zoo/Wildlife Sanctuary
◉ Other Sight

Points of Interest

⊙ Bodysurfing
⊕ Camping
⊖ Cafe
⊜ Canoeing/Kayaking
● Course/Tour
⊘ Diving
⊜ Drinking & Nightlife
⊗ Eating
⊕ Entertainment
♨ Sento Hot Baths/ Onsen
⊖ Shopping
⊕ Skiing
⊜ Sleeping
⊜ Snorkelling
⊕ Surfing
⊗ Swimming/Pool
⊛ Walking
⊜ Windsurfing
⊕ Other Activity

Information

⊕ Bank
⊕ Embassy/Consulate
⊕ Hospital/Medical
@ Internet
⊗ Police
⊘ Post Office
⊜ Telephone
⊕ Toilet
ⓘ Tourist Information
● Other Information

Geographic

🏖 Beach
⋈ Gate
⊕ Hut/Shelter
⊕ Lighthouse
⊕ Lookout
▲ Mountain/Volcano
⊕ Oasis
⊕ Park
)(Pass
⊕ Picnic Area
⊘ Waterfall

Transport

⊕ Airport
Ⓑ BART station
⊗ Border crossing
⊕ Boston T station
🚌 Bus
⊕ Cable car/Funicular
⊖ Cycling
⊖ Ferry
Ⓜ Metro/MRT station
⊕ Monorail
P Parking
⊕ Petrol station
⊕ Subway/S-Bahn/ Skytrain station
⊗ Taxi
⊕ Train station/Railway
⌇ Tram
Ⓤ Underground/ U-Bahn station
● Other Transport

Lázně in the Czech Republic where he lives with his Kievite wife and two sons.

Duncan Garwood

From facing fast bowlers in Barbados to sidestepping hungry pigs in Goa, Duncan's travels have thrown up many unique experiences. These days he largely dedicates himself to the Mediterranean and Italy, his adopted homeland, where he's been living since 1997. He's worked on more than 30 Lonely Planet titles, including guidebooks to Rome, Sardinia, Sicily, Spain and Portugal, and has contributed to books on food and epic drives. He's also written on Italy for newspapers, websites and magazines.

Catherine Le Nevez

Catherine's wanderlust kicked in when she roadtripped across Europe from her Parisian base aged four, and she's been hitting the road at every opportunity since, travelling to some 60 countries and completing her Doctorate of Creative Arts in Writing, Masters in Professional Writing, and post-grad qualifications in editing and publishing along the way. Over the past decade-and-a-half she's written scores of Lonely Planet guides and articles covering Paris, France, Europe and far beyond. Her work has also appeared in numerous online and print publications. Topping Catherine's list of travel tips is to travel without any expectations.

Kevin Raub

Atlanta native Kevin Raub started his career as a music journalist in New York, working for *Men's Journal* and *Rolling Stone* magazines. He ditched the rock 'n' roll lifestyle for travel writing and has written over 70 Lonely Planet guides, focusing mainly on Brazil, Chile, Colombia, USA, India, the Caribbean and Portugal. Kevin also contributes to a variety of travel magazines in both the USA and UK. Along the way, the self-confessed hophead is in constant search of wildly high IBUs in local beers. Follow him on Twitter and Instagram (@ RaubOnTheRoad).

Kerry Walker

Kerry is an award-winning travel writer, photographer and Lonely Planet author, specialising in Central and Southern Europe. Based in Wales, she has authored/ co-authored more than a dozen Lonely Planet titles. An adventure addict, she loves mountains, cold places and true wilderness. Kerry's insatiable wanderlust has taken her to all seven continents – from the frozen wilderness of Antarctica to the Australian Outback – and shows no sign of waning. She features her latest work at https://its-a-small-world.com and tweets @kerrychristiani.

Our Story

A beat-up old car, a few dollars in the pocket and a sense of adventure. In 1972 that's all Tony and Maureen Wheeler needed for the trip of a lifetime – across Europe and Asia overland to Australia. It took several months, and at the end – broke but inspired – they sat at their kitchen table writing and stapling together their first travel guide, *Across Asia on the Cheap*. Within a week they'd sold 1500 copies. Lonely Planet was born.

Today, Lonely Planet has offices in Franklin, London, Melbourne, Oakland, Dublin, Beijing, and Delhi, with more than 600 staff and writers. We share Tony's belief that 'a great guidebook should do three things: inform, educate and amuse'.

Our Writers

Regis St Louis

Regis grew up in a small town in the American Midwest – the kind of place that fuels big dreams of travel – and he developed an early fascination with foreign dialects and world cultures. He spent his formative years learning Russian and a handful of Romance languages, which served him well on journeys across much of the globe. Regis has contributed to more than 50 Lonely Planet titles, covering destinations across six continents. His travels have taken him from the mountains of Kamchatka to remote island villages in Melanesia, and to many grand urban landscapes. When not on the road, he lives in New Orleans. Follow him on www.instagram.com/regisstlouis.

Gregor Clark

Gregor is a US-based writer whose love of foreign languages and curiosity about what's around the next bend have taken him to dozens of countries on five continents. Chronic wanderlust has also led him to visit all 50 states and most Canadian provinces on countless road trips through his native North America.

Since 2000, Gregor has regularly contributed to Lonely Planet guides, with a focus on Europe and the Americas. Titles include *Italy*, *France*, *Brazil*, *Costa Rica*, *Argentina*, *Portugal*, *Switzerland* and *Mexico*. On his travels, he has cycled around Bali, trekked in the Himalayas, repaired his bike with duct tape in the middle of the Wyoming desert and cruised the icy shores of Greenland.

Mark Di Duca

Marc has been a travel guide author for the past 13 years, covering destinations as diverse as Siberia and the Caribbean for Lonely Planet and most other major guide publishers. With over six months experience of living and working on Madeira, Marc can safely say that the island is his favourite destination, bar none. When not downing custard tarts in Funchal or trekking the levadas, Marc can be found near Mariánské

◄——— More Writers ———◄

STAY IN TOUCH LONELYPLANET.COM/CONTACT

AUSTRALIA The Malt Store, Level 3, 551 Swanston St, Carlton, Victoria 3053
☎ 03 8379 8000,
fax 03 8379 8111

IRELAND Digital Depot, Roe Lane (off Thomas St), Digital Hub, Dublin 8, D08 TCV4, Ireland

USA 124 Linden Street, Oakland, CA 94607
☎ 510 250 6400,
toll free 800 275 8555,
fax 510 893 8572

UK 240 Blackfriars Road, London SE1 8NW
☎ 020 3771 5100,
fax 020 3771 5101

 twitter.com/
lonelyplanet

 facebook.com/
lonelyplanet

 instagram.com/
lonelyplanet

 youtube.com/
lonelyplanet

 lonelyplanet.com/
newsletter